DATE DUE

NOV 3 0 2010			
NOV 3 0 2017			

DISCARD

Demco, Inc. 38-293

NOV 1 8 2009

Advertising and Popular Culture

Advertising and Popular Culture:
Studies in Variety and Versatility

Edited by
Sammy R. Danna

Bowling Green State University Popular Press
Bowling Green, Ohio 43403

Copyright © 1992 by Bowling Green State University Popular Press

Library of Congress Catalog No.: 91-77257

ISBN: 0-87972-527-3 Clothbound
      0-87972-528-1 Paperback

Cover design by Gary Dumm

Acknowledgments

In creating this edited volume, many individuals assisted in its preparation. Thanks go to the Popular Culture Association Director, Ray Browne, Ph.D., and his wife, Pat Browne, Bowling Green State University Editor, for their encouragement and direction. Special thanks to all PCA Advertising Area members who worked with diligence and persistence in submitting articles and working on revisions.

For the talents and time of reviewers, editors, and proofreaders, special gratitude goes to members of Loyola University of Chicago Department of Communication members: Michael Cornett, Julie D'Acci, Kay Felkins, Bren Murphy, Marti Tomas, Gilda Parrella, and from the Department of English, Ruth McGugan. Thanks go to Wayne Magdziarz, WLUW-FM General Manager at Loyola University: Dale A. Gadd, Department of Mass Communication Chair, McNeese State University. Thanks are due to Deborah Moore, Secretary and Cynthia Roberts, Administrative Assistant, Loyola University. Thanks go to three priests from St. Peter's Church in the Chicago Loop: Fr. Michael Crosby, Fr. Francis Jerome Gray and Fr. Joseph Windolph. Final appreciation goes to Norman Coco and Betty Danna Gilreath, Monroe, LA. Sincere thanks to the media experts who were interviewed, contributors of photographs and advertising reproductions, and others too numerous to mention who provided moral support and encouragement with open hearts and ears.

Contents

Introduction ix

1. Advertising Is Everywhere 1
Conventional and Alternative
   Advertising Media:
     Two Views, Two Purposes 3
       Sammy R. Danna

*2. Subliminal Perception and Other Comment
and Criticism in Advertising* 22

A Critique of Advertising:
   Stuart Chase on the "Godfather of Waste" 23
     Richard N. Chapman
Postum, Post Toasties and Patriotism 29
   Alfred C. Richard
Images of Yuppies in Popular Advertisements
   of the 1980s 47
     Luigi Manca
Subliminal Seduction: Real or Imagined? 56
   Eric J. Zanot

3. Unusual Advertising Forms and Uses 63

Advertising Trade Cards:
   Nineteenth Century Showcases 64
     Stephen L. W. Greene
T-Shirt Messages:
   Fortune or Folly for Advertisers? 73
     Shay Sayre
Mona Lisa Meets Madison Avenue:
   Advertising Spoofs of A Cultural Icon 83
     Gina Strumwasser and Monroe Friedman

4. Specialized Advertising Forms 93
   and Applications

The Serialized Mini-Drama:
   A New Trend in Advertising 94
     Joanne Morreale and Karen Buzzard
Trends for the Twenty-First Century:
   The Senior Boom 103
     Margaret J. King
Language and Perfume:
   A Study of Symbol-Formation 109
     Tom Zelman
Humor in Advertising:
   It's Funny Business 115
     Marilyn M. Robitaille
The Golliwog:
   Innocent Doll to Symbol of Racism 124
     Robert M. MacGregor

5. Gender and Advertising 133

The Existence and Effectiveness
   of Sexual Content in Advertising 134
     Thomas W. Whipple
Male Parent Images in Advertising 141
   Rita C. Hubbard
Changing Male Image in Advertising:
   An Investigation 146
     Sammy R. Danna

Contributors 160

Introduction

Advertising today, more than ever, is a field filled with change, challenge, and controversy. For about a decade, the Popular Culture Association's Advertising Area has proved to be a forum for a variety of topics that highlight advertising's impact on culture and society. This volume stems from a proposal to collect into a book some of the papers presented at PCA Conferences in the Advertising Area from 1985-1989. Authors represent a variety of interests and research areas. While original plans did not call for any specific topic divisions in this volume, the articles do present variety, though somewhat loosely categorized. In general, these categories fall under the broad umbrella of popular culture studies. Besides the familiar historical and critical presentations, articles of controversy and interest are included, such as subliminal advertising. Some of these articles attempt to debunk previously written pieces and serve as a stepping stone to further discussion.

Subliminal perception debunked, senior citizen advertising comes of age, Mona Lisa goes commercial, and male ad image changes are questioned! These and a host of other insightful, informative essays comprise this volume. Numerous advertising and marketing scholars united to bring the reader some of their most instructive, stimulating and entertaining works.

Eric Zanot explores myths and misconceptions surrounding subliminal perception in advertising. Actually, this piece constitutes a somewhat daring, concerted effort to help explain some of the significant problems and perceptions of this intriguing phenomenon.

Richard N. Chapman examines Stuart Chase's writings. Yuppies in popular advertisements of the 1980s are discussed by Luigi Manca and Alfred C. Richard shows some of the ways companies advertised during American wars.

A bit lighter, but nevertheless still significant, are two essays under the "Unusual Advertising Forms and Uses" heading. Shay Shayre explores the surprisingly potent advertising related communication capacity of the T-shirt. While many illustrations of various kinds and descriptions are commonly employed throughout advertising, one unique area is cited. It focuses on the use of classical paintings to promote products and services. Gina Stumwasser and Monroe Friedman present amusing and informative material on the Mona Lisa's place in advertising. Although not surveying recognized art masterpieces, still Stephen L.W. Greene does investigate and elaborate upon the fascinating realm of late 19th century "trade-card" art.

Thought-provoking and amusing are but two descriptives applicable to Tom Zelman's language and perfume piece. Marilyn Robitaille continues in this vein with her focus on ad humor. Today, more than ever, humor is a prized ingredient in creating TV commercials with the hopes of attracting and holding an audience against "zipping and zapping" tendencies. A bit more serious, but equally interesting and topical, are two other pieces contained in the "Specialized Advertising Forms and Applications" section of this volume. First, Margaret King explores some welcome progress being made in senior citizen advertising, a largely long neglected market niche. Second, Joanne Morreale and Karen Buzzard's mini-drama treatment reveals some novel and notable challenges for advertising. Included in the section is Robert MacGregor's thought-provoking piece on the Golliwog.

What would advertising be without sex? Thomas W. Whipple surveys sexual ad content and Rita C. Hubbard examines male parenting images as revealed in magazine advertising. In a somewhat related category, Sammy R. Danna investigates some of the significant, and perhaps surprising, aspects of the seemingly growing male ad image controversy.

All-in-all, chances are you will find something to amuse, amaze, inform and stimulate in this volume of advertising variety and versatility.

Sammy R. Danna
Chicago

1
Advertising Is Everywhere

Advertising pops up almost everywhere at almost anytime in America. It abounds in conventional print and electronic media and on storefronts and on billboards, on storesides and on roadsides. The vehicle is growing steadily and significantly in alternative ad forms, ranging from sidewalk sandwich-board pitches to blurbs in supermarket shopping cart TV screens. To begin, Danna whisks the reader into ad-land via a whirlwind tour of typical daily persuasive/informative pitches. As the piece progresses he explores a potpourri of popular culture and commercial ad media problems and changes.

Three trucks advertising beverages are visible in this photograph taken in downtown Chicago.

A Chicago bus company advertises atop one of its buses.

A number of signs can be seen in this photograph made in downtown Chicago.

Conventional and Alternative Advertising Media: Two Views, Two Purposes

Sammy R. Danna

Advertising Seeks Us Everywhere: Is There No Refuge?

Each morning millions of people are awakened by a clock radio pouring forth a cacophony of music, news and commercials. Some individuals turn to their television and find countless commercials intertwined with the news and interviews. The morning newspaper delivers even more ads. On the way to work many encounter a multitude of billboards in all directions, and signs on the sides of busses and taxis and in the subway cars.

The barrage continues throughout the business day. Outside the office building, people may be handing out leaflets or product samples to arriving employees. Individuals dressed as lobsters or clowns may be promoting the new seafood restaurant or some other firm down the street. Somebody wearing a sandwich-board announces the grand opening of a new shoe store. Even within the confines of an office it continues. Telephone callers to a business can hear radio station ads when put on hold. The office fax machine can spew out the latest in electronic "junk mail." Professional magazines abound with industry ads. The letter-carrier's pouch is filled with direct mail ads.

Advertising pitches, promotions and persuasion are virtually everywhere. At times we are surprised or distressed by ads that confront us when least expected. However, advertising is a strong part of our culture, business and institutions. Without ads most media could hardly exist. This essay primarily concerns the ubiquity and abundance of advertising. Why do ads intrude into our lives? What are the changes in mainstream, traditional ad media in the 1990s? What relationship now exists between traditional and non-traditional media?

When most of us think of advertising, usually what comes to mind are conventional mass media—newspapers, magazines, broadcasting, billboards, direct mail catalogs and even the telephone yellow pages. Most of us are familiar with a less visible or less noticed second tier of media, from posters, leaflets, bus-stop benches and sandwich-boards to a host of specialty utilitarian items, from matchbooks to pens.

Advertisers desiring to make their messages rise above the clutter use new media made possible by recent technological advances. Fax machines, computers, the growing capabilities of the cable industry and other technological developments have opened alternative avenues in the competition for our attention. Some of these ad pitches are as simple as tacking messages to restroom doors or onto parking meters.

Traditional media and the newer alternative vehicles vie for the same pool of advertising dollars. Conventional advertising methods are still the mainstream employed for the most basic, broad-based advertising campaigns. Alternative ad vehicles generally supplement or complement mainstream media. Many claim that conventional media are faltering or even dying; especially cited is network television. It is true that TV, newspapers and even magazines have experienced some notable problems in circulation, target marketing and profitmaking as the 1990s began.

Television has been affected significantly by audience fragmentation. Instead of the networks realizing over 90% share of the average minute of TV viewers, as was the case of audiences in prime-time during the 1970s, their share is down to about 60% in the early 1990s. Cable TV, independent stations, videotape rentals and the power of superstations have all contributed to this problem. Zipping and zapping constitute more woes. The other broadcast medium, radio, seems as a whole, to be more successful as the 1990s begin. Revenues and listeners, overall, were on the increase according to Radio Advertising Bureau reports. While AM radio was experiencing some downturns during the 1980s, FM radio seems to make up for such deficiencies. As we go into the 1990s AM radio in most areas is trying to find a market with the 17-40 age-group—the people with money to spend.

Conventional Media:
Familiar, Basic and Changing

Advertisers rely upon conventional media to spread their ad messages quickly and efficiently to large audiences. Although specialized media can reach specific, albeit smaller audiences, they often do so at a premium cost. The most economic use of the advertiser's dollar remains with traditional media. The conventional ad vehicles, however, have been going through dramatic changes as their roles are redefined in the contemporary media mix.

Commercial television, independent outlets, super-stations and some cable networks feature a deluge of commercials. Often, successive ads number around a dozen. Brand names pop up as a part of regular dialogue on some shows and are evident in game shows as prizes and promotions. While the networks have become far more lax about this area of gratis brand name inclusion, some network executives and producers feel brand names add a certain realism to programs.[1] The notion is that these trademarks contribute more dramatic impact than do generic product designations.

While television clutter is obvious to most of us and frequently criticized, other conventional media still have their share of this problem. Magazines contain large amounts of ad clusters and whole sections of pitches, as well as a growing number of intrusive inserts. Response-cards loosely placed within the pages are annoying to some readers, but many of these ad ploys do prove to be creative, memorable and effective pitches. In 1985, fewer magazines carried inserts according to a J. Walter Thompson report.[2]

Mass-circulation magazines face the same dilemma as TV networks. They appeal to a somewhat undifferentiated audience which is not what today's marketing people generally want. The mass circulation magazine industry by 1990 was "suffering through a gruesome downturn." Even *Reader's Digest*, the most widely read general interest magazine, in 1990 was down to 16.3 million readers from a high of 18.4 in 1977. During the same time period, *TV Guide*'s circulation dropped by more than four million.[3]

Magazine Publishers of America (MPA), however, points out a significant growth of magazine readers from 1964 to 1989 relative to the national population increase during this time period. In 1989 an adult bought about thirty-six magazine copies a year compared with thirty copies a person ten years earlier, according to MPA. Advertising pages increased 48% from 1979 to 1989 with a 57% increase in magazine subscriptions during the same time period. The magazine publishers call this "a strong indicator of the vitality of magazines."[4]

About 10,000 AM and FM radio stations air countless commercials throughout the day. In order to attract and hold audiences, some enterprising outlets promote "commercial-free" periods. Because of strong competition, most US radio stations scramble to maximize profits while attempting to gain a significant market impact. One may not even have to turn a radio on, for numerous bars, restaurants and other businesses often play select stations over their public address systems. The Radio Advertising Bureau (RAB) touts this major advantage: "Radio offers us the ability to tailor messages to local audiences...to specific target audience segments."[5] In its *Why Radio* pamphlet, the RAB demonstrates that radio is highly targeted, flexible and ubiquitous. It boasts listenership such as: 95% of all cars, 99% of all households, and even 84.3% of walk-along players include radio. In a given week it claims to reach nearly everyone. Americans tune in to the medium, with no appreciable seasonal changes noted in listening patterns.[6]

Like all media advocates, the Radio Advertising Bureau wishes to present its medium as one of success and opportunity for advertisers. Laura Morandin, RAB Communications Manager, points out to this author the following: Radio is a medium widely recognized as having the ability "to target specific consumer groups via its various formats." The benefit of targetability is more important in today's marketing environment than ever before and is playing an increasingly crucial role in the marketing plans of many major advertisers. Radio listeners tend to "tolerate" commercials. In fact, "the 'zipping and zapping' associated with television commercials is not a significant factor in radio listening." This is because the average listener loyally tunes in to only two or three stations, "rather than constantly scanning the dial—quite a contrast to the situation television is facing." Finally, "radio continues to grow steadily at a time when other media are feeling the pinch. The medium grew more than 5.2% and posted another gain in advertising share in 1990."[7]

Outdoor advertising, historically, has been termed the "oldest advertising medium." The outdoor display advertising industry includes not only traditional billboards but many other ad forms such as painted walls, telephone kiosks, truck displays, taxi tops, transit/rail platforms, bus shelters, etc. The Institute of Outdoor Advertising says its medium is the final reminder of a firm's product or service. It bridges the gap between in-home ad messages and out-of-home purchases.[8]

Conventional and Alternative Advertising Media

With more than $1.48 billion in revenues in 1989, local clients represent the largest portion of the industry. Nearly 400,000 billboards dot primary highways in the U.S.[9]

Cities and towns have experienced increases in billboards and signs of all types in recent years. To remain competitive, outdoor display companies try to use highly visible placements, brighter inks, nighttime lighting, unusual eye-catching shapes and moving panels with animation or changing messages. While roadside and, especially, interstate highway billboards usually do not present clutter problems, some difficulties certainly exist within cities and towns. Especially in high-traffic areas, and even more so where billboards can be strategically placed, clusters of advertising vehicles can often be seen. Interspersed with other signs, full-scale billboards can create not only clutter but often confusion and visual chaos.[10]

While there have always been outdoor advertising restrictions, especially on the local level, the 1965 Highway Beautification Act basically requires states to control billboards on interstate and federal-aid primary roadways. In addition, there are sign-limitations, e.g. zones deemed commercial or industrial.[11] In 1991 the Bush Administration proposed even stricter billboard controls. Periodically, state and local restrictions add to billboard placement woes. For example, local neighborhood groups in larger cities have demanded removal or change in billboard messages. There are restrictions to even the basic sign design, for example, to "spectaculars," flamboyant signs which may distract traffic or which owerwise prove to be a visual problem. However, some "spectacular" billboards likely are "grandfathered," since they pre-date restrictive legislation.[12]

OAAA's Burns says:

> Billboards have a special allure to small businesses incapable of affording most traditional advertising. In fact, 64 percent of the advertisers on billboards are local businesses and services that cannot afford alternative forms of advertising. For many advertisers like those involved in tourism, billboards are simply irreplaceable. In 39 states tourism is the number one industry and billboards are the advertising medium of choice for the tourism industry. In 1989 the travel and amusements industry spent a combined total of $217 million on billboard advertising. No business spent more on billboards than the travel/tourism and entertainment/amusements industries.
>
> Results from a recently concluded U.S. Travel Data Center survey reveal that 93% of Americans agree that billboards are important to travelers when looking for travel-related services. Eighty-two percent rely on billboards to locate restaurants, motels, tourist attractions, service stations and other travel-related services. Sixty percent said billboards are their *primary* source of travel information, and 25% said billboards were their only source of information.[13]

During the 1980s and 1990s, some large city neighborhood action groups in New York and Chicago have voiced serious concerns about some of these ad vehicles. They object to billboards touting alcohol and cigarettes, especially when near churches or schools in the poorer areas of a city. As a result of vigorous sustained campaigns, billboard owners did move many of these boards to other, more acceptable areas according to *Chicago Tribune* and *Chicago Sun-Times* articles in 1990.[14] Not content with the above progress on billboard removals, a Catholic priest further urged the city of Chicago to enact tougher measures in this area.[15]

Burns addresses some of these local billboard concerns from the OAAA's official standpoint:

> Ten years ago, tobacco advertising was 40.3% of our industry revenues. The billboard industry's top growth categories last year included entertainment and amusements, healthcare and the media. The outdoor industry estimates that only 10% of its inventory is allocated to tobacco advertising. Our industry has aggressively diversified its category base and relies on many products and services for its livelihood.
>
> We, as individual companies and as an industry, have actively sought the advice of community and national leaders, and they have helped us formulate a voluntary Code of Advertising Practices which effectively addresses community concerns about the advertising of products that may not be sold to minors.
>
> The policy encourages individual OAAA companies to "establish exclusionary zones which prohibit advertisements of all products illegal for sale to minors which are either intended to be read from, or within 500 feet of, established places of worship, primary and secondary schools, and hospitals."[16]

Billboards not only serve as a conventional medium but when used in various forms, sizes and for special purposes tend to become an alternative vehicle as well. Therefore, they undergo numerous applications aside from the traditional roadside-highway free-standing units. As previously noted, they may appear on the sides of buildings, on phone-stands, at transit stops, attached to the sides of trucks and even as mobile or "rolling" billboards. The latter utilize specially built truck-trailers for two-sided displays.

Today, relatively few so-called "spectacular billboards" remain. These vehicles range from lighted to moving-parts displays. In touring New York City's Times Square area, viewers can get numerous glimpses of spectacular billboards. Some are permanent and others come and go, depending on the show or item advertised at one time. One of two eye-catching spectaculars includes a 23 x 32-

foot TV screen, featuring brief entertainment/informational bits. Letters around the sides of the giant video display spell "SONY." Some questions did arise concerning possible interference with normal traffic flow.[17] The other spectacular nearby is a reproduction of Leonardo da Vinci's painting, *Mona Lisa*, appearing 250 times the original size of the work. Van Wagner Communications sponsored the project to celebrate the "renaissance" of the Times Square area, a massive building revitalization program in the 1990s.[18]

Two quite different book-type ad media contrast with the billboard efforts. First, telephone yellow pages (always a generic name—no TM) essentially constitutes an all-ad medium. Sometimes it is multi-volumed. These telephone directories may include business and industry as well as geographic and even tourism information says John Taff, Yellow Pages Association spokesman.[19] Today the yellow pages usually contain special topical guides and indices, making them versatile, practical and inclusive.[20] Even the advertising and promotion of the vehicle has become far more aggressive and competitive since the 1984 AT&T divestiture. This left the all-ad vehicle in the hands of the regional Bell companies such as the Chicago-based Ameritech.[21]

Another traditional medium that consists virtually exclusively of advertising is the ubiquitous catalog. At the start of the 1990s, the quarterly *Catalog Handbook* listed over 5,000 catalogs in America, 300 in gardening alone. Most of them are mailed, often as an integral part of direct mail campaigns.[22] When many of us think of catalogs, the big, general vehicles probably come to mind. Sears and Spiegel volumes are still healthy publications. Rumors abounded in early 1991 that Sears was discontinuing its general catalog. However, this proved false. Responding to such speculation Sears, Roebuck's Chairman and Chief Executive Officer, Edward A. Brennan said: "Reports that we have decided to sell or close our catalog business are false. The company is committed to the profitable growth of the catalog business."[23]

More popular catalogs are in circulation to more potential customers, therefore possibilities for clutter are higher than ever. Perhaps, a good indication of the prevalence of mail-order advertising is the previously mentioned *Catalog Handbook*, the publication aimed at mail-order customers.[24] In 1991, the postal rate hike did hurt catalogs. However, direct mail rivals responded by reducing catalogs, mailing them jointly and targeting their mail more precisely.[25] Also to be noted is that catalogs rely on their unusual array of products. In addition they depend on their availability in the home as a convenient, hassle-free, time-saving means to order desired products. Often, these are hard-to-get items or items not available in local stores.

Catalogs are usually included in the broad direct mail category, along with numerous other printed ads and sample product items. A 1950s term still considered offensive to the Direct Marketing Association (DMA) is "junk-mail." DMA's Chet Dalzell states that today's direct mail advertising is, in large part, targeted. Because so many customers—a record of 98.6 million in 1990—respond to these targeted direct mail offers, "junk" is considered a pejorative term that means different types of advertising mail to different types of people. In fact, DMA claims US surveys in recent years reveal that the average person receives fewer than two pieces of direct mail advertising per day. The association also says the mail medium delivers a much higher percentage of potential customers when compared to other major direct response media. This compares to 2,000 other ad exposures to individuals in a given day. Therefore, actual ad clutter by mail advertising seems less significant than many people may have perceived. In short, DMA claims direct mail, a highly targeted medium, can deliver customers more effectively than other major media.[26]

However, Barbara Mahany in the *Chicago Tribune* (1991) noted that letter-carriers may complain that much of their delivery is direct mail. Common observations have discovered that some recipients feel that they receive too much of this type of mail advertising and that some of it can even prove to be questionable, even deceiving. It is not uncommon to find envelopes containing vague or sometimes even misleading pitches, hoping to entice one to open them. When envelope messages are vague, they can bring into question even exactly who is sending the message. Deception occurs when envelopes are deliberately disguised, e.g. to look like important, official or quite critical correspondence. One magazine firm is notorious for adding: "Urgent and Critical" to its renewal-form envelopes.[27] Postal authorities are working to make it illegal to disquise envelopes containing ads as being government mail.

Alternative Media Emerge:
Innovative, Visible and Questionable

Alternative media—in a wide variety of

vehicles, some old and some new—have made themselves more visible in advertising. Their emergence is significant, for these proliferating vehicles tend to use aggressive marketing tactics, including questionable claims of performance. These non-traditional media tend to supplement or complement conventional (mainstream) vehicles (newspapers, magazines, TV, etc.). Essentially, most of those so-called non-conventional media focus basically on billboard formats (signs, posters, leaflets) and some specialty items (useful aids with ads printed upon them).

Why are we seeing and hearing more of these non-traditional media? The answers are varied and somewhat involved. There is certainly some dissatisfaction with the higher costs, poor targeting and somewhat dwindling audiences of conventional media. Alternatives have capitalized on these and other shortcomings through aggressive marketing claims and tactics to lure potential advertisers to their ranks. These newer media often have emerged for money-making reasons and are often able to begin operation on little capital, believes Roger Baron, a Foote, Cone and Belding Vice President, Chicago. Both traditional and non-traditional ad vehicles are essentially scrambling for the same market.[28]

Numerous newspaper and magazine articles began appearing in the late 1980s and early 1990s stating that alternative vehicles add to the total advertising environment. This helps give rise to the notion that advertising clutter is all around us, leaving few places untouched. In a 1989 *US News & World Report* article, John Leo reports that some New York City taxis are equipped with back-seat electronic message boards that blink hard-sell ads at seemingly defenseless riders. Leo says that traditional media are in "vague disrepute," causing a rush to "cut through the [ad] clutter."[29]

With traditional lines blurring between promotion and advertising, alternative endeavors have mushroomed. These range from the taxi ad message machine to such areas as athletic and concert promotions, even to naming major football bowl games for major firms. Virginia Slims and Volvo sponsor tennis tournaments; Kool cigarettes promotes jazz festivals. Annual college football bowl games also have looked to major corporate association to defray costs. The result is commercial sponsorship of such bowls as: Federal Express Orange, USF&G Sugar, Mobil Cotton, Mazda Gator, John Hancock, Domino's Pizza, Copper and Blockbuster.[30]

While promoters have achieved corporate name exposure at major special events, others tend to employ lesser but still effective vehicles. Some ads have appeared in airline, restaurant and bar restrooms. Enterprising merchants have even taken the traditional business card and turned it into a more viable marketing tool. In addition to name, address and phone number, a few choice product/service notes are included. This is usually accomplished by adding color and sketches or even color photographs.

In a *USA Today* article, James Cox observed that faster than one can hide by switching channels or turning pages, advertisers are discovering new ways to find you by what some might term a "search-and-annoy" mission. Cox claimed that while alternative media can claim only a minute share of the total advertising revenues, they hold enough promise that some major marketers assign in-house teams to investigate their potential.[31]

Alternative Media:
Measurement and Effectiveness Factors

There are numerous reasons for alternative ad media attraction and success besides traditional media shortcomings, such as rising costs and audience-shifting. Increased regionalization of media planning, calling for more focus on local markets has aided alternatives whose forte is in this area. Also important are advances in technology and "the continual drive for innovation." Non-traditional media complement "traditional broadcast and print by extending the advertising message."[32]

Alternative media can be variously viewed as upstarts, exaggerated claims-makers, traditional media replacements, privacy-invaders and complements or supplements to traditional media. Further aiding them is the narrowing of the link or gap between conventional advertising and promotional efforts. Clients hope to build frequency, reach some specific target markets and perhaps even help cut ad clutter, usually viewing alternatives as viable, economical and targeted vehicles. Perhaps ironically, some discover themselves in an escalating spiral to find even more alternative ad possibilities. After all, new ideas tend to breed more new ideas.[33]

Advertisers are cautioned not to turn their "backs to unique or different media ideas" because they may be "bound up by rigid disciplines," says Richard Kostyra, Executive Vice President, U.S. Director of Media Services, J. Walter Thompson. Some measurement questions remain for alternative ad proponents to answer. Specialized media forms should be selected to meet specific communication needs rather than specific cost-per-thousand (CPM) goals. Marketers must be cautious and consider that the newer vehicles usually offer no real basis of comparison with traditional forms. Alternatives should be analyzed carefully but fairly within the context of specific marketing goals.[34]

When the average person is exposed to hundreds of ads per day, and likely remembers only a few, it becomes difficult to grab and hold one's attention. Today's consumer is likely media-sophisticated and has become used to ad-clutter. The result, often, is indifference. Therefore, advertisers look for new and fresh approaches to capture the attention of potential customers. For example, Jeep and GE refrigerators chose to supplement their marketing efforts by advertising, respectively, on Baltimore parking meters and on Arm & Hammer Baking Soda boxes.[35]

Types and Styles of Alternative Media: Some Comments and Concerns

Videotapes have become a notable competitor to broadcast and cable TV outlets as an advertising vehicle or at least as a factor in marketing. In the 1980s, many advertisers (e.g., Pepsi and Coke) began placing commercials with movies and other related opportune media. Some patrons object to this practice but some advertising executives defend the growing medium because it allows for targeting of specific demographics.[36]

Alternative pitches even appear sandwiched among the "exchange material" accessed by phone-line connections, all contained on computer bulletin board services. These usually tout goods and services of interest to the highly targeted computer enthusiast market. Other unusual forms are facsimile-transmitted flyer-type ads and unsolicited telephone calls promoting certain goods and services. These are often computer handled calls using sophisticated databases and technical equipment. Even "900" type phone calls (time, weather, etc.) for which the caller pays a premium often include commercials interspersed in their messages.[37]

While free-sample distribution and product demonstrations have traditionally been in-store functions, these have also taken to the streets and to TV. Observing the Chicago Loop for two decades, 1970-1990, a broad general pattern emerges. Typically, in more recent years, free samples consist of edibles, but in the 1970s and early 1980s when cigarette give-away campaigns were launched, samples were generously handed out to all who asked. Often new product brands make their debuts but reinforcement for established products also has been a frequent goal.[38]

Smartfood Marketing Team, or "SMUT," managed to attract considerable attention in the Chicago Loop during the summer of 1990 with ambitious and flamboyant promotional handouts, one of which became a hit. It featured performances of people dancing on truck-tops and sidewalks, donned in black-and-yellow plastic popcorn bag outfits, culminating with the distribution of free Smartfood Pop Corn samples to all takers.[39]

Several SuperCuts Hair shops have taken advantage of the inexpensive but seemingly effective sandwichboard ad vehicle. Mobile billboards occasionally make an appearance in the Chicago Loop and adjoining Near Northside. These consist of two-sided large, colorful posters carried on specially built "uni-body" trailer-truck vehicles. Camel Cigarettes has been one of the more prominent Chicago advertisers with their Old Joe camel mascot image featured.[40]

Larry Anthony, head of Mobile Media, Inc., Milwaukee, says his firm has created a special copyrighted design for its mobile advertising vehicles. They use a patented poster panel interchange which allows advertisements/products to be changed within ten minutes. In addition, a specially designed fluorescent lighting system illuminates the mobile ads at night.[41]

Mobile Billboards, Inc., with a Chicago area office in Michigan City, Indiana, is headquartered in Huntington, California. Its president, John "Buckeye" Epstein, notes that the mobile media industry consists of more than billboards on wheels. In addition, there are specialized motor vehicles created in the form of a beer can, for example. In the past, some may have been familiar such as a hot dog wagon advertising effort.[42]

During the summer of 1990 the *Chicago Observer*, a specialty newspaper, placed dozens of unconventional-looking newsboxes, featuring 3 x 4-foot poster displays on the entire fronts of the rectangular frames. These vehicles created two controversies. One was that they were generally considered "eyesores"; and two, they contained a McDonald's mini-billboard, giving the impression the giant food firm was a major advertiser. In addition, serious questions arose relating to the ad vehicle's legality. While many passers-by obviously thought the giant fast food firm was a formidable supporting advertiser, closer examination revealed different facts. Actually, the McDonald's poster merely referred to a local McDonald's ad appearing in the *Chicago Observer* newspaper, contained in the same display-case with the ad poster. Even

Examples of rolling billboards. (Reprinted with permission of Mobile Media, Inc., Milwaukee).

10   **Advertising and Popular Culture**

An Illinois Bell advertisement on a Chicago bus.

An example of humor in advertising.

Utility poles are frequently used for advertising purposes.

Conventional and Alternative Advertising Media 11

A woman passes out handbills in downtown Chicago.

The Chicago skyline is cluttered with advertisements.

An example of the use of space above the streets of Chicago for advertising.

the *Wall Street Journal*'s headline to a story on this topic implies a more positive McDonald's affiliation: "McDonald's Ads on Mini-Billboards Irk Some Chicagoans."[43]

The estimated 520 *Chicago Observer* mini-billboards—news-boxes (combined unit) were ordered removed in April, 1991, after the City of Chicago won a Seventh US Circuit Court of Appeals order. The city had been fighting for such removal since the displays first appeared in the Chicago Loop/Near Northside in mid-1990.[44]

Another advertising pitch sailed to unfavorable response during the summer of 1990. An oversized electronic billboard floated around in the Chicago River (Chicago Harbor area), operated by Lakeview Advertising. While the effort was relatively short-lived since city officials soon stopped the enterprise, Lakeview appealed the case in court. In late April, 1991, US District Judge James B. Zagel threw the appeal out, denying any First Amendment violations, as the firm had alleged.[45]

Ad benches can be found just outside the immediate Chicago Loop and in many outlying areas of the city. They sometimes are placed in groups, cluttering street corners, particularly at busy bus stop points. In late 1990 the Chicago City Council passed an ordinance to restrict the numbers of such ad benches, including provisions for possible "bench-free zones" on a ward by ward basis.[46] In the spring of 1991, ad bench companies became gravely concerned that the city officials' estimates of the numbers of ad benches were much too high, and more pointedly that the city was preparing to curb the number of benches allowed to carry advertising.[47]

The skies are certainly not immune from advertising. Sky-writing has all but disappeared because of the tedium of creating the message and its somewhat brief life. More usual today is the airborne banner. A light plane pulling a large banner over a football or baseball stadium will gather thousands of impressions. Albeit expensive, the Goodyear Company has built a sports tradition with its blimp. Not only does the company make thousands of impressions on the fans present at the sporting event but it gains free publicity from the television broadcast by furnishing a flying scaffold for television cameras. Epstein, head of Mobile Billboards, Inc., boasts that his firm offers helium-filled remote-controlled indoor balloons. This ad vehicle encircles large arenas. In addition, the firm owns both manned and unmanned blimps for ad displays.[48]

Before delving specifically into in-store alternative media, a few comments from an advertising agency executive should prove helpful. Baron, (Vice President, Director of Media Research, Foote, Cone & Belding, Chicago), emphasizes the notion that alternative media are primarily billboard, sign, poster and leaflet oriented. Other variations, especially technical versions, are becoming more evident with each passing year especially in retail store promotions.[49] The next section focuses, in detail, on a number of major in-store alternative ad vehicles. Many of these feature rather advanced sophisticated technology.

In-Store Alternative Media:
A Specialized World

While a deluge of alternative vehicles has appeared in retail stores, usually supermarkets, during the 1980s, the trend of growth continues into the 1990s. One of the more successful pioneers is ActMedia Shopping Carts, established in 1972. Its major ad device consists of an 8 x 10-inch ad attached to special display units placed on both the inside and outside of shopping carts in participating grocery stores. ActMedia, a unit of Dallas-based Heritage Media, anticipated spending by 1992 between $60 and $75 million installing TV monitors in 5,000 grocery stores. Checkout Channel, associated with Turner Broadcasting System of Atlanta, features live TV news, supposedly the first in-store system of its kind.[50] ActMedia (AisleVision) makes 20 x 30-inch ad space available on overhead aisle directories. Each contains two four-color pitches to identify selected products sold on aisles of participating stores.[51]

The TV screen is making its way into grocery stores for additional applications. One is IRI's VideOcart, consisting of mini-TV screens attached to grocery store carts. Some 5,000 stores are expected to participate by 1994. The 6 x 9-inch screens are equipped with infrared sensing devices that signal their location in the store. In each aisle the device promotes selected products with 10-second ads and price information. VideOcart noted in 1991 that units would not be in stores until about 1992. The reason for the delay is that it is working with IBM to redesign a shopping cart display unit.[52]

Coupon Solution is a computerized target-marketing system designed to issue coupons at grocery store checkout points. Featured in 1,500 stores in 1988, its premise is based on customer purchases at the checkout counter. Another firm, Top Image Resource, tested a similar vehicle, Audio Coupon Dispenser, that automatically delivers

Conventional and Alternative Advertising Media

cents-off coupons and a thirteen-second audio pitch when a customer approaches.[53]

POP Radio, a departure from these two types of devices, is a customized musical programming setup targeted to over 10,000 drug and grocery store customers. Ads interrupt disc-jockey hosted music and entertainment shows at specified times. At the other end of the spectrum is "SilentRadio," composed of three-foot by eight-inch high screens. Flashing words and phrases, along with simple graphics and formed LEDs, constitute the messages viewed. Segments of news, weather, sports and entertainment are custom-packaged for different establishments. These places usually consist, however, of bars, restaurants, hospitals and bowling alleys. Most cities feature ads interspersed with the editorial content, according to Carmen Ulloa, Regional Sales Manager for Chicago. As of early 1991, 7,000 such boards appeared throughout America with 300 in Chicago alone.[54]

Perhaps, most of us do not usually associate motion picture screens with conventional advertising, a medium often scorned by patrons and even movie studios. However, there are a number of life-long movie theatre patrons who not only associate ads as an acceptable segment of their viewing but who seem to like them as a rule. Screenvision, a national network of first-run movie theaters, has been distributing made-for-cinema commercials since 1976. As of 1988, it had contracts with 1,800 movie houses, representing 5,000 screens, displaying commercials.[55] In addition, there are many products highlighted in a growing number of motion pictures. Examples are Pepsi in "Back to the Future II" and Reese's Pieces in "E.T."[56]

Even the health club offers no respite from ads. Numerous exercise facilities—notably the largest, Bally—began in 1991 to feature Health Club TV (HCTV). In addition, there is Health Club Radio Network (HCRN). In short, these ad vehicles consist of dozens of TV monitors or speakers throughout specified areas of participating health clubs. Programs of interest to workout enthusiasts, such as music videos, are interspersed with commercials.[57]

Channel One, Special Reports Magazines/TV: Unique Targeted Alternatives

Whittle Communications of Knoxville, Tennessee, is often considered America's best known large-scale multi-alternative media proponent. Its Channel One, unveiled in the spring of 1990, is the most publicized, best remembered and most controversial of its offerings. Aimed at high school students, this is a daily, twelve-minute satellite-transmitted television series. By March of 1991, Channel One boasted a teenage viewing audience of more than 3.8 million in over 7,000 high schools across America, noted Gary Belis, Corp. Relations, Whittle Communications. News, public affairs, features and entertainment segments attempt to stimulate and educate youngsters for ten minutes. However, commercials occupy the remaining two minutes. These ads are light, breezy and colorful in style, usually containing a flare for interest and entertainment, notes Belis.[58] Despite criticism that it "force-feeds" advertising to teenagers, Channel One had a relatively strong first year.[59]

Another Whittle Communications innovation targets elementary, high school and college students. The medium consists of one-piece folding wall-boards measuring 60 x 45-inches. These quite colorful, richly illustrated posters attract attention because of Whittle's claims that they are appealing, interesting and informative formats. The top 75% of the layout consists of feature material and the lower 25% is devoted to three equally divided ad segments. Pitches represent mostly beverage, food and grooming products.[60]

"Special Reports" is another Whittle innovation, this one aimed at patients waiting to see their physicians. Recorded television programs with health themes directed to young female adults are presented in the waiting rooms. Also present are high-quality four-color magazines. Several editions center on various topics from entertainment to psychology. The TV programs and magazine articles are aimed at women eighteen to thirty-nine years of age and provide a very controlled environment for commercials. Nielsen Marketing, during 1990-1991, checked ad recall at Whittle's request. Patrons who were exposed to these two physicians' waiting room media were questioned to determine the effectiveness of the ad messages. Initial results, according to Belis, were encouraging.[61]

Referring to Whittle's aggressive target audience media projects, Belis emphasized that when individuals fail, for whatever reason, to come to the medium, then the medium must be brought to them. This includes whatever editorial content and ads are designated to target these specific groups.[62]

Traditional Media Response: Strong Defenses and Aggressive Offenses

While the advertising industry has seen such a phenomenal growth in the use of non-traditional or alternative media, the fact remains that traditional vehicles continue as the mainstay of most advertising campaigns. There is a good reason for that—traditional media deliver large audiences at an attractive cost. That is not to say that some alternative vehicles cannot do the same. Primarily it is simply that measuring their effectiveness and reach can be difficult, and in some cases, impossible. Although technology and changes in our society are altering some of our accepted thinking about advertising media, advertising executives are quick to point out that you cannot argue with the proven track record of the major media. Len Feldman, TV Bureau of Advertising, correctly maintains that although television audiences have been fragmented and audience levels are lower than they were in the 1970s, the medium still remains the most viable for advertisers: "If the advertiser does not use TV for his or her basic initial reach," Feldman asks, "what other major media are really left from which to choose?"[63]

The TV Bureau spokesman reminds us that television advertising is now dispersed. Some viewers have switched from the networks to cable, independent stations and the like. In short, there exists today, fragmentation. Many of these TV vehicles are quite narrowly targeted, primarily serving specific interests. For instance, if one advertised on CNN, one would reach a certain audience. Clients would then need to supplement this with other broader-based ad coverage potentials. This example holds true even more so for alternative media reach prospects.[64]

How much are fragmentation, zipping and zapping, audience-shifts, ad clutter, audience media sophistication, as well as some questionable programming, hurting the major TV networks? Feldman acknowledged that these factors do have an effect on the television medium. However, he felt that as of 1991 these still were not overly significant. Specific negative fallout is still too uncertain and too difficult to measure accurately: "First of all, these and all other media out there are competing for a certain basic pool of ad dollars," Feldman said. Any major expenditures for these non-traditional vehicles will have some negative effect on television and other mainstream media. At present (1991) however, this does not seem to be too threatening.[65]

Feldman noted that the forte of the newer media is targeting—filling in for the traditional advertising vehicles: "However, the non-traditional vehicles are quite costly and yield somewhat limited results. They certainly do, however, have their place in the overall scheme of service and product promotion," the TVB spokesman noted. Feldman reminds us that while targeting is an uppermost goal for many advertisers, it may be even more important to combine this tactic with other broad-based strategies. He concluded that, as of 1991, alternatives did not seem to be having any overall negative effect on television or any of the other major traditional media.[66]

The TV Bureau spokesman relayed some significant statistics taken from his research files. The total ad volume for TV indicates that from 1990 to 1996, a continued steady increase from over $30 billion in 1991 to over $43 billion by 1996 will likely occur. The average number of TV viewing hours during the first half of 1990 was six hours and fifty-six minutes per TV home per day. However, this was down twelve minutes from the posted seven hours and eight minutes during the first half of 1989. Nevertheless, these figures still are an encouraging sign for the continued success of network TV, related Feldman.[67]

Finally, the Bruskin Associates' 1990 "Media Comparisons" report, published by the TV Bureau, notes some of the major advantages of television usage. The report claims that 89% of all adults watch TV, more adult patronage than any other medium. More time is spent with television than all other media combined. This is true for every major demographic group. Specifically relating to TV advertising, three categories received praise: Most Authoritative—57% of adults felt TV was the most authoritative medium in advertising; Most Exciting—76% opted for TV commercials; Most Influential—81% chose TV advertising.[68]

Lucille Luongo, Senior Vice President, Corporate Relations, Katz Communications, supported much of what Feldman related. Furthermore, she questioned alternative media's marketing values, noting that many advertisers use such vehicles either when they cannot afford television or when they are seeking some specific target or supplement to their regular advertising efforts: "Someone is trying to prove the thesis that alternative media are equal to TV," Luongo said, "and this is simply not true." Conceding that daytime TV audiences have changed for numerous reasons, she said that new viewers have moved in to take their places. While zipping and zapping problems still exist, according to Luongo their effects on TV audiences are too difficult to measure as of 1991: "It's simply not as bad as some would have you to believe." Luongo said, "Make no mistake about it, network TV is very much alive."[69]

Baron of Foote, Cone & Belding, Chicago, basically agrees with both Luongo and Feldman and adds a few salient points of his own. He leads off by pointing out that TV's share of total advertising dollars is unchanged between 1980 and 1990, at 21% (McCann-Erickson). Even television's reach-potential is unchanged in that time-period, still holding at 98% of the total US households. In reality, all that has happened is that the audience has fragmented into various vehicles: network, cable, syndication, independent stations and the like. Simply put, this means that fewer people watch any one ad. For instance, in November 1985, the average network prime-time program was viewed in 16.9% of US homes. In November 1990, this decreased to 12.6% (A.C. Nielsen). To achieve 100 gross rating points (the commonly used measure of media height), it now takes nine spots versus six in the past.[70]

"In my opinion," Baron said, "the growth of many alternative media is being pushed essentially by entrepreneurs. These individuals often create a business with relatively little capital and sometimes little notable media background." Like Luongo, Baron feels that many advertisers seek alternatives when they cannot afford TV. Although the coverage is highly targeted, the audience figures are often questionable and cannot be compared to the closely scrutinized research available from traditional media. Also, the media have more than mass appeal to offer. They present advertisers with the ability to deliver in-depth messages with generally wide appeal, and that is a potentially serious problem with most alternative ad vehicle formats. Thus far, Baron repeats: "Most have appeared in 'billboard' forms, i.e. simple card, poster and related styles, placed in the potential customers' environment."[71]

According to Baron, no matter how selective alternatives try to be, advertisers cannot count on them to do the core of their promotional tasks. In order for a plan to succeed, it must rely primarily upon mass media and upon alternative vehicles. "This leads us to thinking of non-traditional vehicles as supplements, as adding that certain 'sizzle' to the standard plan. One could say this is a 'dash' of A-1 sauce on the steak; that is, a nice addition."[72]

Baron says that "In reality, what we are seeing is the new, the innovative and the trendy getting attention out of proportion to their actual value." He further states: "Make no mistake about it, while the relatively new media alternatives can supplement the basic, traditional vehicles, no one should have the distorted picture that they are replacing them."[73]

Part of television's problems lie in difficulties facing the mass media of the 1990s, such as the need to hit specified audiences more accurately. Like other media, TV is being prodded to present more complete data on its audience composition. "Delivering tons of undifferentiated audiences to advertisers" is no longer a sufficient goal for TV and magazine operations, noted Joshua Levine, (*Forbes* 17 Sept. 1990). "Mass Media are going to have to become less mass; today's marketers want to target their messages." By the start of the 1990s the magazine industry (along with network TV) was experiencing notable downturns. The decline can be seen even in the number of new magazine introductions, dropping from around 600 in 1989 to around 500 in 1991.[74]

According to NBC's Nicholas Schiavone, head of the major networks' research arm, CONTAM (Committee on National Television Audience Measurement) New York, each of the three networks has coverage of 98% of US households. No other medium can claim such depth, not even independent or super-stations. During a typical seven-day week, the three networks get into nine out of ten households with unequaled coverage and reach. To illustrate the effectiveness of network television power, Schiavone noted that if you put one spot simultaneously on NBC, ABC, CBS—say, Tuesday at 8 PM EST—you would reach over 40% of American households. The TV medium thus offers unique, unequaled opportunities in marketing and efficiency for advertising agencies and sponsors alike.[75]

Schiavone admits that the total TV audience the networks now enjoy during an average minute of prime time had declined (62% in 1991 vs. 92% in 1978). However, the same percentage of the population tunes to the networks today, as did twenty years ago, but it stays tuned somewhat less in time. He uses a hypothetical party as a metaphor. People are still coming to the network party; but as previously noted, they are spending less time there. Television still reaches—according to Nielsen figures—98% of all US households. On average, the typical household spends more than three hours per day, viewing the three networks for over twenty-one hours during a seven-day week.[76]

Fragmentation does exist and the network share of the overall audience has declined. This is based on a given average minute survey. The hypothetical party the networks are throwing finds just as many people attending as twenty or thirty years ago, but the total time spent is less. While the network viewing time decline certainly is real, it is not the entire story. To repeat, Schiavone relates that the usage is the same: 98% of US households.

The clutter problem affects all in the media, not merely television. Clutter may be a perception of seeing TV ads, per se, anywhere, e.g. independent and super stations, cable networks, local stations. It is certainly no more a network problem today, than it was twenty years ago.[77]

In scientific surveys, Schiavone has consistently discovered that over eight out of ten people feel that advertising is a fair price to pay to watch free TV to avoid paying money for sports and other cable programming. A much smaller percentage also favors ads included with cable viewing as a fair price to pay for TV viewing—given what is already paid in cable subscription fees.

It is socially acceptable to criticize advertising. People say "yes" automatically when asked if there are too many ads on TV; "it's their perception." Schiavone stressed his core point that if one looks at an advertising schedule on network TV, the problem of a decline in time spent affects frequency of exposure and not reach. One needs to bear in mind that people have to be reached a certain number of times for the ad to be effective. Because these individuals are spending less time watching network television, it takes more spots now than in years past to persuade/inform the viewers. However, one may not actually need more to get one's effective reach.[78]

Yes, zipping and zapping do have effects and can pose a challenge. However, for the present, in 1991, there is no real quantitative basis for alarm. If one zips through the TV dial, one is bound to hit upon a commercial one otherwise would not have come upon, agreeing with Katz's Luongo. As far as zapping is concerned, the networks have warned advertisers and their agencies alike that they must make their ads as interesting as the programs carrying them. Herein lies the real challenge that the networks face. Relating to advertising clutter, there is no more commercial time on the networks than there was previously. The perception is that there is an overall clutter of ads on cable networks as well as super and independent stations.[79] Gadd responded to this problem by expressing this observation: "Could TV ad clutter be related, at least in part, to the perception caused by the shortening of commercial lengths? Now, there are six where there used to be two or three."[80]

Schiavone notes that there are two other factors causing decreased network viewing: tape-rentals and video games, not to mention increased cable and satellite channel potential via pay-per-view. Increased cable channels mean increased competition, of course, and that is the name of the game. So far as videotape rentals are concerned, the degree of defection may likely be somewhat higher on Saturdays, but this could change in the future. Video games such as Nintendo, for that matter, may already be affecting the networks or other TV sources. The suspicion is that this is "extended usage," that is, extra employment of the TV set, aside from regular viewing. One theory is the active playing of games competes with the passive viewing of television.[81]

Relating to measurement, the Nielsen people-meter controversy is far from satisfactorily being resolved by 1991. The current system is questionable in terms of both design and execution. It must be repaired or replaced, Schiavone states. He claims that CONTAM operation has tried for nearly thirty years to bring about a more accurate and reliable TV audience measurement system. So called "lost viewers" found by ABC and the other networks were never lost, but were merely those "non-home" TV fans such as the college population. TV viewing in bars and other public places is largely unmeasured and is an approximate 3% "bonus" to advertisers. CONTAM is most concerned, however, with getting an even more accurate, reliable and perhaps, more useful measurement of the other 97% of the TV audience, the household audience.[82]

Mass Media Problems:
The 1990s See Some Changes

Richard Zoglin notes network television is "no longer the only game in town" the basic reason for the decline in the last decade. According to Zoglin, the major nets "are victims of a 'changing TV universe.'" In the past, they have made repeated denials of the VCR's adverse effect or that of cable and direct-to-station program syndication. However, zapping out commercials on time-delayed program viewing does hurt especially when combined with the growing video rental/purchase market. The TV set remote-control unit brings about active channel changing known as "grazing." Even technology advances such as high-definition, satellite-direct-to-home view and other new wonders offer future threats to the networks, according to Zoglin.[83]

In a later piece for *Time* in 1990, Zoglin notes that the total share of the TV audience dipped for the networks, and even valiant, well-publicized new programming, as a whole, failed. The networks began to realize they need to adjust to a "new, more competitive game." There was talk of networks adopting the strategy that if huge audiences were no longer possible, then the right ones should be sought. These, of course, are the more defined audiences that ultimately attract the most advertising dollars.[84]

Conventional and Alternative Advertising Media

As of the beginning of March, 1991, "ABC, NBC, CBS...tallied their combined share of the nation's television-viewing audience, this time [at] 62 percent." The February 1991 sweeps period result ended up haunting the "big three," for it was "the lowest ever recorded." The days of 92% of the total TV audience figures of the late 1970s seemed gone forever. In a *Chicago Tribune* article, media writer Kenneth R. Clark noted that "despite frequent network predictions that cable soon will plateau and grow no more, its multiple channels are robbing the network audience bank at an unprecedented rate."[85] While the TV Bureau of Advertising reported TV advertising revenues showed a 6% increase in 1990 to reach a record $22.6 billion, ad revenues for the combination of ABC, CBS and NBC dropped 2.2% during the fourth quarter compared with the same period of 1989.[86]

TV technology advances can further threaten the TV networks. Besides the proposed HDTV and cable innovations, there are several sophisticated satellite ventures. These include satellite transmitted direct-to-home channels and pay-per-view channels such as the proposed Sky Cable, an NBC-Rupert Murdoch venture restructured in early 1991. That same year Paramount Pictures and MCA joined forces for the satellite venture, TVN Entertainment Corp. TVN is a system that allows people who have home satellite dishes to order movies by telephone and receive them via satellite. The revised system was expected to expand from four to ten channels by mid-1991. In May, 1991, TVN became fully operational. Its goal, according to leader Stuart Levin, is to reach the fifteen million homes in rural cableless America. Also in 1991, Time-Warner, Inc., an entertainment and cable company, announced plans for a sophisticated cable TV system that will allow viewers to interact with their sets to order movies or other services.[87] Clearly, these and other related ventures can ultimately prove to be a competitive threat to network television.

Billboards seem to continue their woes along with newspapers' problems of rising costs and further decline of afternoon editions. Since the late 1960s, billboards have come under continuous attack as blights and visual polluters of the American landscape. Billboards once a reasonably viable alternative to TV ads banned in the early 1970s, now feel the sting of increased attacks from neighborhood groups. Dodger Stadium in Los Angeles had already limited billboard ads when the structure was built in 1962. Wrigley Field (Chicago Cubs) banned beer billboards around 1980.[88] While Chicago eighborhoods campaign against billboard cigarette and alcohol ads, citizens groups have demanded that such pitches not even appear along city transit lines. Rev. Michael Pfleger, Catholic Priest in Chicago, received specifically national publicity in USA Today, Aug. 28, 1991. The article, among other things, emphasized his determined efforts to rid poorer economically affected Chicago neighborhoods of all alcohol and cigarette billboard advertising. Other larger cities across America had witnessed similar campaigns during 1991. Previously discussed are related outdoor ad incidents: governmental and neighbor groups opposing standard-size billboards, mini-billboards and sidewalk ad bench numbers all scheduled for review during 1991.[89]

At the Chicago Stadium, home of the Chicago Black Hawks and the 1991 world champion Chicago Bulls, "rotating" wall-type billboards appear. These consist of a series of 3 x 5-foot sign-panels extending for seventy feet along the facing of the scorer's table and another ten feet along each of the baselines. A single advertiser's message is displayed on polyvinyl sheeting, housed on rollers in each of the modular panels. During the game, on computer command, the messages are scrolled through the game to reveal the next ad image. The ad exposure coincides with TV shots of the game action.[90]

The rise of more alternatives will not likely cause the death of the mass media as we know them, but the 1990s could easily see great transformation and modification of many of the major media. While we will still be watching and hearing ads in abundance, many simply may present themselves via different media, with different appeals and approaches and perhaps with unique values.

The Future:
Two Ad Executives Respond

Two executives from a pair of highly respected advertising agencies prognosticate on advertising's future. Kostyra told a conference in Canada in 1990 that magazines are expected to contain fewer ads than in the 1980s. However, ads placed on prerecorded videocassette programs are expected to have more impact. The primary reason is that videocassette programs can readily provide the means to target specific groups, such as men, eighteen to twenty-four, or parents of young children.[91]

According to Kostyra, increased commercialization and clutter will continue to trouble the advertising industry in the 1990s "as we search for a solution that advertisers, the media and the consumers can all live with." On the other hand advertisers and their agencies cannot afford to turn their backs on unique media ideas because they "are bound up by rigid disciplines." Taking advantage of new things "is exciting," Kostyra exclaimed. He added: "I think there's a lot to be said for traditional mass vehicles. Even with highly publicized audience fragmentation, the sheer size of audiences of major media vehicles continues to be impressive." Finally, new media must meet product and service needs demographically, geographically and psychologically and with relative cost-effectiveness.[92]

Michael Drexler is Bozell Advertising's first Executive Vice President, Worldwide Media Director. In a 1990 speech to the "Asociacion Mexicana de Agencias de Publicidad" (AMAP) in Mexico City, Drexler said:

New media technologies continue to splinter audiences, and the overall amount of advertising clutter has become overwhelming. Pressure on advertising costs is forcing harder negotiation to lower media prices, and multi-media packaging is creating alliances between companies that never dreamed of working together before.... An atmosphere of competitive cooperation is establishing the worldwide environment of the '90s.... The '90s will be the time to rethink traditional ways of doing business and to create new relationships among advertisers, agencies and media that can produce greater marketing impact.[93]

In 1990 ABC productions decided to sell made-for-TV films and series to NBC and CBS as well as cable services. CNN and *USA Today* are jointly selling cable time and newspaper space.

Bozell was the architect of a two to three-year agreement beginning in 1991 between the Chrysler Corporation and media conglomerate Time-Warner that will include sixteen-page inserts in six Time Warner magazines, plus full sponsorship of special issues of *Fortune*, *People* and *Life*. In addition, promotions with Time-Warner video, recording companies, and book clubs as well as Chrysler product-placement in upcoming Warner theatrical films are part of a deal: "These developments...are a portent of things to come. And they're beginning overseas as well," Drexler said. He reminded his audience that the 1992 European community unification of marketing economy add to this changing media revolution.[94]

"International agency media departments are responding to these changes and in many cases are developing new initiatives," said Drexler. New TV shows are being developed by agencies for their multinational clients. The US is headed toward more integrated communications programs. This allows agencies to reach customer targets from many different directions, using both conventional and unconventional media/marketing tools, including promotions, advertising, direct mail, public relations or special marketing events.[95]

For instance, Bozell works with several media companies to create multimedia programs that cut across their entertainment and information disciplines. Drexler believes that in the 1990s agencies must open their minds to new practices and not allow themselves to be bound by media measurements that are worn-out tools of conventional thinking: "We need to create alliances with the media that can provide innovative solutions to problems of increasing clutter, shifting audiences, and rising media costs," concludes Drexler.[96]

Conclusions: Some Pros and Cons on Conventional and Alternative Media

Advertising, especially in urban America, seems to be practically everywhere we go. As if conventional media, newspapers, magazines, TV and radio did not hit us with enough ads, the alternative media add even more opportunities. Many pitches seek us out in our own environments using alternative media ranging from match covers and sidewalk signs, to grocery store carts with TV screens, and street corner ad benches. Some people feel that advertising may have gone too far by seeking them out in places where they would least expect ads to appear, from physicians' waiting rooms to public rest rooms. How serious is the accusation of privacy intrusion? Should there be, as some have suggested, "ad-free zones"?

Alternative media proponents have made the enthusiastic claim that they are major competitors to the faltering established conventional vehicles, notably broadcast TV. They tout their innovativeness, their uniqueness and their abilities to intercept potential customers and target specific audiences. However, their optimistic forecasts may rest on fragile assumptions. Media do not die; they merely change. Television is now a prime example of a medium in notable flux, mainly via fragmentation into various areas (network, independent stations, cable, etc.); adding to this are audience-shifts, zipping and zapping and the videotape recorder's many applications. Yet, TV, overall, is still very much alive.

The 1990s will likely witness further changes and shifts not only in television but in magazines and newspapers as well. Alternative media will continue to grow and to change, finding their niches in the scheme of advertising. Their main forte is to supplement as well as to complement the conventional vehicles. Conventional vehicles, on the other hand, excel in serving as the primary means to cover broad-based markets. They generally present ad messages with significant depth and impact. Each media form has its own fortes and failings and must be considered accordingly.

Many alternative media claims may be quite legitimate. However, some seem to be exaggerated, overly optimistic and even possibly unfounded. Yet, when properly evaluated and placed, generally in concert with traditional vehicle deliveries, non-traditional media can truly become that complement or supplement. This makes them especially valuable to advertising as a whole. Conversely, some of the propositions favoring conventional media also are probably overstated and may even disregard much of the value of alternatives. Pointedly, this refers to network TV whose cause have been highly touted by leading advertising agencies and the prominent industry representatives. While the case for conventional media's continued effectiveness has been forcefully and even eloquently stated, perhaps it is a bit overstated.

There have been exaggeration, evasion of some notable facts and simply over-insistence that TV's overall performance is really unchanged. Specifically, potential dangers seldom have been fully acknowledged, such as the previously mentioned zipping and zapping, fragmentation and overall audience shifts and less time spent viewing network shows. The major TV audience share by 1991 had sunk to 62%, an all-time low. The glory days of the 1970s are gone, i.e. those when ABC, CBS, NBC claimed over 90% of the total TV audience.

Regardless of media changes, however, the average consumer can still certainly expect to see and hear at least as many commercials as he/she did in the 1980s. They may be more spread out, shifted or placed in different media, but they still likely will be present. Truly, one will probably find ads almost everywhere one goes. Some pitches will continue to seek you out in your own environment. Ad-free zones will probably exist no more than they did in the 1980s. While this may seem a bit hard on advertising, in reality it is just an attempt to paint a reasonably realistic and honest picture. On the other hand, most of us either will tolerate or appreciate ads much of the time. Advertising is not only essential for business and commerce and the economic survival of many media entities, it is far more. Advertising is well entrenched, and it is an integral part of our popular culture. Somehow, while we may criticize, attempt to avoid or become indifferent to advertising, we usually see another side of it: the amusing, the entertaining, the cultural and informative/persuasive aspects which, in the end, can prove quite vital to all of us Americans.

Notes

[1] Joanne Lipman, "Brand-Name Products Are Popping Up in TV Shows," *Wall Street Journal* 19 February 1991: B1.

[2] "Magazine Inserts: 'Stop, Look and Listen,' " J. Walter Thompson, Media Resources and Research, September 1989: 1, 2, 3; Debbie Solomon, Vice President, J. Walter Thompson, Chicago added notes.

[3] Joshua Levine, "The Last Gasp of Mass Media?" *Forbes* 17 September 1990: 178.

[4] *The Magazine Handbook*, Magazine Publishers of America, 1990-91, 59: 2, 3, 6.

[5] "More Agencies Lead Clients to Radio," *Radio: The Most Effective Marketing Solution of Offset Newspapers' Eroding Circulation*, Radio Advertising Bureau (New York 1990) 9.

[6] *Why Radio*, Radio Advertising Bureau, (New York, undated) first five pages, unnumbered; *Radio Facts for Advertisers 1990*, Radio Advertising Bureau (New York 1990) 3, 14.

[7] Laura M. Morandin, Communications Manager, Radio Advertising Bureau, New York, letter to the author, 2 April 1991 (sentence-structure slightly altered for ease of reading and summary-type desirability).

[8] *Outdoor Advertising—Marketing Strategies*, Institute of Outdoor Advertising (New York, undated) 2; "Outdoor, the First Medium," *Outdoor 101*, Institute of Outdoor Advertising (New York, undated) 2.

[9] *Billboard Basics*, Outdoor Advertising Assn. of America (Washington DC, undated) 6, 10.

[10] Kippy Burns, Director of Public Relations, Outdoor Advertising Assn., Washington, D.C., telephone interview, 20 March 1991.

[11] *Billboard Basics* 19, 20.

[12] "U.S. Challenge to Billboards," *New York Times* 19 Feb. 1991: C-8; Burns interview 20 March 1991.

[13] Kippy Burns, Director of Communications, Outdoor Advertising Assn. of America, letter to the author, 26 April 1991.

[14] Carol Jouzaitis, "Billboards a Battleground," *Chicago Tribune* 30 April 1990: 3: 1, 7; "Campaign Against Billboards Continues," *Chicago Sun-Times* 11 November 1990: 26.

[15] Alf Siewers, "Priest Prods City on Stalled Billboard Bans," *Chicago Sun-Times* 7 March 1991: 20.

[16] Burns letter, 26 April 1991.

[17] James Barron, "Catching Times Sq.'s Eye, in a Flash," *New York Times* 16 January 1991: B-12.

[18] "Mona Lisa, I Outdoor You," photo caption, *Chicago Sun-Times* 1 February 1991: 37.

[19] John Taff, *Link*, Associate Editor, American Assn. of Yellow Pages Publishers, telephone interview, Chesterfield, MO, 17 June 1991.

[20] Kathy Pomaville, Media Relations Specialist, Ameritech Publishing, Troy, MI, telephone interview, 18 Feb. 1991; Pomaville, letter to the author, 18 Feb. 1991.

[21] Ameritech News Release, Troy, MI (undated); Alan D. Fletcher, *Yellow Pages Advertising*, rev. ed., American Assn. of Yellow Pages Pub. (Chesterfield, MO, 1987) 5; Advertisement: "Down South. It's Here or Nowhere." (TM), BellSouth Advertising & Publishing Corp. (BAPCO) 1990; Pomaville interview; Pomaville letter.

[22] *Catalog Handbook*, Spring 1991, Enterprise Magazines, Inc., Milwaukee.

[23] Charles A. Brennan, Chairman and Chief Executive Officer, Sears, Roebuck and Co., Sears News Release, Chicago, 30 Jan. 1991.

[24] *Catalog Handbook*, Spring 1991: front-cover, 154; Cindy LaFavre Yorks. "Tabletop Shopping," *Chicago Sun-Times* 27 February 1991: 43.

[25] "Postal Rise May Cancel a Direct-Marketing Edge," *New York Times* 19 February 1991: C-8; Ellen Neuborne, "Catalogers: Adopting to Soaring Costs," *USA Today* 19 February 1991: 2B.

[26] Chet Dalzell, Public Relations Director, Direct Marketing Assn., New York, telephone interviews, 1 March 1991, 24 April 1991; Chet Dalzell, notes to author, 25 April 1991.

[27] Barbara Mahany, "Special Deliverer," *Chicago Tribune* 17 February 1991: 5: 1; Sammy R. Danna, Research and Advertising I Class Presentation-Discussion, Spring 1991, Loyola Univ. of Chicago, Water Tower Campus.

[28] *The New Advertising Media*. J. Walter Thompson, September 1988: 1, 2: Roger Baron, Vice President, Director of Media Research, Foote, Cone & Belding, Chicago, telephone interviews, 30 Jan. 1991, 19 April 1991.

[29] John Leo, "The Proper Place for Commercials," *US News & World Report* 30 October 1989: 71.

[30] "Bowl Line," *USA Today* 31 December 1990: 1E; *Blockbuster Video Magazine* December 1990, back-cover (promotional ad); Sammy R. Danna, Chicago Loop—Near Northside Checks, 1990-1991.

[31] James Cox, "Ad Attack: No Place to Escape," *USA Today* 22 March 1988: 1B; Tom Vercruysse, Chicago Businessman, interview, 14 March 1991; Cox 1B-2B.

[32] *The New Advertising Media*, J. Walter Thompson, September 1988: 1, 2.

[33] *The New Advertising Media* 1, 2; James Wagner, Katz Communications Representative, Chicago, interviews, 24 Jan. 1991, 15 March 1991.

[34] *The New Advertising Media* 2; Richard Kostyra, Vice Pres., U.S. Director of Media Services, J. Walter Thompson, "Communications in the Future: The Changing Media Environment," Speech: "90/90 Vision" Seminar (Canada), August 1990: 7.

[35] Cox 2B; Gary Belis, Corp. Relations, Whittle Communications, telephone interview, 4 February 1991.

[36] Kostyra 4; Kay Felkins, Associate Professor, specialist in Organizational Communication, Dept. of Communication, Loyola Univ. of Chicago, interview, 25 Jan. 1991.

[37] Dale A. Gadd, Head Dept. of Mass Communication, McNeese State Univ., Lake Charles, LA, telephone interview, 26 Jan. 1991, letter to the author, 30 Jan. 1991.

[38] Sammy R. Danna, observations, 1970-1990.

[39] William Spain, "Tagged, Bagged and Snagged," *Advertising Age* 27 August 1990: S-12.

[40] Sammy R. Danna, Observations, Fall 1990, Chicago Loop-Near Northside, SuperCuts Store visits, employee interview, 15, 17 October 1990, Chicago.

[41] Larry Anthony, head, Mobile Media, Inc., Milwaukee, letter, 6 April 1991, telephone interview, 14 February 1991.

[42] John "Buckeye" Epstein, Mobile Billboards, Inc., Huntington Beach, CA, letter 28 May 1991 and telephone interview 24 May 1991.

[43] Andrew Patner, "McDonald's Ads on Mini-Billboards Irk Some Chicagoans," *Wall Street Journal* 29 June 1990: A: 6E; Sammy R. Danna, observations, Summer 1990, Chicago Loop—Near Northside.

[44] Rosalind Rossi, "Court Upholds Ban on Large Newsboxes," *Chicago Sun-Times* 6 April 1991: 5.

[45] John McCarron, "Group Calls Billboard on River an Advertisement for Trouble," *Chicago Tribune* 24 August 1990: 2C: 6; "Ban on Ad Ships in Harbor Upheld," *Chicago Sun-Times* 26 April 1991: 16.

[46] Fran Spielman and Ray Hanania, "Ad Bench Curbs Win Backing of City Panel," *Chicago Sun-Times* 4 December 1990: 3; "Number of Ad Benches Limited," *North Loop News* (Chicago area newspaper) 27 December 1990: 1.

[47] Pamela Sherrod, "Bench Curb Doesn't Sit with Firms," *Chicago Tribune* 9 March 1991: 2: 1.

[48] Epstein, telephone interview, 8 April 1991.

[49] Baron, telephone interview, 24 January 1991.

[50] The New Advertising Media 5; Joann S. Lublin, "In-Store Ads Are Getting Harder to Ignore," *Wall Street Journal* 16 October 1990: B6 (w); Alison Fahey, "Advertising Media Crowd into Aisles," *Advertising Age* 18 June 1990: 18.

[51] *The New Advertising Media* 7.

[52] Martin Wolk, "Shopping Carts Enter Computer Age," *Chicago Tribune* 11 November 1990: 7: 10D; "Hard-Sell Shopping Carts," *Newsweek* 18 July 1988: 46; "IRI's 'VideOcart' Out of Test, Set for Rollout," *Promo*, October 1990: 28, 33; *The New Advertising Media* September 1988: 10; Anita Manning, "High-Tech Advances in Food Aisles," *USA Today* 25 April 1991: 1D, 2D, VideOcart Loss Widens as Fallout Is Delayed, Chicago Tribune, Nov. 4, 1991, 3, sect 4.

[53] Fahey 18; *The New Advertising Media* 11.

[54] *The New Advertising Media* 9, 14; Carmen Ulloa, Regional Sales Manager, Chicago, SilentRadio, telephone interview, 22 February 1991; Silent Radio Information Booklet, 1990, unnumbered.

[55] *The New Advertising Media* 22.

[56] Sammy R. Danna, Advertising I class interviews with select students, Loyola Univ. of Chicago, Water Tower Campus, 28 Feb. 1991; Gadd interview 26 Jan. 1991.

[57] "Health Club Media Networks," J. Walter Thompson, "For 'ImMEDIAte' Consideration" (News Release), January 1991.

[58] Whittle Communications, News Release, 26 November 1990; Gary Belis, Corporate Media spokesman, Whittle Communications, telephone interview, 4 February 1991.

[59] Michaelle Healy, "Despite Static, Channel One Has Strong First Year," *USA Today* 5 March 1991: 4D.

[60] Belis interview; Sammy R. Danna review of three wall-board media: The "Big Picture" for elementary school, "Connections" for high school and "Campus Voice" for college students, 2 Feb. 1991; Whittle Communications Media, News Release 7 Nov. 1990.

[61] Belis interview; "Special Reports," Whittle News Release, 13 Nov. 1990; Sammy R. Danna, Examination of five issues of "Special Reports Magazine," 2 Feb. 1991, for months in 1990/1991.

[62] Belis interview.

[63] Len Feldman, TV Bureau of Advertising, Media Specialist, telephone interview, 13 Feb. 1991.

[64] Feldman interview.

[65] Feldman interview.

[66] Feldman interview; Feldman telephone interview, 29 April 1991.

[67] Feldman interview; TVB: *A Research Trend Report*, "Trends in GNP, Ad Volume, TV Ad, Volume 1960-1996," TV Bureau of Advertising, Research Dept., New York, November 1990: 1; TVB: *A Research Trend Report*, "Trends in Viewing," TV Bureau of Advertising, Research Dept., New York, July 1990: 2.

[68] TVB: *A Research Report*: "Media Comparisons," Bruskin Associates, 1990, TV Bureau of Advertising, Research Dept., New York, 1990: 3.

[69] Lucille Luongo, Corp. Communications Senior Vice President Katz Communications, New York, telephone interview, 5 April 1991.

[70] Baron interviews, 24 Jan. and 19 April 1991.

[71] Baron interview, 24 Jan. 1991 and letter, 31 Jan. 1991.

[72] Baron letter, 31 Jan. 1991.

[73] Baron interview, 24 Jan. 1991; Baron letter.

[74] Levine, *Forbes* 177, 178; "Fewer Magazines Launched," (graphic) *USA Today* 8 Feb. 1991: 1B.

[75] Nicholas Schiavone, NBC and CONTAM, telephone interviews, 7, 8 March 1991.

[76] Schiavone interviews.

[77] Schiavone interviews.

[78] Schiavone interviews.

[79] Schiavone interviews.

[80] Gadd, telephone interview, 18 June 1991; Notes, 16 June 1991.

[81] Schiavone interviews.

[82] Schiavone interviews.

[83] Richard Zoglin, "The Big Boys' Blues," *Time* 17 October 1988: 57-60 (cover story); Wagner interview.

[84] Richard Zoglin, "Goodbye to the Mass Audience," *Time* 19 November 1990: 122-23.

[85] Kenneth R. Clark, "Networks Show Another Decline As Cable Climbs," *Chicago Tribune* 3 March 1991: 7: 1.

[86] Wayne Walley, "TVB: Ad Revenues Up 6%," *Electronic Media* 11 March 1991: 3.

[87] Michael Lev, "Paramount and MCA Invest in Satellite Movie Venture," *New York Times* 15 March 1991: 5C; Michael Lev, "Media Impresario Is Selling Movies, via Satellite Dish," *New York Times* 23 June 1991: 3: 5.

[88] Nancy Ryan, "Stadiums New Arena for Ad Debate," *Chicago Tribune* 11 March 1991: 4: 1, 4.

[89] Siewers, *Chicago Sun-Times* 20; Sherrod, *Chicago Tribune*: 2: 1; Rossi, *Chicago Sun-Times* 5.; Marthat Moore, "Communities Fight Alcohol, Cigarette Ads" *USA Today*, 28 August 1991, 1B.

[90] Bruce Buursma, "Rotating Ads New Backdrop for Game," *Chicago Tribune* 25 November 1990: 7: 1.

[91] Kostyra 3-5.

[92] Kostyra 5-7, 9.

[93] Michael Drexler, "Surviving in a Changing World," *Bozell Opinion*, Bozelle, Inc. 4 (Winter 1991): 7.

[94] Drexler 7, 8.

[95] Drexler 9, 10.

[96] Drexler 10.

2
Subliminal Perception and Other Comment and Criticism in Advertising

Ethical and professional comment and criticism in advertising helps to enlighten consumers. In the Stuart Chase essay, Chapman presents a critical stance on advertising germane to the problem of waste and advertising, a persuasive vehicle. Richard's study is filled with humorous examples of American advertising ingenuity during World War I and World War II. Manca discusses the image of yuppies, the consummate consumers of the 1980s. Subliminal perception in advertising arouses one of the most controversial and interesting topics in the field, and has been especially heightened during the past 20 years. Allegations of subliminal messages in ads abound in frequency as well as conflict. Such disputed claims range from sex symbols and words sketched on ice cubes in liquor ads to single-frame messages contained in a film or video picture-sequence. Even the Camel Cigarette mascot "Old Joe" is not free of an alleged sexual symbol. Zanot's concerted, up-to-date scholarly efforts constitute some of the most illuminating and provocative insights and assertions made in recent years regarding the subliminal advertising topic.

A Critique of Advertising: Stuart Chase on the "Godfather of Waste"

Richard N. Chapman

It has become a cliché to say that advertising has shaped American consciousness and molded American popular culture. According to historian David Potter, advertising "compares with such long-standing institutions as the school and the church in the magnitude of its social influence." Advertising supposedly "dominates the media" and has "vast power in the shaping of popular standards." In *Channels of Desire*, a breezy and slightly hysterical polemic, Stuart and Elizabeth Ewen treat advertising as a "bald mechanism of social control," the fundamental means of reconciling popular "demands for a better life and the general priorities of corporate capitalism." Advertising, in other words, is the institution that perpetrates the consumer culture.[1]

What is often ignored by critics of the consumer society, such as Stuart and Elizabeth Ewen, is resistance and opposition to the power of advertising. That resistance, as historian Warren Susman has written, "is a cultural fact of profound significance too seldom explored."[2] The distortions and exaggerations of advertising have always invited attack. In the early years of the twentieth century, groups urging "truth-in-advertising" campaigned for the elimination of misstatements and deliberate untruths. The "truth-in-advertising" movement, however, was concerned more with protecting reputable advertisers than with shielding customers from fraud. Larger questions about the importance of advertising in promoting conspicuous consumption and a consumer culture were rarely raised.[3]

During the 1920s, a decade when advertising became ever more pervasive in American life, social critic Stuart Chase formulated an analysis of advertising as an institution that went beyond earlier concerns about dishonesty and deception. Like Thorstein Veblen, his intellectual mentor, Chase examined the role of advertising in facilitating waste and in furnishing fantasies for the masses. As perhaps the most widely-read social and cultural critic of the twenties, Chase's theory of advertising reached large numbers of Americans.[4] The public distrust of advertising that he fostered helped place the industry on the defensive, especially after the beginning of the Great Depression. As one observer of advertising recalled:

During the thirties only Herbert Hoover and the banks received more abuse than advertising. Its voice had been the voice of business and industry that had lured people into debt with bright promises and gaudy pictures of a false Utopia. It was the cause of lost jobs, breadlines, foreclosures, and want. It had promised the moon, had delivered dust, and should be destroyed. It almost was.[5]

Of course, it goes too far to claim that advertising was "almost destroyed" during the thirties. Nevertheless, that such a statement could be made suggests some measure of public suspicion and hostility. As this essay will show, Stuart Chase played a major role in arousing and channeling popular resistance to advertising.

The Early Life and Career of Stuart Chase
In order to understand the sources of Chase's critique of advertising, it is necessary to consider briefly his background.[6] He was born March 8, 1888, and came from an old New England family. During his childhood, he lived for long periods with his grandfather, a retired shoe manufacturer and country banker of "mugwumpish" opinions. Grandfather Chase, like other "men of the Mugwump type," despised the "crass materialism" of the Gilded Age and communicated to his grandson an aversion for the cruder forms of avarice in late nineteenth-century America.[7] Stuart Chase remembered his grandfather taking the *Review of Reviews*, a famous magazine of the day, and patiently clipping out all of the advertisements before beginning to read. Business dealings, in Grandfather Chase's view, should be built on a solid personal relationship between producer and buyer, not on the deceptive and insincere appeals of

advertising. The lesson taught by the grandfather was not lost on the grandson.[8]

Sojourns with grandfather became less frequent once Stuart Chase's father finally attained financial success. Now it was the father who exerted the dominant influence, and he wanted his son to become a certified public accountant. In accordance with his father's wishes, Stuart attended M.I.T. for two years to receive technical training, and then he attended Harvard for two years to become acquainted with the genteel culture of the time. In 1910 he graduated from Harvard—a member of the illustrious class that included John Reed, T.S. Eliot, and Walter Lippmann. After college, Chase went to work for his father's accounting firm in Boston. At this point he began to challenge the conventional values of his middle-class surroundings. He became, in dizzying succession, a Henry George single-taxer, a Fabian socialist, an outspoken advocate of women's suffrage, a member of the Socialist Party of America, a determined opponent of U.S. entry into World War I, and from 1917 to 1920, a federal price regulator. However, his political views were too unorthodox for him to remain in government. During the post-World War I "Red Scare," he was discharged from the federal service as a dangerous subversive.

"Versailles and...reaction," Chase later wrote, had drowned every hope that the end of World War I might lead to a transformation of society and the international order.[9] In a mood of despair, Chase took consolation in the Bolshevik revolution. He considered becoming a communist, but his experiences since 1911 had made him wary of all creeds and doctrines, and communist ideology seemed the quintessence of dogmatism. Moreover, the American socialist movement had disintegrated into a bewildering variety of factions. Disgusted by sectarian and ideological quarrels, Chase lapsed back into an independent, skeptical, and idiosyncratic socialism.

The war years had defeated Chase's hopes for social change, but they were crucial to his intellectual development. In the United States, the wartime coordination of industry, agriculture, and transportation had permitted huge increases in production. Impressed by that achievement, Chase concluded that technology could "treble the standard of living" for ordinary Americans "if society could only organize for peace as it had once organized for war."[10] The theories of Thorstein Veblen, the caustically irreverent sociologist and economist, reinforced Chase's conviction. In 1918 and 1919, Veblen's articles on "The Vested Interests," and "The Engineers and the Price System" appeared in *The Dial*, and Chase immediately perceived their significance. Veblen stressed the waste inherent in existing economic institutions and the conflict "between 'business' (profit-seeking ownership) and 'industry' (maximum production of goods and services)."[11] Much of Veblen's work, especially its disdain for vendibility, either explicitly or implicitly condemned advertising and salesmanship as waste—that is, activities that do not "serve human life or human well-being on the whole." Indeed, in one of his more savage asides, Veblen labeled advertising "capitalized inefficiency" and placed it in the same category as "saloons, gambling houses, and houses of prostitution."[12]

Chase absorbed the teachings of Veblen firsthand at the New School for Social Research and became a disciple of the man he later called "the greatest economist this country has produced."[13] In 1921, Chase found a job as economist and statistician with the Technical Alliance, a group of technicians and engineers "who had taken Veblen seriously," as Chase put it. During his brief association with the Technical Alliance, Chase was also exposed to the principles of scientific management, which converged with socialism, Veblenism, and the lessons of World War I to form his critical outlook during the 1920s.[14]

Advertising and Waste

Persuaded by those influences of the irrationality and inefficiency of the business system, Chase in the early 1920s inaugurated an important career as a social, economic, and cultural critic. As a demolisher of the pieties of business, he had few peers. He undertook a study of the American economy in the hope that "the documentation of waste could lead to its elimination."[15] The result of this endeavor was a series of articles entitled "The Tragedy of Waste," which appeared in the *New Republic* in August 1925 and then in book form later that same year.[16]

Following Veblen, Chase argued that business throve on waste in manpower, natural resources, and useless, harmful, or adulterated products. That wastefulness condemned millions of Americans to live below a minimum level of health and decency. The "godfather" of the waste in consumption was advertising:

It is the life blood of quackery [Chase wrote] and the patent medicine industry. It enters largely into the output of super-luxuries, fashions, commercialized recreation. It is an invaluable adjunct in mobilizing a nation for war.[17]

A Critique of Advertising

Chase believed that technological innovation in the late nineteenth and early twentieth centuries had created an industrial plant "capable of producing goods a great deal faster than purchasing power has been released to absorb them." As a consequence, business had shifted its emphasis "from producing to selling." The problem confronting businessmen in the 1920s was "how to dispose of the volume of articles which mass production...made possible." The perverted solution dictated by the profit system, Chase declared, was "the higher salesmanship, advertising, sales quotas....[even] the discovery of Jesus of Nazareth as the first advertising man."[18] Advertising commercialized and trivialized human emotions and frailties: envy, "shame, cupidity, fear, vanity, curiosity, [sexuality]...superstition, and mother love," wrote Chase, were all exploited by advertising agencies that used applied psychology in order to sell a "superfluity of goods."[19] Perhaps the worst thing about advertising was that it relentlessly stimulated a hunger for material possessions at the expense of non-material aesthetic, intellectual, and moral concerns.

Chase also recognized that advertising supplied illusions for ordinary Americans that provided "a certain sense of escape in a machine age." Advertising

creates a dream world [Chase wrote]: smiling faces, shining teeth, school girl complexions, cornless feet, perfect fitting union suits, distinguished collars, wrinkleless pants, odorless breaths, regularized bowels, happy homes in New Jersey (15 minutes from Hoboken), charging motors, punctureless tires, perfect busts, shimmering shanks, self-washing dishes—backs behind which the moon was meant to rise.[20]

This dream world existed, Chase went on, to sell a deluge of "things which we do not wear, which we lose, which go out of style, which disappear ...endless jiggers and doodads and contrivances." Dreams and illusions sold those mainly non-essential goods, and those dreams and illusions sustained the profits and power of those who ruled.[21]

Chase's theory of advertising provoked a spirited rejoinder from the targets of his diatribe. During the 1920s, advertising men tried hard to convince themselves and the public that their activity was an authentic profession providing an essential service to society.[22] For an upstart critic like Chase to dismiss their purported profession as "artificial stimulation which would make Cleopatra blush" and ninety percent waste incited screams of outrage.[23] Indeed the editors of the *New Republic* were surprised at the passionate reaction to Chase's article on advertising:

The *New Republic* [the editors wrote] has received many protests against Mr. Stuart Chase's analysis of the art of advertising in his series on economic waste. He has been variously called a Puritan, a bigot, a misguided economist, a detractor of progress, and has come perilously close to being accused of blasphemy.[24]

One protestor solemnly declared that advertising was the only thing that kept the United States from sinking back to savagery and heathenism. It was, this writer insisted, "the greatest force for good in America today—more subtle and persuasive than the church, the theatre or the newer liberal magazines."[25]

Other protestors registered more serious if less bombastic complaints. First, they claimed that Chase failed to grasp the technical function of advertising in the modern economy. It facilitated a high velocity of flow in the purchases of goods by consumers. Advertising amplified the amount spent on consumer goods by eliminating sales resistance and encouraging Americans to devote a larger share of their incomes to consumption. Advertising was not wasteful, in this view, because it constituted the essential lubrication of the economic system.[26] Actually, Chase never denied that advertising performed such a function, which he defined as encouraging Americans to abandon habits of thrift. Advertising's "lubrication" of the economic machinery was a result, Chase declared, of the bad design of the economic mechanisms.[27]

A second claim presented by his critics was that Chase had unfairly ignored the efforts made by advertisers to eliminate abuses. The "truth-in-advertising" movement and efforts to professionalize the industry, so the argument went, had ended the worst practices. In fact Chase had not neglected the "truth-in-advertising" movement, which he admitted had "made great strides in eliminating bold-faced lying." However, his indictment went beyond concerns about dishonesty to the role of advertising in promoting planned obsolescence and artificially-stimulated wants, and in furnishing illusory escape for the masses. Perhaps "truth-in-advertising" would eradicate "baby-killer" patent medicines, Chase noted, but it would do little or nothing about that dream world of "svelte lines, motor cars, and skins you love to touch."[28]

What his detractors only dimly perceived was the depth of Chase's hostility to the emergent culture of consumption in the 1920s. While he was not, as one adversary claimed, "an old-fashioned idealist who wanted to abolish material things," Chase plainly disliked the obsession of Americans and their culture with money and things.[29] Advertising in the United States encouraged the consumption of "stuff," Chase wrote, "but it is largely ugly, depressing, mean, or swanky stuff. It carries little nourishment for the human organism. This is no triumph of human intelligence. This is the defeat of human intelligence."[30] A "billion dollars' worth of advertising and publicity a year," Chase continued, led to a "disposable society" where consumers were induced "to throw things away before they are worn out, and buy a new model." He wrote in disgust how natural beauty was defaced by the steady spread over "the country, urban and rural," of the "most sublime exhibit of offscourings and litter upon which the sun has ever shone."[31]

Your Money's Worth and the Founding of Consumers Research

Believing that "America is too fine a land to be...drugged by the infantile slogans and dazzled by the glittering gadgets of shoddy speculators," Chase sought an antidote to the narcotic of advertising and the dazzle of unnecessary, useless, harmful, and mediocre goods.[32] He found a like-minded ally in Frederick J. Schlink, an engineer who had compiled data on products that did not fulfill the claims of their producers. Chase and Schlink collaborated on a book entitled *Your Money's Worth*, published in 1927.[33] Aiming this vivid piece of muckraking directly at consumers, the authors documented the manipulation and defrauding of the American public. Advertising, Chase wrote, had created "a Wonderland of conflicting claims, bright promises, fancy packages, soaring words, and almost impenetrable [consumer] ignorance." The purpose of *Your Money's Worth*, Chase declared, was to explore the Wonderland and "to indicate a path which may lead out of it—if and when its glamor, its romance begin to fade." Chase did not underestimate the attractions of advertising's fantasy world—the escape it provided, he wrote, was "the next best thing to going to the movies"—but he did hope that some Americans might wish to find their way back to solid reality. His prescription for that return to reality was "in no sense revolutionary." Instead, it was simple and practical. He advocated "the principle of buying goods according to impartial scientific test, rather than according to the fanfare and trumpets of the higher salesmanship."[34]

Your Money's Worth became a best-seller, with over a hundred thousand copies sold. As "the 'Uncle Tom's Cabin'" of consumer protest, it is credited with beginning the modern consumer movement in the United States. Hundreds of people wrote the authors to ask for information about the defects of particular products. Encouraged by the eager public response, Chase and Schlink founded Consumers Research Incorporated, a consumers' testing service and the forerunner of Consumers Union. The new consumers' organization provided members with objective information about products, and it grew rapidly, as indicated by the subscriptions to the Consumers Research *Bulletin*, which soared from 565 in 1927 to 42,000 in 1932.[35]

Not surprisingly, advertisers reacted somewhat differently than the enthusiastic recruits to Consumers Research. Disturbed by the public antagonism that Chase and Schlink had either tapped or aroused, and annoyed that Chase had once again made them the villains, the advertising agencies struck back. The two major trade journals, *Printer's Ink* and *Advertising and Selling*, ridiculed the charges contained in *Your Money's Worth*. The International Advertising Association hired Charles E. Carpenter to write a rebuttal defending the industry. Carpenter's book, entitled *Dollars and Sense*, concluded that *Your Money's Worth* was communist propaganda. Irate advertising men agreed with that verdict. One blasted Chase as an un-American, possibly demented, "soap box red."[36]

Spokesmen for the advertising industry fumed, but the success of *Your Money's Worth* and the growth of Consumers Research indicated a rising public skepticism about advertising. "Anyone with two eyes in his head can see that the public is getting restive," warned an advertising agent.[37] Chase had encouraged that restlessness by formulating a scathing critique of advertising and by channeling public distrust into the organized consumers' movement. To Chase, both the critique and the organization were fundamental protests against advertising. He considered consumer testing a means to dissolve the dream world in which consumers moved. Someday, he wrote, advertising's "Wonderland would well-nigh cease to be."[38]

Such high hopes for consumer testing reflected Chase's distaste for the culture of consumption. It is not without irony that the testing service Chase helped establish later evolved into a source of advice and assistance for those who participated in the consumer culture. Nevertheless, if Chase's expectations for the fledgling consumer movement were not entirely fulfilled, his contributions to that movement were still significant. The public response to his work should remind the critics of consumption that not all Americans in the late 1920s and early 1930s were putty in the hands of the

A Critique of Advertising

advertising agencies. Doubtless advertising was powerful, but Americans still retained capacities for resistance to the shaping of consciousness by advertising.

Notes

[1] Keith L. Bryant, Jr., and Henry C. Detholff, *A History of American Business* (Englewood Cliffs, NJ, 1983), 184, 195; David M. Potter, *People of Plenty: Economic Abundance and the American Character* (Chicago, 1954), 167; Stuart and Elizabeth Ewen, *Channels of Desire: Mass Images and the Shaping of American Consciousness* (New York, 1982), 36-37. See also Daniel J. Boorstin's discussion of advertising and "consumption communities" in *The Americans: The Democratic Experience* (New York, 1973), 89-164.

[2] Warren Susman, *Culture as History: The Transformation of American Society in the Twentieth Century* (New York, 1984), 255-56.

[3] Poyntz Tyler, "Social and Economic Effects," in *Advertising in America*, ed. Poyntz Tyler (New York, 1959), 141-42; Sidney Ratner, James H. Soltow, and Richard Sylla, *The Evolution of the American Economy* (New York, 1979), 382-83; Roland Marchand, *Advertising the American Dream: Making Way for Modernity, 1920-1940* (Berkeley, CA, 1985), 8; Norman I. Silber, *Test and Protest: The Influence of Consumers Union* (New York, 1983), 1-4.

[4] Arthur Schlesinger, Jr., in *The Crisis of the Old Order* (Boston, 1957), 201, called Stuart Chase "perhaps the most widely read of liberal economists." David Riesman thought that Chase had done more than almost anyone else in the 1920s to teach Americans about the distortions of the business system. See David Riesman, *Thorstein Veblen: A Critical Interpretation* (New York, 1953), 94. Much of the general public, William J. Barber writes, was exposed to criticisms of the prevailing business system through the works of Stuart Chase. See William J. Barber, *From New Era to New Deal: Herbert Hoover, the Economists, and American Economic Policy, 1921-1933* (Cambridge, England, 1985), 44.

[5] Tyler, "Social and Economic Effects," *Advertising in America*, 143.

[6] There is no satisfactory study of Stuart Chase's life and career. The following accounts are of some use: James C. Lanier, "Stuart Chase: An Intellectual Biography, 1888-1940" (unpublished Ph.D. dissertation, Emory University, 1970); James S. Saeger, "Stuart Chase: At Right Angles to Laissez Faire," *The Social Studies* 63:6 (November 1972), 251-259; Stanley J. Kunitz, ed., *Authors Today and Yesterday* (New York, 1933), 153-55; Maxine Block, ed., *Current Biography, 1940* (New York, 1940), 162-64.

[7] Richard Hofstadter, *The Age of Reform: From Bryan to F.D.R.* (New York, 1955), 139-40.

[8] Lanier, "Stuart Chase: An Intellectual Biography," 4.

[9] Stuart Chase, "Portrait of a Radical," *The Century Magazine* 108:3 (July 1924), 300.

[10] Chase, "Portrait of a Radical," 302.

[11] "Thorstein Veblen," *International Encyclopedia of the Social Sciences*, ed. David L. Sills (1968), 16: 305.

[12] Quotations from Joseph Dorfman, *Thorstein Veblen and His America* (New York, 1935), 177-78, 280. See also David Riesman, *Thorstein Veblen: A Critical Interpretation* (New York, 1953); Thorstein Veblen, *The Engineers and the Price System* (New York, 1921), and *Absentee Ownership and Business Enterprise in Recent Times* (New York, 1923).

[13] Quotation from Dorfman, *Veblen*, 509. For Veblen's influence on Chase, see "Portrait of A Radical," 300-02; Schlesinger, *Crisis of the Old Order*, 201; Silber, *Test and Protest*, 6-7; Joseph Dorfman, *The Economic Mind in American Civilization*, v. 5 (New York, 1959), 511; William E. Akin, *Technocracy and the American Dream: The Technocratic Movement, 1900-1941* (Berkeley, CA, 1977), 14-26, 31.

[14] Quotation from Chase, "Portrait of a Radical," 302. For Chase's thought during the 1920s, see Richard N. Chapman, "Ambiguities of Technology: Stuart Chase on Men and Machines," paper delivered to the Society for the History of Technology, Cambridge, MA, November 3, 1984, copy in possession of the author.

[15] Akin, *Technocracy and the American Dream*, 42.

[16] Stuart Chase, *The Tragedy of Waste* (New York, 1925). Chase also wrote *The Challenge of Waste* (New York: League for Industrial Democracy, 1922).

[17] Stuart Chase, "The Tragedy of Waste: III. The Wastes of Advertising," *New Republic* 43:559 (August 19, 1925), 342. Chase called advertising "a sort of godfather" to the wastes in consumption. See Chase, *The Tragedy of Waste*, 31.

[18] Stuart Chase, "Six Cylinder Ethics," *Forum*, 79 (1928), 24.

[19] Chase, "The Wastes of Advertising," 343-44.

[20] Chase, "The Wastes of Advertising," 345.

[21] Chase, "The Wastes of Advertising," 344. See also Stuart Chase, *Men and Machines* (New York, 1929), 323.

[22] Marchand, *Advertising the American Dream*, 1-9, 25-32, 83.

[23] Quotation from Chase, *The Tragedy of Waste*, 42.

[24] "The Wastefulness of Advertising," *New Republic* 44:565 (September 30, 1925), 139-40.

[25] Charles C. Baldwin, "The New Religion," *New Republic* 44:561 (September 2, 1925), 47.

[26] Lanier, "Stuart Chase: An Intellectual Biography," 53-56; Marchand, *Advertising the American Dream*, 1-2, 9, 29.

[27] Chase, "Six Cylinder Ethics," 22-34; Chase, "The Wastes of Advertising," 343. See also Chase, *Men and Machines*, 193, 209, 216, 322-23. The American economy, Chase wrote in *Men and Machines*, was "the economy of a madhouse," which created the "foolish and expensive antics" of advertising and "high pressure salesmanship."

[28] Quotations from Chase, "The Wastes of Advertising," 344-45. See also Lanier, "Stuart Chase: An Intellectual Biography," 57.

[29] Quotation from Lanier, "Stuart Chase: An Intellectual Biography," 56.

[30] Stuart Chase, "My Great-Great-Great-Grandfather and I," *Nation* 123:3191 (September 1, 1926), 192.

[31] Stuart Chase, "The Mad Hatter's Dirty Teacup," *Harper's Magazine* 160 (April 1930), 581, 585.

[32] Quotation from Stuart Chase, "Declaration of Independence," *Harper's Magazine* 164 (December 1931), 36.

[33] Stuart Chase and F.J. Schlink, *Your Money's Worth: A Study in the Waste of the Consumer's Dollar* (New York, 1927).

See also Lanier, "Stuart Chase: An Intellectual Biography," 52; and Silber, *Test and Protest*, 17.

[34]Quotations from Chase and Schlink, *Your Money's Worth*, 2-3, 260.

[35]Silber, *Test and Protest*, 17-18. See also Joseph Gaer, *Conumers All* (New York, 1940), 112; and Chase and Schlink, *Your Money's Worth*, 238-257. According to Rhoda H. Karpatkin, executive director of Consumer's Union, *Your Money's Worth* is usually considered "the 'Uncle Tom's Cabin' of the consumer movement." See Rhoda H. Karpatkin, "Memo to Members," *Consumer Reports* 51:3 (March 1986), 139.

[36]Quotation from William H. Gesell to Mr. Bell, December 11, 1931, folder for Consumers Research, 1928-31, box 2, Chase papers, Library of Congress. For controversy over *Your Money's Worth*, see Stuart Chase to Macmillan Company, April 29, 1927, and C.B. Larrabee to Stuart Chase, February 9, 1954, box 1, Chase papers, Library of Congress; and folder for Consumers Research, 1928-31, box 2, Chase papers, Library of Congress. See also Lanier, "Stuart Chase: An Intellectual Biography," 56; and Marchand, *Advertising the American Dream*, 82-83, 314.

[37]Marchand, *Advertising the American Dream*, 314. See also Tyler, "Social and Economic Effects," *Advertising in America*, 142-44.

[38]Silber, *Test and Protest*, 17.

Postum, Post Toasties and Patriotism

Alfred C. Richard

For many who served on the home front or on overseas battlefields during WWII the Coca-Cola and Camel ads featured in the pages of *Life, Look* and the *Saturday Evening Post* are as easily recalled as are the familiar refrains of Glen Miller's "In the Mood." "Have a 'Coke'—Soldier, refresh yourself." The accompanying color illustration of an American GI willingly answering the command as he stood on a makeshift "Main Street" carved across an unidentified Pacific island obviously enjoying this touch of home was simple and effective. Coca-Cola, Camel, and Chesterfield frequently fought to occupy the back covers of the most popular weekly magazines throughout the war years. Their presentations were patriotic and designed to identify their product with a united effort for national defense and with the nation's survival.[1]

This form of advertising reached its zenith during WWII. It would be difficult to find a major magazine that did not devote a significant proportion of its total advertising copy to defense oriented ads. The most popular weeklies, *Life, Saturday Evening Post, Look* and *Collier's*, frequently allocated more than fifty percent of their total half and full page ads to the crusade against the Axis. Capitalizing on current events was both patriotic and profitable for America's corporations.[2]

More recent generations are unfamiliar with this Madison Avenue manifestation which achieved its most intensive and generalized use during WWII. Neither the Korean "police action" nor this country's participation in the Vietnamese civil war produced any patriotic advertising. It has not really been employed since that time. A historic survey of this patriotic practice tempts one to use it as a barometer to gauge the popularity or public support offered by Americans for the more militant conflicts their nation has experienced.

There is little evidence that the Civil War generated any specific patriotic product identification advertising. *Harpers Magazine* carried a few small ads for "officers watches" at seven and nine dollars which claimed to be exact imitations of $100 units used by the "Royal Engineers" of the British army. In May of 1865 the B.T. Hayward Co. advertised for sale a "new Richmond medal...in the true likeness of General Grant" and a "Memorial Badge...in memory of Abm Lincoln," but little else is easily found in the popular press.[3]

Spanish-American War:
Patriotic Product Identification Begins

By 1898 the print media experienced a significant expansion: newspapers publishing a daily edition had soared from 387 in 1860 to more than 2200 by the end of the century. The weekly and monthly press had grown in like proportion.[4] The Spanish-American War provided this increased media with the opportunity for exploiting its potential power. The story of the Hearst and Pulitzer rivalry is a familiar one. Not so well known is that others also sought to capitalize on this growth and the aggressive war sentiment generated by the yellow journalists. It was at this time that advertisers made their first real attempts to identify their products and services with their nation's destiny. The outpouring of patriotism bubbled over into the business world. Before the actual outbreak of hostilities, Hoff's malt extract was offered to a "strong people" by an Uncle Sam with soldier and sailor at his side. More aggressively, W.C. Loftus illustrated in a small ad that he was ready to fire a cannon "into the enemy's ranks to assure victory." He claimed that his suits were the "ammunition" by which his company was "reducing the ranks of higher price tailors."

At the same time, Wanamakers encouraged people to join their History club by offering the new Ridpath, *History of the World*, which dramatically showed "Spain's grip on America" passing into more progressive hands. The slick copy read: "Bit by bit [Spain's] American soil has been wrenched from her till now her trembling fingers clutch on little else than Cuba...if you would estimate the chances of the Cuban war read...." McKinley's ultimatum was delivered the following day with the overwhelming approval of the American public.[5]

29

The reaction of some merchandisers to the call to arms was immediate: O'Neill's of Sixth Avenue was ready with flags and patriotic copy: The "Star Spangled Banner...[is] that symbol of freedom which typifies the letter of spirit of our Great Republic...may it wave forever to perpetuate the splendid government it represents" and while customers were singing and saluting they could "judge" the store's own patriotic contribution: "American wool bunting flags...12 by 20 feet...$10.98. Hosiery and underwear were also offered."[6]

As the *Times* editorialized in praise of the growing number of volunteers, Frederick Loeser and Co. of Brooklyn, in a four-column ad expressed a more personal concern for the soldier's well-being, noting that they were well stocked with "those needful things for the men who [would] go to the front." This was no empty promise. They offered as an incentive "especially low prices to the National Guardsmen on shoes, underwear, flannel shirts...drinking cups and knives." For those not so fortunate as to be able to serve actively but who wished to do their share, flags could be purchased at "little price" for display "from every flagpole and house window in every borough." And whereas life still continued for those at home, there "was also a 40% savings on dishes, a beautiful selection of silks and some palms and jardiniers."[7]

Two weeks after the outbreak of hostilities the Wanamaker Store expressed concern for its country and its customers in an editorial-like ad titled "Business and Belligerency":

War is happily an abnormal condition and will pass, but the needs of the individual are constant and never ending. There will be eating and drinking, and dressing and homemaking, whatever the news from the Philippines or Caribbean. We shall not mix belligerency with business. The store will go on, brighter, bigger than ever. If the conditions shall occasion price-lowering in certain lines—a public profit through private misfortune—we shall enable you to gain by it.

The statement was a clever, if not genuinely altruistic, reassurance to their buying public, a unique combination of capitalistic concern and patriotic promotion.[8]

This new merchandising practice was not reserved to the major metropolitan dailies; in reality, it was much more the province of smaller cities and towns.[9] Many small merchants pioneered the practice of patriotic product identification, although at times in questionable taste. Two separate merchants in the *New London Day* used the flag as a backdrop. One sold shoes the other stoves. Yet, the great majority of the new ads were clever blends of product and patriotism. A New London eye doctor claimed that "poor eyesight" was the cause for "the rejection of the majority of recruits at Camp Haven," and suggested that a visit to his office would increase chances of being able to serve.[10] The Leonard Mallory company declared war on Cuba sometime before Congress, featuring a stern Uncle Sam rolling up his sleeves with a caption that was something of an oxymoron: "Peace by Jingo, if I have to fight for it." But the message was clear. The United States was standing up to Spain and calling on her to halt the "Cuban atrocities." They also asked their customers to inspect their plumbing and roofing should it need repair. "Prepared for Action...The Cannon Ball Special [and] the Harvest of death in Cuba" were other variations employed throughout April and May in the service of product and country.[11]

By mid-month the *Day* demanded that the "Spanish Barbarians" be driven into the sea. William W. Winchester's home repair company expressed a similar request with a double-entendre:

Give Us your business, we are at
Liberty and promise
*Or War*ant the best work.

They used a similar technique in the following week for another message:

Don't Be taken in with cheap material...
Afraid Of The extra cost of the best material...we are the
Enemy of high prices, as well as poor stock.[12]

The war's hero was quickly recognized by the business community. The Ewen McIntyre company of New Haven demanded a great "Hurrah!" for Commodore Dewey while C.E. Longley offered pictures of the "Hero of Manila" for sale. Another merely used the name in bold print to catch the attention of prospective customers. Gratitude for the heroic exploits was boundless. The Walter L. Main Circus named one of "the first elephants" born in American captivity "Dewey" and used the *New York World's* article describing the incident to promote their show. Hundreds of similar ads, some more serious, more humorous, more bizarre appeared throughout the northeast. What first began as part of a patriotic outpouring of support for the government's expansionist policy in 1898 would experience an explosive growth itself during the Mexican crisis. Advertisers' exploitation of war fever reached new heights with the Tampico incident sixteen years later.[13]

Postum, Post Toasties and Patriotism

*Tampico Crisis, 1914:
Business Responds Immediately*

The Mexico of 1914 was troubled; three years of bitter civil war had created divided loyalties and rival factions. Huerta, Carranza, Villa and Zapata each commanded loyal supporters. Thousands were killed in the struggle between Huerta's Federalists and the Constitutionalists in Mexico. It was impossible for the North American republic not to become involved. With part of the Atlantic squadron guarding American interests at Tampico, it was only a matter of time before they did.

The Tampico incident began on April 9, 1914 when President Huerta's soldiers mistakenly arrested a few American sailors who had come to shore for supplies. The men were immediately released and apologies were offered by the government's representatives. Admiral Mayo (another Vermonter in Dewey's tradition) demanded more; he wanted a twenty-one-gun-salute fired to remove what he considered to be a significant insult to the American flag. The nation's honor was at issue. President Wilson supported his commander and within days American troops took and occupied the port of Vera Cruz. Nineteen American and more than two hundred Mexican lives were lost. The Mexican dictator had refused to salute.[14]

Historians have generally ignored the American public's reaction to this incident preferring to discuss official diplomatic decisions, but in so doing they have missed what was a truly unique expression of national spirit. Although some historians have argued that there was little support for an aggressive policy, it is clear that the majority of Americans were ready for war with Mexico in April of 1914. Some advertisers quickly sensed the nation's mood. Anti-Mexican and patriotic copy appeared immediately after the first news reports of the arrests reached the home press. Newspapers from every section of the United States editorialized for redress. From Fairbanks, Alaska to Atlanta, Georgia, Bangor, Maine to El Paso, Texas, the demand for an apology from Mexico was backed by the offer of thousands of volunteers ready to march to Mexico City. The advertisements which appeared in hundreds of these papers indicate similar support from the business community.[15]

One might expect the border states to be interested in the possibility of war with Mexico; they were. Newspapers throughout the southwest overwhelmingly praised the President's order to take Vera Cruz. The following day, April 21, Webber and Savage, a department store in Tucson announced "War with Mexico" and a "5% discount for cash." In Phoenix, Hanny's, a haberdashery, told their customers that if they wanted to fight, they could "Join the Army," but they were open for business if any wanted to shop before leaving for Mexico. H.G. Edwards wished to make sure that every one had read "about the war" and their own great "slaughter of furniture prices."[16]

There was no less excitement two thousand miles away. The patriotic aggressiveness displayed in one cigar ad carried by the *Bangor Daily News* expressed this clearly: Smokers should "enjoy the BFA cigar and watch the Mexican fur fly. Still only 5 cents." If one preferred a ten cent cigar, the Blackstone could be found in any army camp "from Maine to Mexico." Rumford Falls was a small pulp-mill town hidden in the "piney" woods of central Maine, citizens there read the local *Times*. In May, well after the crisis period had passed, that paper ran an intriguing ad disguised as a news story announcing that the "War [would] begin next Wednesday...not in Mexico but at George Elias's Department Store." The advertising copy exhibited more than a passing acquaintance with the leading characters in the ever-changing Mexican drama. It read like a script from a dime novel: "The price of every article [had] been slashed as deeply as Villa would slash Huerta if he could get his hands on him...the regular prices at the store [had] no more chance of escaping the knife than Huerta [had] in escaping death." These are not merely random examples selected as humorous curiosities; they represent but a few of the many similar advertisements employed by New England and Atlantic Coast businessmen in their local newspapers.[17]

The situation was the same on the Pacific coast. The enthusiasm for aggressive action against Mexico generated hundreds of patriotic ads. As far north as Fairbanks, Alaska, where news had to be transmitted by telegraph at significant expense, the *Daily-News Miner* carried three such ads in one edition. The Big White Store proclaimed that "War was Hell...alright [sic], but while the fleet [was] punching holes in Mr. Huerta's little hand made republic," it would be business as usual. Hall's bookstore asked all who were "enlisting for the war with Mexico" to stop by "before the first shot was fired." As did many other stores throughout the nation, Gordon's "declared war" on high prices. These personalized declarations of war, overtly against high prices, subliminally against Mexico, were the most frequently used technique to identify with the conflict. Not unfamiliar in 1898, the practice was common in the Tampico crisis but would not be as popular during WWI.[18]

The Spanish-American War had helped hide the "bloody shirt" and heal the wounds inflicted by the Civil War: North and South had been reunited against a common foe. In 1914 the almost ritualistic reaction against Mexico welcomed America's new immigrant population to join in common effort. The Irish, Greeks, and Poles all offered volunteer companies to the President for active service. In Los Angeles the German American Bank provided its depositors with a "Mexican War Map...an authentic map of the entire war zone."— only one to a customer. Almost every major metropolitan daily throughout the nation did the same. The *Boston Post* even included a "War Game" with their map: "You can move a pin and work out the Mexican campaign in your own home, All nationalities could participate."[19] Similar maps would be offered in both World Wars.

Two days after the occupation of Vera Cruz the *Los Angeles Examiner* carried a quarter page ad for the F.P. Newport Excursion Company. After a detailed explanation of how vital the harbor would be for this country's success in the war, "when every minute might hold the destiny of [the] nation within its sixty seconds," it was sure that the government would place the harbor directly under its control. Before that happened, a round trip sightseeing tour of all the naval installations and other harbor sights was still only twenty-five cents.[20]

"Colorado's greatest newspaper," the *Rocky Mountain News*, declared hostilities with a full-page ad announcing that "War [had] started in peaceful Denver....[The] aggressive policy of the Lewis Store condoned nothing in the way of inactivity...[Their] generals and lieutenants in common [had] fretted with impatience long enough." This ad copy, designed to sell everything from dresses to writing paper, was a less than oblique criticism of Woodrow Wilson's earlier "watchful waiting" policy which many Americans considered weak and frustrating. Now was the time for action. Two thousand miles away in Keene, New Hampshire, the C.C. Beedle Piano Co. expressed the same sentiment: The eyes of the world were now focused on the U.S. Navy. "Watchful waiting" had been "succeeded by energetic action."[21]

As was the case in many ads throughout the country, another mile-high city merchant took his words directly from the demand made by Admiral Mayo on Huerta's government. "War was declared," but the ladies still had to "salute" the owner of Budd's shoe store for the great opportunity of purchasing his product. The National Order of Cowboy Rangers was based in Denver. They used the crisis to recruit new members, but reassured the Secretary of War by telegram reprinted in the *News* that they would "raise a regiment for Uncle Sam to serve in Mexico."[22]

All of this activity took place within two weeks, a remarkable example of American ingenuity and enterprise. It was the same throughout the entire nation, in the *Chicago Tribune*, the *Enid* (Oklahoma) *Daily Eagle*, the *New Orleans Times-Democrat and Daily Picayune*, the *Portland Sunday Telegram* and the *Moosup* (Connecticut) *Journal*, advertisers and merchants realized that patriotism could be profitable. There is no implied criticism here for the business community. "The business of America is business": these ads were genuine expressions of support for the administration, and for the nation against an apparent aggressor. It must have been a pleasure to express one's patriotism and hope to share a profit simultaneously.[23]

Advertisers became aware that national events could have a positive profit potential during the Spanish-American War. The Mexican crisis nationalized the practice, but it did more than that. Now national brands experimented with its use. Hart, Schaffner and Marx allowed local merchants to adapt their ad copy to home areas, and they did so. The ad in the Los Angeles area pictured mean-looking Mexican revolutionaries in bold face copy exclaiming: "3,000,000 Volunteers"..."something like 50,000 men are ready to march into Mexico. Sixty-nine times that many Americans wear [our] suits." Brannen's Daily Bulletin, in the *Tucson Citizen*, merely emphasized that "neatness...played a very important part in the impressiveness of Uncle Sam's army." They carried the line for the southwest.[24]

Buick made its first use of this new adaptation during the two-week crisis, but would use similar ads in both world wars: "Sturdiness and strength ...fearless under fire....War brings no qualms of fear to the hearts of us who live beneath the outstretched wings of the American Eagle....These things are fundamental American characteristics— and these principles are incorporated in every Buick." Young soldiers were pictured in a charge with rifles at the ready—very effectively identifying the product with the youthful aggressiveness of the national character.[25]

Events in Mexico moved too quickly for most of the monthly national magazines to use in self promotion, *Collier's* ordered its "Land and sea forces...to Mexico for action," but the fighting was all but finished once their formidable squad of "scribblers" arrived.[26] Yet one very popular journal was fortunate enough to have a young adventurer, John Reed, covering Villa's struggle against Huerta,

Postum, Post Toasties and Patriotism

as American bluejackets were taking Vera Cruz. In daily newspapers nationwide, *Metropolitan Magazine* asked in bold headlines "What will happen when we invade Mexico?" They claimed that Reed had produced the first "pen picture of the Mexican soldier in battle" which described "the kind of fighting our soldiers [would] face in their march on to Mexico City."[27] The *Worlds Work* promoted Wm. Bayard Hale's personal interview with Huerta. The former minister had been sent by Wilson to evaluate the Mexican dictator. Hale's report might not have been as exciting as Reed fighting side by side with Villa's men, but his characterization of Huerta as a "brandy drinking ape" would be quoted in thousands of news articles, and eventually, in the history books.

Nationwide Brands Enthusiastically Endorse Government Policy

Postum, Post Toasties and Encyclopedia Britannica provide the best examples of patriotic product identification during the Tampico incident. In March of 1914, before the outbreak of hostilities, Britannica began a major nationwide promotion. Five major leads were employed to sell the product. Usually not more than two of the variations appeared in any individual newspaper, but beginning in early April, the entire series was used in the *Atlanta Constitution*, one every few days in half-page attractive and intelligent ads. Military action across the border changed that immediately. The week after the occupation only one ad was featured. It asked the timely question "What has brought about the present condition of affairs in Mexico?" and offered a full-page of "splendid articles" reprinted from their new edition, which promised to fully explain "the troubles which have finally resulted in the armed intervention of the United States in Mexico." The informative message appeared in hundreds of newspapers nationwide. One must admire the aggressiveness and speedy action which produced this copy for publication within less than a week after the actual incident.[28]

The Postum people reacted even faster, their ads prior to the action were simple and straight forward: if you don't like coffee, "drink Postum." Three days after the hostilities, new copy appeared for national distribution. It portrayed bluejackets and 13-inch guns on an American battle cruiser with the words: "Good Eyes! Steady Nerves! There's a Reason." It was not a difficult message to understand.[29]

The Post Toasties "Fight or Frolic" ad was the most reproduced throughout the national daily press. It was used in all parts of the country between the 24th and the 30th of April. Sailors were pictured hard at work. The caption explained that the drawing was taken "from an actual photograph, April 17, 1914. Our bluejackets loading Post Toasties on U.S. Flagship *Virginia*, Rear Admiral Beatty commanding at Charlestown Navy Yard, preparatory to possible war with Mexico." The drama continued in the copy beneath: "Up and down our seacoast Battleships, Transports and Destroyers have been waiting the President's word. At Portsmouth, Charlestown, Brooklyn...the Big Ships that carry the Flag have been loading food for the guns and food for the men." This ad represents the best example of how far some ad men had come in their attempts to identify their product with the national purpose and presidential policy. The two were united in common effort. The enemy now was Mexican. Later, it would be German and Japanese, but the techniques developed by these early advertisers would differ little from those employed in 1918 or in 1945.[30]

Within two weeks the crisis passed, few if any believed that mediation would result in a definite settlement. Many Americans still supported direct intervention as the only solution to the Mexican problem. Internal pressures forced Huerta to resign in July a few days before Germany's ultimatum to Serbia. But in that last summer of peace, America's attention remained focused across the Rio Grande.

The last of the "Tampico Crisis" ads appeared in early May when the peace talks started. Advertisers would not utilize the European war until America joined the Allies in 1917. Nevertheless events in Mexico and border incidents continued to supply some advertisers with material for patriotic promotions. One such ad stands out. Elgin watches had used the *Literary Digest* as a medium for many years. In August of 1914, as part of their "Elgin Wonder Tales," they featured a lithograph showing two Mexican revolutionaries in sombreros and bulletbelts holding a railroad conductor at bay. The caption was to the point: "Wear an Elgin— or be shot!" It was signed Emiliano Zapata. Further copy explained the circumstances which had prompted the ad. In the taking of Salazar, Zapatistas had been disappointed with the poor quality of the "cheap" watches taken from their victims. Upon leaving the town, Zapata had posted the above notice. It was "a severe ultimatum—conclusive evidence that the leaders of insurrection-torn Mexico know the watches which serve best in war and peace," at least as far as Elgin was concerned.[31] Companies are quick to use wars to advertise their products. The ads have a patriotic theme and appeal to the emotions.

War's test is the test of tests—and particularly so in the desolate wastes of old Mexico

And there the chainless Packard is Uncle Sam's efficient burden bearer.

One hundred and twenty-two strong—Packards are showing what trucks can do under the most adverse conditions.

They stand the test.

And now the third big repeat order has come to us.

Army officers specify Packards for the severe Mexican service, because:

(1) Their power and endurance have proved equal to every demand.

(2) Their maintenance, replacement and repair charges are down to minimum.

(3) Their simple, enclosed, protected working parts and noiseless, chainless drive are proof against alkali dust and dirt—are dependable under every combination of bad roads and over-loads.

You can't know what a motor truck will do for your business until you have thoroughly investigated the Packard chainless truck. Why not let our transportation experts talk the matter over with you—now?

Packard Trucks

In 1916 Pancho Villa "invaded" the United States. Although immediate pursuit took place on horseback, the need for mechanized calvary was quickly realized. Packard was only one of many truck companies which helped make the transition from horse to motorized carrier. Packard continued to use this participation in Mexico well into WWI as proof of the reliability of their product and their contribution to making the world safe for democracy.

Postum, Post Toasties and Patriotism

Have a Coca-Cola = Eto Zdorovo
(HOW GRAND!)

To visiting Russian and British allies it's good news to see fighting planes pouring out of American plants. And it's good to see our flying friends respond to the everyday American invitation *Have a "Coke"*—a way of saying *We're with you*. Coca-Cola wins a welcome from those who come from Moscow or Manchester. And in your home, there's always a welcome for "Coke" out of your own refrigerator. Coca-Cola stands for *the pause that refreshes,*—has become a symbol of friendliness in many lands.

* * *

Our fighting men meet up with Coca-Cola many places overseas. Coca-Cola has been a globe-trotter "since way back when". Even with war, Coca-Cola today is being bottled right on the spot in over 35 allied and neutral nations.

Coca-Cola -the global high-sign

It's natural for popular names to acquire friendly abbreviations. That's why you hear Coca-Cola called "Coke".

COPYRIGHT 1944, THE COCA-COLA COMPANY

Not unlike Camels, Coke dominated its field. No other soft drink used more ad space to identify its product with the war effort than Coca-Cola. In other ads they claimed that their product was not only consumed on the homefront but by thirty-five nations, neutral and Allied. Coke was secure enough to recognize Russia's war contribution.

Throughout the war Camel used hundreds of different color ads to promote their product and identify it with the war effort. Camels were shown to be smoked on every front, in every theater, by all the service groups, and in almost every action that took place. This ad campaign, combined with the creative invention of the T-Zone and their claim that most doctors who smoked used their product, helped to make them number one in sales throughout the decade of the 40s.

Postum, Post Toasties and Patriotism

Although the watchmakers displayed some knowledge of the now famous Plan of Ayala, its catch words were "Land and Liberty." The implication that the Plan made reference to Elgin watches was the product of a creative ad man's imagination.

From actual photograph, April 17, 1914, our Bluejackets loading Post Toasties on U. S. Flagship Virginia, Rear Admiral Beatty commanding, at Charlestown Navy Yard, preparatory to possible war with Mexico.

Fight or Frolic

Here's a Food that, like our Navy, Is Always Ready

Up and down our seacoast, Battleship, Transport, and Destroyer have been waiting the President's word.

At Portsmouth, Charlestown, Brooklyn, League Island, Washington, Norfolk, Pensacola, and New Orleans; at Mare Island, Bremerton, and our other Naval Stations the Big Ships that carry the Flag have been loading food for the guns, and food for the men.

Post Toasties

—ready-to-serve delicious bits of toasted white corn—a food that Uncle Sam and his men both like—has been a favorite aboard ship for many a year. Grocers sell them everywhere in tightly sealed packages that bring them to YOUR table factory fresh.

If you like good things to eat and want to get into action, order a package of delicious POST TOASTIES from the Grocer—

Although there were earlier local examples of patriotic produce identification, the "Fight or Frolic" ad was the first and most widely used national brand to employ this practice. Considering that the Tampico crisis was first reported on the 10th of April, the decision to employ the incident had to have been made before it became a full blown crisis on the 20th.

In the weeks before the crisis, the Postum ads employed housewives in aprons preparing meals for their businessmen husbands. With the fleet in Mexican waters and engaged in taking Vera Cruz, the ads changed in less than a week to the above naval motif.

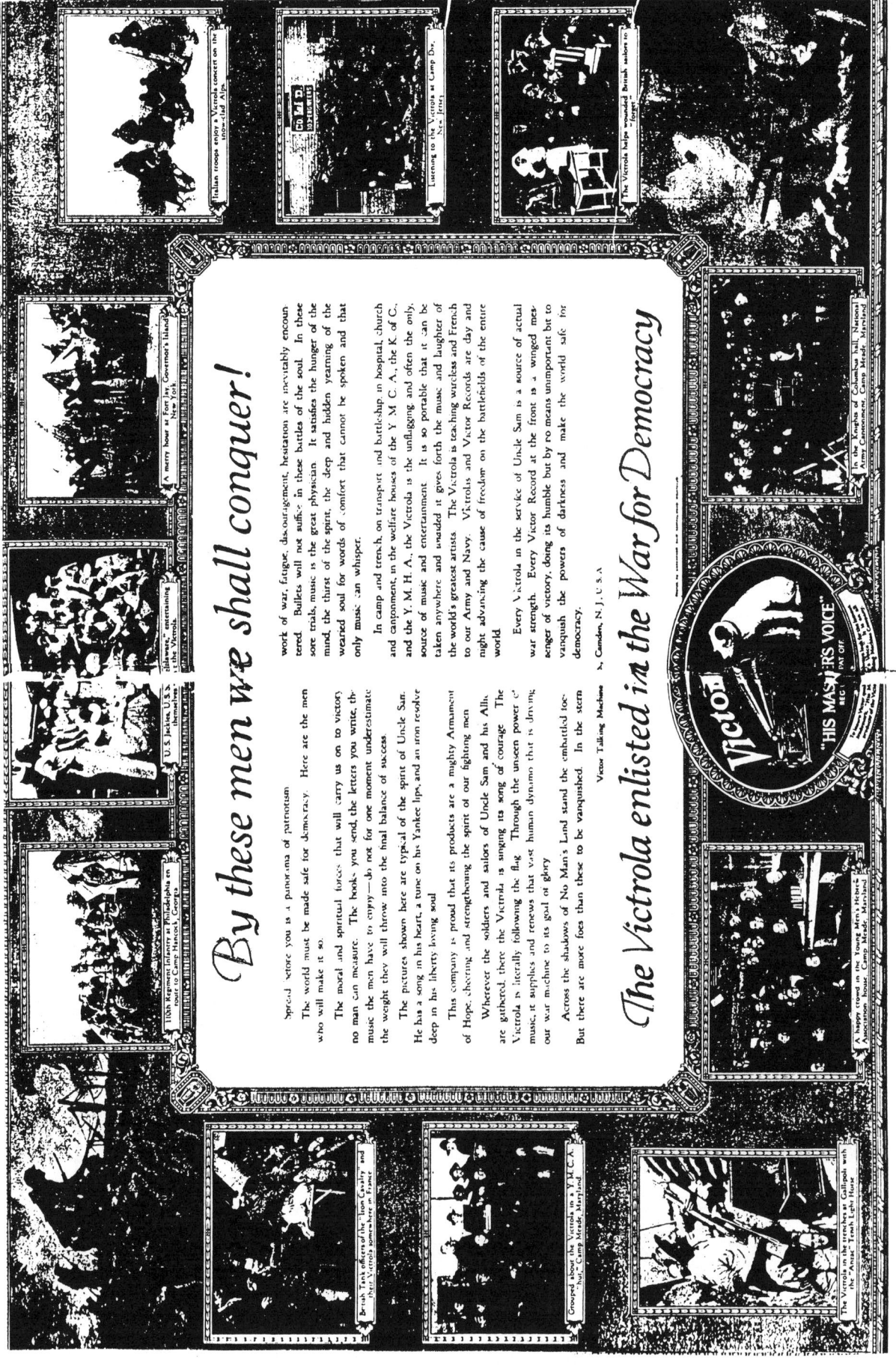

RCA's parent company produced as patriotic and effective an ad without the government's help: "Every Victrola in the service of Uncle Sam" was the "source of actual war strength." In 1918, Germany was the "Evil Empire" with the "powers of darkness" that Victor Records would help vanquish "and make the world safe for democracy."

Postum, Post Toasties and Patriotism

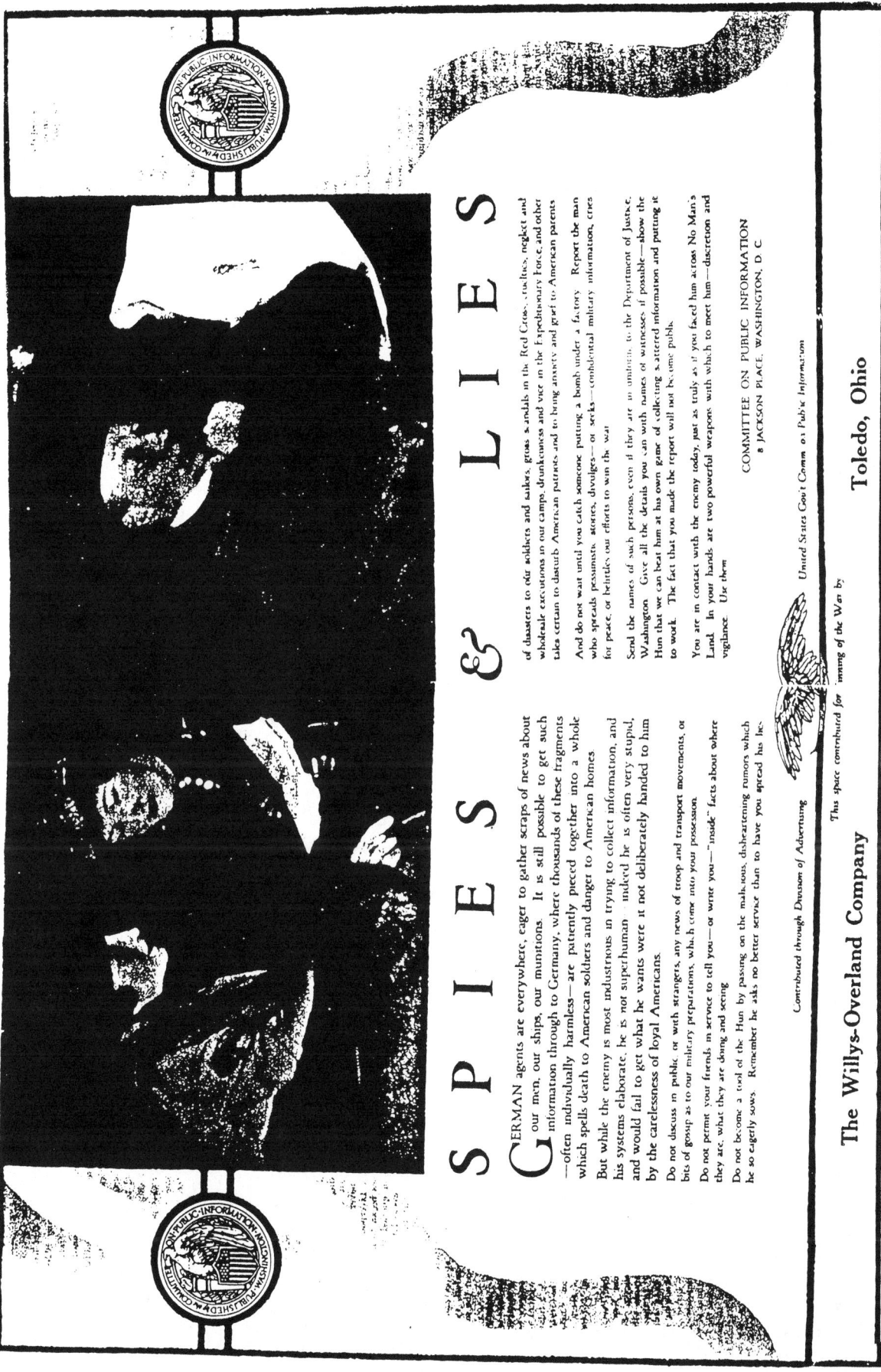

This ad is an excellent example of the close cooperation that existed between some in the business community and the government's war effort. The Committee on Public Information was headed by George Creel and was Woodrow Wilson's chief propaganda agency during WWI. Willys-Overland profited by contributing their ad space for this important public information message designed to helped win the war.

Ads Generated by Villa Crisis

A new opportunity occurred when in March of 1916 Pancho Villa's disenchantment with the Wilson administration exploded into the infamous raid on Columbus, New Mexico. The President responded by sending Pershing in a futile attempt to capture the revolutionary "Dead or Alive." Some ad men went along. The Wrigley's Spearmint people asked the public to empathize with their troops on the border: "If you were one of Uncle Sam's soldiers miles away in the cactus— temperature a hundred in the shade and no shade, dusty, tired, canteen empty...you'd give a good deal for a cool [chew]." A cavalry man was shown smiling as he opened his pack of gum.[32]

This "fight" may not have been a "frolic" for some, but old campaigners went along. Although in no way as aggressive as in the prior action, the New Post Toasties were there on horseback, armed and with welcomed reinforcements: "United States troopers [knew] a good thing....[All] along the Mexican border you'll find Grape-Nuts...one of the favorite foods of fighting men...wherever big things are to be done." Soldiers were shown preparing their breakfast by pouring it out of a familiar box.[33]

Border duty was, at best, boring. The early excitement generated by the prospects of a heroic and quick capture soon faded with unfulfilled headlines. But before the dreariness of the daily routine dampened the soldiers enthusiasm, 'Bull' Durham volunteered. This time, the ad men had a plan. In a smaller ad which was for coast to coast distribution, they claimed to be "alive with national spirit," but in the newspapers of the southwest the big campaign unfolded.[34] A small news story with an appropriate photograph in the pages of the *Bisbee Daily Review* was typical of the first action. The Tobacco Company of California announced that it had received orders from the parent company to pay all their employees "in active service on the border" full wages. They were further ordered to distribute their product to all men serving there. Five days later, on the 20th of July, they used half-page ads announcing their contribution: " 'Bull' Durham shipped in carload lots to Mexican border...from seasoned campaigner to newest 'rookie,' every American soldier 'rolls his own' with 'Bull' Durham."[35]

Some of the ads unconsciously reflected the passing of an era: four legs were giving way to four or more wheels. Mechanized cavalry would make its first "hot pursuit" in Mexico. Buda Motor Company advertised in the *Scientific American* that "northern Mexico [was] an awful test for a truck motor, but when Uncle Sam had to go into Mexico on Villa's Trail," he chose Buda to give him the ride.[36] In a full-page ad, Packard trucks illustrated much the same message: "War is the test of tests...and particularly so in the desolate wastes of old Mexico...[but] one hundred and twenty-two strong Packards [were] showing what trucks could do under the most adverse conditions....Army officers [had] specified Packards" for service in Mexico. As late as 1918 in an ad promoting Caterpillar tractors usefulness in France, that company still made reference to "when General Pershing went into Mexico in 1916...no roads existed....Caterpillar was there."[37]

Growth and Elaboration During the First World War

It is not too much to say that the "Mexican crisis" prepared many advertisers for the challenges of the first world war. The techniques developed during that time were merely refined, elaborated upon and expanded during the great war, but basically they remained the same. There was a significant difference in that many more national advertisers used the war as a basic theme to promote their products and that their advertisements also appeared in the weekly and monthly journals. The expressed goals were more lofty than the mere demand for a "salute" or an "apology," but Pershing still needed Packards. Now they were serving "over there...where they would prove their stamina on every battle front in Europe."[38]

New forces invaded the advertising world in 1917. George Creel's Committee on Public Information provided censorship service for many of the national ads. The Committee presented "Pershing's Crusaders" at local motion picture houses and advertised them as such in the national press.[39] Creel was also responsible for innovating practices that would be used in WWII. Companies were asked to donate their advertising copy for public service. And they responded: Corporations as diverse as Prudential, H.J. Heinz, and Goodyear Tire and Rubber encouraged the public to support bond drives and "National War Savings Day[s]." More dramatically, the Willy-Overland automobile company paid for two page ads in the *Literary Digest* warning Americans against "Spies and Lies" and that "German Agents were everywhere." The company's name was only briefly mentioned.[40] If one did not know what a "spy" was, the *Scientific American* offered a book that answered 2000 questions about the war: Is an enemy alien that gives information a spy? Is a woman of German

Postum, Post Toasties and Patriotism

birth a spy if she accidentally learns something of importance and tells of it? and most important, "What must a person do to be shot as a spy?"[41]

American Telephone and Telegraph saw their first active service in a series of ads entitled "The Miracle of the Marne in the Nation's Service" and "Lafayette, Here We Are." It was for us, "The Great Democracy," to rally all our might to the support of our army and allies. Only one brief line in small print identified the product as an essential industry in the national effort.[42]

The great majority of WWI ads served the dual purpose of public service and private profit. John Philip Sousa had written the music for the Spanish-American War. Now it was rearranged and replayed for American soldiers in Europe. "First in France" was the Marine Corps slogan, but it was also used by Columbia's Grafonala which sailed with them, if somewhat naively, "to help pass the time in camp and help them laugh in the trenches under shellfire." Not to be out done, another pubescent record company enlisted in the "War for Democracy." The two-page international panorama of patriotic pictures featured in the "Victrola in the trenches with the ANZAC'S at Gallipoli [and] with Italian troops enjoying a concert on the snow clad alps." The other ten photos were of American boys for which "bullets would not suffice...the Victrola [would sing] its song of courage" and fight right along side these brave young men.[43]

Many of the advertisers who enlisted in WWI are still familiar household names: Gillette and EverReady offered military shaving ["khaki"] kits for service men. Other companies reminded those who stayed behind of their duty. Eastman Kodak's product was marketed with a photograph of soldiers reading letters as the cure for "the homesick boy at the front." Parker fountain pens suggested their new "Trench Pen—non-self-filler, in case of injury" as a Christmas gift most desired by service men. To get our boys "Ready for the Huns—and for his French comrades, too," the Funk and Wagnalls Company offered the "Soldier's Service Dictionary." Westclock agreed that "food, bullets and dollars were vital factors in winning the war" but advised that "time" was even more important. "The clock" would be the final judge. Expressing an egalitarian spirit, they explained that "time was the only thing" that both "rich and poor alike" could give. Hart, Schaffner and Marx, in this conflict, encouraged all to "buy clothes only when needed." Campbell Soups reminded everyone that "when the Eagle fights, every American is glad to help. America was in this war "to the last ounce of energy, the last dollar, the last man." That included "woman...the bravest soldier of all."[44]

The changing role of women would be more evident in the patriotic advertising of WWII, but it began in 1917. While her man was away the woman became the forceful protector of her family when she purchased an Iver Johnson Revolver. Other women became industrial workers: "In larger numbers than ever before, women and girls [were] invading American industry" declared the "Standard" Plumbing Fixture Company. To help solve the problem this created in the work place, they offered manufacturers their booklet on "factory sanitation."[45]

Removed by nearly three-quarters of a century from the food shortages and "meatless days" of 1918, present day readers might consider some of the war's patriotic attempts to promote public service humorous, if not bizarre. Isbell's advertised a "War Garden Special" as an opportunity to help win the war. To promote the sale of pork products, the National Agricultural Society prepared a booklet for the WWI public and claimed that "fat may win the war" and that a pig was as "good as a bond." The choice was simple; it was "Pigs or Prussians." Anyone with a "pig in the back yard [was] to get a good grip on the right end of the question...Pigs, Patriotism and Profit." Readers were asked to mail in the coupon for an informative booklet.[46]

A few advertisers exploited less altruistic public spirit in an attempt to discredit competitors. Some ad men tried to capitalize on anti-German, anti-alien emotion. In response to such attacks the Pebeco toothpaste company mounted an offensive and counterattacked: Do not be the "Dupe of a Patriotrick." A patriotrick was a swindle by which "patriotism was twisted to serve the selfish interests of another." It usually took the form of spreading a rumor "that a certain brand...was in the control of 'Alien Enemies'." Pebeco claimed to be the victims of such a campaign and publicly assured all their customers "that all their officers and directors" were American citizens and no foreign capital was used to produce their goods.[47]

By 1918 ad agencies themselves promoted the profit potential of war advertising. In a series for the *Literary Digest* the Massengale Agency of Atlanta, Georgia pointed out to perspective subscribers that Dixieland was like a great battlefront. Because of its semitropical climate, the United States government had selected it as "its main field for war fighting preparation." There were more units south of the Mason-Dixon line than in all other states put together. The presence of these "big bodies of troops" meant "enormous and incalculable increase in the number of circulating dollars." They listed more than a hundred camps and locations by name along with more than forty newspapers they represented which would be "ideal" for advertising campaigns. Creel's watchdogs must have let this one slip through the cracks.[48]

With the Armistice, the militant tone of American advertising ended, it was time to capitalize on more peaceful themes. The war ads did not resurface until after Pearl Harbor. This form of advertising reached its zenith during WWII. All of the more popular magazines and journals used ads which reflected a particular product's contribution to or support for the nation's war effort. Advertisers did their share in promoting what was truly a popular cause.

Korea and Vietnam:
No Support from the Ad World

Although it is impossible to arrive at any precise formula, it can clearly be postulated from a survey of the source material in this study that there was a positive correlation between the popularity of a particular conflict and the amount of advertising produced by the nation's ad men to support it. A few companies, Boeing, Nothrop and North American Aviation, used the Korean police action to promote new aircraft such as the Saber Jet, but the ads were almost totally restricted to trade journals, like *Popular Science* or *Popular Mechanics*.[49] The *National Geographic Magazine* had been a medium for hundreds of patriotic ads during WWII; none were used to promote the Korean action or the conflict in Southeast Asia. Not one of the popular journals mentioned in this study did so. As late as 1952, the *Saturday Evening Post* was still publishing stories reliving the heroics of WWII: "We Escaped in an Outlaw U-boat—an amazing untold saga of WWII."[50] The telephone company was promoting the use of "the book," men wearing fancy shirts were sporting an eye patch. And in the late sixties, some women who smoked had one eye blackened, not in defense of their nation but for refusing to switch brands. International Harvester was not using a "till the Japs say 'uncle' "—or any other Asiatic epithet—in their ads.[51] And there were no pictures taken of Post Toasties being loaded on the Enterprise preparatory to possible war with "Veet Nam."[52]

Notes

[1]"Have a 'Coke'," *Life* August 28, 1944, back cover.

[2]This does not include a significant number of quarter page and smaller ads which appeared as frequently and were as patriotic.

[3]"Army and Memorial Badges," *Harpers Weekly* January 7, 1865, 15.

[4]Alfred M. Lee, *The Daily Newspaper in America* (New York, 1937), 715.

[5]"Nation's Honor," and "Into the Enemy's Ranks," *NYT* April 12, 1898; "Spain's Grip on America," *NYT* April 13, 1898.

[6]"Ready with Flags," *NYT* April 22, 1898; "The Panorama Shifts Daily," *NYT* April 25, 1898.

[7]"That Eternal Question Why," *NYT* April 24, 1898.

[8]"Business and Belligerency," *NYT* April 24, 1898.

[9]In New Haven, for example, the Robert Cunningham Company, which sold everything from "up-to-date bicycles" to "dress" shoes, featured a stern Uncle Sam spanking a screaming Spain with a small "Cuba Libre" flag in the background. It was entitled "Spain Chastised." *New Haven Register* May 2, 1898. Thompson and Belden sold paint supplies with an ad announcing that Uncle Sam was out with his "war paint" and was as ready as they were. Two others followed later, "Our Battery," and the "Results of a Brush," which changed the map of the Caribbean. *NHR* May 18 and 23. Simpler one line formats, "High prices—like Spanish rule—must go," were used beneath a waving American flag by the McIntyre [dry goods] Company. Although others would do it in a more polished fashion in later conflicts, this use of military terms was an obvious [none too symbolic] identification with the Cuban war: "For years we have kept up a constant cannonading. Many of the old Forts have succumbed. Our up-to-date assortment of the choicest goods, our small profit system of doing business and our little prices are a Fleet that cannot be equalled and will win every time, no matter how strong Old Fortifications are. Talk of 13-inch Rifled Guns! Read about these projectiles and come and see them. No other navy, fort and country can produce their equal." *NHR* May 19, 1898. Possibly because of their name, Londonderry, this Litha water company, claimed to be "intensely American." The watchword now was "American products for Americans." *NHR* May 18, 1898.

[10]"For good service...," *New London Day* April 12, 1898; "A gas range ready to fire," *Ansonia Citizen* May 9, 1898; "Poor eyes at Camp Haven," *NLD* May 17, 1898. This ad appeared above that of Chas R. Stadden's which featured an Uncle Sam with spy glass standing on the quarterdeck of an "overly" armed destroyer. It was entitled "Uncle Sam is on the Lookout." The small insert read "Columbus 1492, the United States 1898."

[11]"Prepared for Action," *New London Day* April 13 and 16, 1898. "The Cannon Ball Express...is pretty certain to make a change in the political division of the Western Continent," April 20, 1898. "Harvest of Death,...500,000 Cubans starved to death by Spanish rule," April 26, 1898. "Monkeying with the Maine Hornets Nest...has brought Spain to her present plight...monkeying with inferior material will [ruin your home]," May 3, 1898.

[12]"Give us liberty," *NLD* April 15, 1898; "Don't be afraid," April 29, 1898.

[13]" 'Hurrah' for Commodore Dewey and his brave men. Let us celebrate by singing the Star-Spangled Banner," *Ansonia Citizen* May 10, 1898; variation of same in *New Haven Register* and *New Haven Times Union* May 2, 1898. " 'Dewey' did it by having good material...use the same for your house," June

Postum, Post Toasties and Patriotism

14, 1898. "One of the first elephants..." *Ansonia Citizen* June 8, 1898. Later that month the circus moved to New London and advertised in the *Day*: "Remember the Main [sic] is the show;" they did not fail to mention the "baby elephant," June 8, 1898.

[14] The entire incident is covered in a superior monograph: Robert Quirk, *An Affair of Honor* (New York, 1967), Ch. 2.

[15] For reasons which are not completely clear to this reporter, Wilson's major biographer, Arthur Link, in his three volume work and his *Woodrow Wilson and the Progressive Era*, has written that the nation was not for intervention or with Wilson in the Tampico case. In a long footnote (footnote 40, p. 124) he explains that peace groups, socialists, ministers and others were opposed; this is true enough, but these groups represent only a fraction of those who would have warred with Mexico. In an article for *Connecticut History*, "The Tampico Incident: Connecticut Almost Goes to War" (November 1987) and two papers (for the Association of Connecticut Historians and the Duquesne Forum, 1988), I presented the results of a study of more than four hundred New England and nationwide newspapers which leave no doubt in this researcher's mind that Wilson could have had war with Mexico for the asking at any time in April of 1914 and right up to the outbreak of WWI. There was significant dissatisfaction with the administration's lack of action and lack of preparation prior to the Great War.

[16] "War with Mexico," *Arizona Daily Star* April 22, 1914; "Branner's Daily Banner," *Tucson Citizen* April 27, 1914; "Join the Army," *Arizona Republican* April 22, 1914. The *Republican* also offered: "*The True History of Mexico*...all nations are today watching unhappy Mexico, where bullets are more potent than ballots," April 22, 1898. A similar offer was made by the *Daily Eastern Argus*, a newspaper in Portland, Maine.

[17] "The Eagle..." *Bangor Daily News* April 27, 1914; "In camp and field...".

[18] "War is hell," *Fairbanks Daily News-Miner* April 20, 1914; "U.S. volunteers," "War declared on high prices," "War, war, war," "Uncle Sam is after Huerta's goat," April 23, 1914.

[19] "Mexico War Map," *Los Angeles Examiner* April 17, 1914. "This instructive map printed in colors...will familiarize you with places where history is in the making and will entertain the whole household. One person can play it, or two or three." *Boston Post* April 29, 1914.

[20] "War with Mexico," *Los Angeles Examiner* April 22, 1914.

[21] "War has started..." *Rocky Mountain News* April 12, 1914. Two thousand miles away in New Hampshire, the Keene Evening Sentinel, the C.C. Beedle Piano Co, expressed the same sentiment: "Watchful waiting, succeeded by energetic action....The eyes of the world are now focussed on the U.S. Navy....Peremptory presidential orders for such big sea fighters as the Florida, Connecticut [she was there already as Admiral Mayo's flag ship], New Jersey...to hurry to Mexican waters shows that Uncle Sam is in earnest and will not be trifled with...." April 28, 1914. This ad for Autopiano's was another of the many that appeared in the Northeast; they were, it seems, either very patriotic or in a hurry to get their music makers into Mexican waters: "Lying at anchor in New York's harbor is one of the United States' mightiest fleets, the North Atlantic...120 vessels." They pictured the fleet "passing the Autopiano factory in New York" and claimed that there was an "Autopiano on every warship at Mexico." *Portland Daily Press* April 24, 1914. "National order of..." *Rocky Mountain News* April 21, 1914.

[22] "Budd..." *Rocky Mountain News* April 24, 1914. "In every walk of life you'll find good old 'Bull' Durham...men of action, men with red blood," April 26, 1914. This ad had a wide distribution in many different newspapers.

[23] The *Moosup Journal* and the *Litchfield Enquirer* were very small town weeklies in Connecticut whose main concern was listing "who and when had come to visit where and what." Their features were very local, preserves, cows, feedstores, but the Tampico affair put national news in their pages. Weir Brothers, a meat store, even produced an ad: "The war scare...." The Outlet in the *New London Day* advertised "one week of battling prices, a chance to salute the styles. War declared, May 1, 1914." "War is hell," *Ansonia Citizen* April 24, 1914. *New Orleans Times-Democrat and Daily Picayune* April 27, 1914. "War, it has come to this," *Enid Daily Eagle* April 23, 1914. On the 24th, the *Lawrence Telegram* advertised a small volume of war songs, but many larger papers used full page ads as subscription promotions for their war songs: "Songs of war and patriotism...and one great song that grew out of our first Mexican War, 'The field of Monterey!'" *Portland Sunday Telegram* April 26, 1914. The *Boston Post*'s song book helped answer a question which perplexed many North Americans: "Songs that cheered our troops to victory...in the first Mexican War...'Green Grow the Rashes O!' was heard so much that the natives called Americans 'gringos'." April 26, 1914.

[24] "3,000,000 Volunteers," *Los Angeles Times* April 21, 1914; *Tucson Citizen* April 27, 1914.

[25] It was a formidable group: Jack London "is our war correspondent with General Wood [still in the United States making speeches] and General Funston [in Texas preparing to leave for Vera Cruz]." Jimmy Hare, "our own war photographer of the Spanish-American War...Henry Reuterdahl, America's foremost naval artist [and] Arthur Ruhl, authority on Central America and South American problems, [are] at Vera Cruz." By the time this ad appeared in the *Scientific American*, the fighting was over, the occupation had begun, an occupation that proved to be too dull to keep many of the war correspondents there beyond the first reports of the German mobilization in August. May 9, 1914.

[26] "Buick," *Los Angeles Examiner* and *Los Angeles Times* April 26, 1914; "War is on in southern California," by the Moreland Motor Truck Company, ibid.

[27] For example the *New York World*, the *Boston Post*, the *Bridgeport [Connecticut] Post* and the *Los Angeles Examiner*, to name a few, used the ad April 23, 1914; "...Hale," *Boston Herald* April 24, 1914.

[28] *Atlanta Constitution* April 13, 15, 20, 27, 29, 1914; *Chicago Tribune* April 28, 1914; *Los Angeles Times* April 30, 1914; *Rocky Mountain News* April 30, 1914; *Boston Post* April 28, 1914.

[29] For the regular Postum ad: *NYT* April 28, 1914. War ad: *Providence Evening Bulletin, New Haven Union, Birmingham [Alabama] News, New Orleans Times-Democrat and Daily Picayune* April 28, 1914; *Penny Press* [Middletown, Connecticut], *NYT, Los Angeles Examiner* April 29, 1914.

[30] *NYT, New Haven Union* April 24, 1914; *Boston Post, Willimantic Daily Chronicle, Birmingham News* April 25, 1914; *News Orleans Times-Democrat and Daily Picayune* April 27, 1914; *Los Angeles Examiner* April 29, 1914; *Bisbee Daily Reporter* April 30, 1914.

[31] *Literary Digest* August 8, 1914, 243.

[32] *New London Day* September 9, 1916. At times the connection was a little thin. Rexall used a soldier to underscore the need to *guard* the home against biliousness and constipation. *Winstead Evening Citizen* April 18, 1916.

[33] "The Real Thing," *Bisbee Daily Review* August 10, 1916; "U.S. Troopers know a good thing," August 9, 1916. A week later they reinforced the message by identifying themselves with the technological marvel of the century: "In Mexico or Panama...or wherever Americans must endure the torrid heat, there you will find the tasty food Grape-nuts. In building the Panama Canal thousands of workers kept brains clear and bodies fit...so [too] with our fighting men along the Mexican border." August 13, 1916.

[34] "Alive..." *New London Day* March 10, 1916.

[35] "Joys of 'Bull' Durham invade ranks of Uncle Sam's soldiers," *Bisbee Daily Review* July 15, 1916; " 'Bull' Durham being shipped..." July 20, 1916.

[36] "When I had to go into Mexico on Villa's trail," *Scientific American* June 3, 1916, 603. The Jeffrey Motor Truck Company also used a Mexican motif: "Over mountain passes and desert trails," and "War's test is the test of test's." They used a full-page photograph titled "With Pershing in Mexico." ibid., 571. Clarence C. Clendenen, an old campaigner himself, discussed the problem of purchasing these trucks in the immediate confusion after the raid in his *Blood on the Border*: "According to tradition, they [the Secretary of War and his border commander] moved boldly and practically seized a shipload of trucks on the docks...awaiting shipment to Europe...Whites, Jeffreys, Macks, Packards..." ibid., 225.

[37] "When General Pershing went into Mexico in '16, no roads existed for either trucks or mule teams....desert trails were quickly whipped into deep ruts...but, the U.S. Corps of Engineers rushed 'Caterpillar' tractors to the border by special express trains....they kept communication lines open for...the troops...far to the south," *Literary Digest* July 13, 1918, 59. The big machines had made the front page of the *Bisbee Daily Press* August 12, 1916: "Giant tractor used by troops on border irons out roads."

[38] "Army's Packards," *Scientific American* March 9, 1918, 225; "Pershing's hand is set to help win the war," *Independent* January 19, 1918.

[39] "Pershing's Crusaders," "the government's own film," *Literary Digest* June 7, 1918, 1; July 28, 1918, 55. Prudential: *Independent*, February 9, 1918; Heinz, June 15, 1918, 79.

[40] "Spies and lies," "German spies are everywhere, eager to gather scraps of news about our men....do not wait until you catch someone putting a bomb under a factory...[do not help in spreading] lies of disasters...grow scandals in the Red Cross...drunkenness and vice in the Expeditionary Force-....send the names of such persons to the Department of Justice." *Literary Digest* June 28, 1918, 49-50.

[41] "What is a Spy?" *Scientific American* May 11, 1918, 444.

[42] *Independent* March 9, 1918, 423; April 13, 1918; May 11, 1918, 259; October 12, 1918. The *Outlook*, *Review of Reviews*, *Current Opinion*, and *Scientific American* carried the same ads.

[43] "First in France," *Literary Digest* April 20, 1914; "By these men we shall conquer," May 18, 1918, 523.

[44] "EverReady Army Razor," *Literary Digest* April 6, 63; "For Active Service," *ibid.*, 103; "Why do so many of Uncle Sam's boys use Gillette?" *Scientific American* March 9, 1928, 261; "There's Cheer in the Pictures From Home," *Independent*. Another version in the *Review of Reviews* December 1917, 83. "Keep the Home Fires Burning," Literary *Digest*, April 6, 1918, inside cover; another version, *Independent* November 7, 1918. The Waterman Ideal Fountain Pen Company also served "Making and Writing History," *Scientific American* May 4, 1918. "Ready for the Huns," *Literary Digest* September 21, 1918, 60. In answer to the question "What Shall I Send Him Now?" the *Independent* Corporation suggested a Roth Memory Kit. March 30, 1918. The American Bible Society wanted to help put a "Khaki Testament in every Soldiers Kit," *Independent* October 20, 1917. "Time and the War," *Literary Digest* August 17, 1918, 1; "When the Eagle Fights," *ibid.*, 43.

[45] "Women in factories," *Literary Digest* May 18, 1918, 94; "Now You Won't Feel Afraid," March 1918, 455; "The Girls Can Do Their Share: It's Easy to Farm With a Straude," ibid., April 20, 1918, 47. One of the most observable features of WWII advertising is the emergence of the modern American woman and the ever increasing role that she was playing in helping to win the war. "The girl behind the man behind the gun...," is only one of hundreds of such ads. *Life* September 18, 1944, back cover.

[46] "Fat May Win the War," *Literary Digest* May 18, 1918, 2.

[47] "Are You the Dupe of...," *Literary Digest* June 6, 1918, 63.

[48] "Army Camps, Aviation Fields...," *Literary Digest* April 13, 1918, 6-7; "How Dixieland is helping to win the war," ibid., June 29, 1918, 8-9.

[49] Caterpillar, in *Newsweek* (May 14, 1951), did use an insert of American fighting men, but it is impossible to tell where they were or even if they were involved in conflict. Boeing advertised its C-97 strato-freighter showing what it could do in time of need, but there was no mention of the war. Although the Korean action may have enjoyed some degree of popularity for those who viewed the world in a "Cold War" context, for a brief period after the successful Inchon invasion, it seems obvious to this reporter that the advertisers sensed that there was no general feeling of popular support for the conflict, certainly not one strong enough for one to capitalize on. Although the fighting which took place between 1964 to 1973, a significantly longer period than 3 weeks in April of 1914, would cost more than 50,000 American lives, it would be impossible for anyone familiar with the advertising used during that time to even be aware that their country was involved in so costly a conflict.

[50] *Saturday Evening Post* November 22, 1952.

[51] "Till the Japs Say Uncle," *Saturday Evening Post* April 21, 1945; "Getting Ready For the Japs," "How to Keep a Jeep in Shape for the Japs," ibid.

[52] A pronunciation popularized by President Johnson.

Images of Yuppies in Popular Advertisements of the 1980s

Luigi Manca

Preface:
Some Theoretical and Methodological Assumptions

In this paper I attempt to analyze a sample of twenty magazine advertisements from the 1980s that may help to illustrate the emergence of the yuppies as Madison Avenue's new and formidable role models for American consumers.

The concept of "yuppy" used in this paper is derived exclusively from popular advertising images and has no necessary correlation with real yuppies in the real world, if indeed there are such people. In other words, the paper deals with Madison Avenue's images of yuppies and not with yuppies themselves. The term "yuppy" is defined here as referring to young and successful professionals in their thirties or early forties exclusively devoted to the pursuit of happiness in business, family, sex, and private affairs.

American consumers regard the pursuit of happiness as an inalienable individual right. They hold a very pragmatic and somewhat materialistic view of what happiness is, and they see the open marketplace as the great equalizer that allows all citizens to get a fair shake in their individual quest to satisfy personal needs and desires. Perhaps as a reflection of this important trait in consumer culture, the pursuit of happiness has been for many decades a fundamental theme in American advertising.[1]

In the 1980s, the pursuit of happiness continued to influence both the American way of life and the content of popular advertisements. Yuppies emerged as an important consumer force in the marketplace and, in the political arena, Ronald Reagan captured the imagination of millions of Americans by promising that one's self-centered pursuit of happiness was, in fact, the best way to help others. (The reasoning went pretty much like this: Only when people are free from government interference as well as from their own sense of guilt about the less fortunate can they build a strong economy that will take care of everybody—including those who can't or, as in the case of the "poor by choice," don't want to help themselves.) Madison Avenue has both reflected and exploited these changes in the public mood. During the Reagan years, many popular advertisements were encouraging people to pursue selfish needs and desires even more than in the past. The yuppy thus became an important role model for the American consumer.

The popular images we get about the yuppies, their devotion to the pursuit of happiness, and their formidable spending power perhaps may be exaggerated and may not square with some of the statistical evidence.[2] The yuppies of the 1980s may be just as much a myth as, indeed, the huge American middle class of the 1950s and 1960s might well have been. Yet, the myth has helped shape the whole consumeristic society of the 1980s just as the middle class ideal helped shape the consumer society of the 1950s and 1960s.

This paper investigates the consumer culture of the 1980s by simply looking into the advertising mirror. The original data for the investigation are provided by an in-depth analysis of twenty popular advertisements from this period chosen to represent the advertising industry's depiction of the new yuppish role models for the pursuit of happiness. Before I begin the presentation of the findings, I need to discuss the limitations of the research as well as the theoretical and methodological assumptions underlying the study.

First, the study was designed to simply *illustrate* certain theoretical principles about the pursuit of happiness in advertising and in American culture—but not to *demonstrate* their validity or reliability. Both the selection and the analysis of the twenty advertisements clearly reflect the researcher's own subjectivity; another researcher would probably not produce the same data. While this type of study may not claim to provide indisputable evidence, it may offer some intuitive insights into the subject. I believe that these insights are very important in the study of the mass media and their impact on consumer consciousness.

A fundamental assumption which has guided my research (even though I am aware that I might never be able to demonstrate it) is that, overall, the images portrayed in the most common advertisements reflect the consumers' collective unconscious. I am proposing that advertising functions as a sophisticated cultural mirror, capable of bringing to light images of the American consumer's most intimate motives and desires, secret aspirations, and forbidden fantasies.[3] I submit that the American consumer is not a passive target of Madison Avenue's manipulating appeals, but rather a formidable co-conspirator. I submit also that, as a whole, advertisers are only acting as catalysts in bringing out the public's true feelings and emotions. Ultimately it is not up to the advertisers to determine what will and what will not sell. Consumers make that decision by rewarding only those images and appeals that they like. Therefore, only those images and appeals that are consistent with people's however peculiar needs and desires would tend to survive and prosper. To be sure, American consumers are being manipulated by Madison Avenue's hidden persuaders, and they are not even very aware of what is happening to them. At some subconscious level, however, the advertisers are the ones who are calling the shots.[4]

I believe these theoretical propositions to be very important and I intend to expand on them by relating the insights generated through my analysis of the twenty advertisements depicting various examples of Madison Avenue's use of the "pursuit of happiness" themes. According to the method I have devised, advertisements may be read within three levels of analysis: spoken, unspoken, and unspeakable.

At the spoken level of analysis, we consider that portion of the advertisement's content which consumers would be able to articulate without much probing. We postulate that at this level consumers are aware of what is happening to them and are able to tell why. The analysis of the advertisement deals strictly with facts or with obvious common-sense interpretations of facts.

At the unspoken level of analysis, the advertising content cannot be easily put into words. At this level, consumers may not be aware immediately of the message. When probed, they may be able to make some general and vague statements about whatever they are experiencing but would find it difficult to describe exactly what is happening to them. At this level, our analysis of the advertisement deals with somewhat more subjective interpretations of what is going on in the picture. In our analysis, we need to treat the advertisement as a work of fiction (like a novel, painting or motion picture) and attempt to probe the feelings and emotions of its fictional characters as well as our own responses.

Finally, at the level of the unspeakable, the analysis focuses on that portion of the advertisement's content which is assumed to be repressed within the reader's subconscious. We assume that not only are the consumers not aware of their true feelings, but they would not speak of them even if they knew of them. The analysis of an advertisement's unspeakable content almost inevitably deals with controversial inferences about cultural and personal taboos that may be evoked by the picture. We need not assume that the people who made the advertisement were necessarily aware of the unspeakable content, just as an artist may not be conscious of whatever hidden message the critics discover in his or her work.

Liberty and the pursuit of happiness are often tied with one another in popular advertisements

In American advertising, the notions of freedom and happiness are closely tied together. For several decades, for example, the Marlboro cowboy has been riding throughout the rugged west finding his happiness only in knowledge that he was asserting his free will in his eternal struggle against the punishing unforgiving environment. In a typical Marlboro advertisement [© 1983], we see a close-up of a cowboy's face. It is the face of a freedom fighter. His eyes show unstoppable, indestructible conviction. He will keep on fighting for his freedom as long as there's life in his lungs.

At some unspeakable level, his fight is one against cancer and even against the Surgeon General who determined that smoking is a health hazard. Against all odds, our Marlboro man will not give up the cigarette which is the symbol of his freedom. The concepts of "Marlboro Country" and the "Marlboro cowboys" were created back in the 1950s, decades before the rising of the yuppies, and they are still successful today because of their extraordinary universal appeal to both the working class and the professional elite.

An advertisement introducing Classic Visa cards [© 1984] proposes a freedom appeal quite different from that of Marlboro. In a very elegant and expensive restaurant, a young upper-middle class couple is portrayed at the end of what we may infer was an enjoyable dinner. The waiter, wearing a black suite and tie, is walking away from the picture, holding in his hand a silver platter with the bill and a Classic Visa Card. "You made Visa a classic," the ad says. But even more important, in the lower right corner, it concludes in smaller type: "You can do it. We'd like to help."

The card is presented as an obvious symbol of yuppy freedom. It is shown as the ticket that allows the couple to go everywhere. Many readers (the ad appeared in *TV Guide* and was thus aimed at a predominantly middle class public) feel intimidated by fancy restaurants; they feel out of place. They are afraid that they may embarrass themselves, as regularly happens in television sitcoms. Most of all, they fear the haughty waiter who will be judging their every move and won't hesitate to castigate them in front of all the other diners for the slightest transgression. Our couple, however, has just what it takes to keep him in his place: the Classic Visa card. Although the waiter's face is virtually cut off from the picture, we can see that he is smiling approvingly.

In the 1980s, many advertisements aimed at women have also kept the notions of happiness and freedom tied together. For example, the Virginia Slims advertisements of the 1970s and 1980s have been proposing their cigarette as a symbol of liberation and happiness. An indignant yet humorous condemnation of the old days when women were not allowed to smoke, a touch of chic liberation, and a promise of beautiful slim body just like that of a glamorous fashion model have provided the trademark of the Virginia Slims advertisements throughout the 1970s and 1980s. Also, the slogan "You've come a long way, baby" has remained unchanged all these years. In a two-page advertisement from *TV Guide* [Virginia Slims, © 1988], we are presented with a caricature-like vision from our repressive Victorian past. A crowd of well-to-do men and women are posing against a white gazebo in the middle of a park. The men are tacky, pompous and oppressive; the women share an expression of sorrow and resignation. The copy below the old-days photograph tells us that in 1903 women weren't allowed to smoke. Then, on the other page, we see a much larger picture of today's yuppy woman—an elegant and slim fashion model who is celebrating her freedom as she looks with a confident smile into the camera. The slim cigarette she holds in her hand is the symbol of a beautiful person free from the oppression of men. Since she has come a long way, Philip Morris has made a cigarette just for her so that every time she lights one she can celebrate her inalienable right to smoke and to show off her beautiful slim body.

It is interesting to note that, at some unspoken or even unspeakable level, the Virginia Slims cigarette is the symbol not only of a woman's freedom from man's domination but also from body fat. The very name of the cigarette, "Slims," and the selection of slender models to be highlighted in the ads seem to combine to suggest the unspeakable proposition that smoking helps today's woman stay trim.

Another example of Madison Avenue's appeal to women's fantasies of freedom is an advertisement for Gillette Daisy Twin Blade Shavers [© 1983]. The ad proposes an unlikely graduation scene in a woman's college. In a crowd of disapproving yet envious white-gowned graduates, one free-spirited student dares to show off her beautiful legs. "When you shave with Daisy, you go a little crazy," the copy explains. On the surface the women in the crowd seem to be embarrassed only by the Daisy user's exhibitionism. Deep down, however, they are ashamed because their own legs are not so hairless and beautiful.

On the one hand, the graduation theme is used to display conformity and oppression in an Orwellian fashion. All the women in the picture experience real discomfort and feel inhibited because of their hairy legs. They are passively resigned to their fate and, symbolically, the college from which they are graduating becomes the place where they have been trained to repress their desire for freedom—and for beautiful legs. They have learned to be another anonymous—and leg-less—face in the crowd. On the other hand, graduation may also be a symbol of a student finally seeing the light. In this sense, only one graduates in this group. She is the bright one; she is creative. She does not accept the oppression and discomfort of hairy legs. She finds a brilliant solution that allows her to be free, to express her own self with confidence, knowing that her legs are no longer an object of shame to be covered up but one of beauty to be shown off.

An advertisement for Vanderbilt perfume [© 1987] proposes an interesting and quite peculiar liberation appeal to women. It offers an enchanting photographic composition: below a close-up of a young and beautiful woman's face next to that of her lover is a picture of a majestic swan about to take off from the blue waters of a lake. "Let it release the splendor of you," the copy says. The ad evokes a fairy tale along the lines of Swan Lake theme. The swan is the symbol of a woman's inner grace and beauty and of her very freedom. To be sure, this is not the same kind of freedom as that proposed in one of those ads for Marlboro or Camel cigarettes.

The woman's free energy is not directed outward toward a tough and competitive world, but inward toward a peaceful and enchanted world of her own. The advertisers of Vanderbilt perfume promise an escape within an inner magical dimension where the woman/swan takes off on her exhilarating flight to freedom above the enchanted waters of the lake.

In advertisements featuring yuppies success is tied to the pursuit of happiness

Yuppies seem to have readily accepted into their way of life a fundamental trait of American culture—namely the belief in success and in the individual's ability to achieve it. For the yuppies, however, success is more a means for pursuing happiness than an end in itself. The thrill of struggling head-to-head to beat the competition and the quest for higher social status and power do not seem to capture the yuppies' imagination—at least in the eyes of Madison Avenue—in the same way as the pleasure of cashing in on one's hard work and skills.

During the 1980s, many advertising campaigns have been stressing images of people enjoying their success rather than struggling to achieve it. Moreover, they have been making relatively little use of those symbols of status or power which are normally associated with success. Instead, these advertisements have been stressing personal pleasure and a certain amount of physical, economic and emotional security. In this, Madison Avenue seems to have slightly modified the American ideal of success, which was traditionally associated primarily with hard work, tough competition, and continuous challenges through which the fittest eventually assert their will. Advertisements featuring yuppies have often depicted success as the achievement of self-realization. Rather than showing people competing with one another, these ads have proposed images of people doing their own thing in a virtually stress-free environment.

In the mid-1980s, Vantage cigarettes launched an advertising campaign featuring several young, affluent and self-motivated men and women realizing their dreams. The Vantage ads told stories of successful professionals such as artists, dancers, filmmakers, fashion designers, architects, journalists. They also told stories of people finally getting the antique luxury car or the new boat they had been coveting in their yuppy hearts. And in all these ads the copy read: "Vantage. The taste of Success."

In one of these advertisements [Vantage, © 1984], a man and a woman are having a picnic at the construction site where their new home is being built. All the workers are gone and this allows the two some quiet and privacy as they celebrate the realization of their dream. There is no trace of stress or uncertainty in this advertisement. The man and woman are savoring a piece of their wonderful future together in their new home. Their future is symbolically represented by the solid foundation of the house being built, which makes up the entire background of the picture. They know that nothing can take their happiness away from them.

Here is another example of the advertising industry's exploitation of the yuppies' particular fascination with success:

"I promised her the glow of gold for Christmas," says the husband in an advertisement for International Gold Corporation [© 1984]—and he delivered. Now, in the golden light of the fireplace, he allows himself a relaxed and triumphant smile as his fortunate wife sits on his knee with her arms around his neck and an equally triumphant smile of her own. She is wearing her new outstanding real gold necklace and still holds in her hand the box it came in. It is interesting to note that while the man is looking with confidence—and maybe even arrogance—at the camera to show off his satisfaction with his many accomplishments, the woman's eyes look away as she celebrates her happiness in a more private and inner fashion.

An ad for Children's Tylenol [© 1988] provides a good example of how success and happiness are combined with a strong feeling of security in many advertisements featuring yuppies. Through a door into the nursery we see a young mother in a rocking chair gently holding her child who is sleeping comfortably and safely in her arms. The light is soft and gentle; the room is quiet and protected from whatever evil might lurk in the outside world. The ad says: "She is a pediatrician. When her child has a fever, there's only one medicine she trusts." Then the ad concludes: "Children's Tylenol. The one most pediatricians give to their own children."

All the components of the ad combine to convey a strong sense of safety. First, images of a mother with her child are most often loaded with feelings of security and protection. They tend to evoke in the readers archetypal images of a mother's warmth, safety and comfort. Moreover, in this ad a mother's loving protection is brilliantly combined with the expert and competent protection a doctor can give. It is interesting to note that in order to make this combination even more believable, the advertisers chose to sacrifice another formidable claim: Children's Tylenol may also be the one most pediatricians give to anybody's children.

If safety seems to be the dominant claim, the Children's Tylenol ad also stresses personal success. The archetype of a mother holding her child is reproposed in this ad in a more contemporary fashion. The mother is unmistakably a yuppy Unlike the archetype of the Virgin Mary who was poor and a full-time wife, our mother is a well-to-do successful professional. She carves out her career in the competitive outside world, yet also has the time to nurture her child in the comfort of the safe and protected environment she has built for herself and her family.

The sexual suggestions tied with Madison Avenue's promises of happiness have become more sophisticated

Madison Avenue's exploitation of the consumer's sexual desires and fantasies is such an obvious feature of American advertising that even the least perceptive critic would easily be able to point it out to us. Many advertisements from the 1980s, however, have abandoned blatant sexual appeals in favor of somewhat more subtle (and sometimes kinkier) suggestions.

In the very early 1980s, a series of magazine advertisements for Barclay cigarettes began proposing a confident, distinctive and mysterious man as a role model for millions of American smokers. The ads showed a close up of this impeccably dressed man either lighting a cigarette or holding it. A woman's hand was also shown in the picture, holding sometimes a drink, sometimes a cigarette, sometimes even a lighter. The colors were predominantly dark. The copy read: "The pleasure is back." In one of these "The pleasure is back" advertisements [Barclay, © 1982], the man is wearing a dark business suit and tie and is about to light his Barclay cigarette with his gold lighter. The woman's hand is holding a cocktail glass. He is looking at her with an almost inscrutable expression. Perhaps we are to infer that he is pleased, but it is not clear whether he is pleased with his cigarette, with the woman, or with himself.

The ad is able to create two unspoken associations. The first one is obvious: it connects the Barclay cigarette with the man, providing the male reader with a powerful role model. The second association, less obvious, is between the cigarette and the woman. Our hero seems to become aware of the woman's attention just as he is about to light his cigarette. The male reader is thus vicariously offered both the cigarette and the woman.

An advertisement for Amaretto di Saronno claims "Not for love or money. Simply for taste" [© 1984]. Against a black background, the ad introduces three peculiar but also elegant and sophisticated yuppy characters. The first is a glamorous sexy brunette holding a light Amaretto di Saronno glass. She is wearing a fur coat but still manages to show her naked shoulders and a knee. The second character is an elegantly dressed blonde holding a red rose; her smile is bitter, almost a frown. The third character is a man in a black tuxedo holding a more masculine glass with Amaretto di Saronno on the rocks. He has a confident and pleased smile as he looks straight to the first woman's knee. It is clear enough that the makers of the ad are trying to establish an association in the reader's mind between their liqueur and the sophisticated and kinky games of the rich and beautiful people.

The ad seems to have been composed so as to be open to all sorts of unspeakable interpretations. First, the copy of "Not for Love or Money. Simply for Taste" seems to give us a clue that the story we are about to be told is one of a high class tart with taste and a strong vocation. Moreover, the blonde holding the red rose is directing her attention not to the man but to the other woman. She is turning her shoulders toward him and her hidden left arm must logically be around the brunette's shoulders. If we mentally pictured a man standing exactly in the same position as the blonde (i.e., with one hand on the other woman's shoulder and the other holding a red rose), we would have very few problems in admitting that this man is actually propositioning the brunette. Since we see a woman instead, we repress or quickly dismiss this unspeakable inference.

This is just one of the several kinky stories we might infer from the clues were are given: The brunette is a high-class prostitute who cannot be won simply by love or money. The blonde is trying to proposition her by offering a red rose, but the prostitute has her eye on the man in the black tuxedo, and he has his eye on her propositioning knee. The blonde is obviously disappointed.

Another interpretation of this peculiar triangle could be that the blonde is a jealous wife who is very annoyed at her husband's attentions to the tart and is offering her rival a poisoned red rose just like the bad witch offered Snow White a poisoned red apple.

Of course, what is really happening in this picture is that three professional models are posing for a studio photographer. However, our interpretations of advertisements such as this one should not be simply dismissed as subjective and invalid inferences. Advertising is not photojournalism; advertisers do not have to tell true stories.[5] They create illusions with whatever tools they have to appeal to the reader's unspoken and even unspeakable fantasies. As millions of consumers react to advertising images, these fantasies constitute a legitimate and fascinating field of inquiry and can generate invaluable insights into our culture.

Here is another example of how sexual suggestions can be introduced with extreme discretion, making use of the reader's own imagination. An advertisement for Raynal French Brandy prescribes "Raynal & relax" [© 1987]. The ad tells a story of a man and a woman, although they do not appear at all in the picture. All we can see is a close-up of some objects they left behind on the coffee table against a dark background lighted only by the warm glow of the fireplace. A bottle of Raynal, the man's glass with the ice cube still unmelted, the woman's glass lying on its side still holding some brandy, and a pearl necklace carelessly draped over a pencil and an unfinished crossword puzzle provide us all the clues to reconstruct what has just happened. Thus, in a rather discrete way, we get a glimpse of a romantic moment in the life of this rich and glamorous couple. She was doing her crossword puzzle, sipping her brandy. He suddenly appears, puts his glass on the table, nibbles the nape of her neck, and sweeps her off her feet. Now they are probably in each other's arms, out of the picture and safe from the indiscrete eye of the reader.

Another scene from the romantic life of a young, rich and sophisticated couple is proposed in an advertisement for Remy Martin Cognac [© 1987]. He holds the cognac glass close to her so she may smell—with her eyes almost closed—the wonderful aroma that seems to awaken her sensuality. The copy reads "Indulgent. The sense of Remy" as the man and the woman share their feelings toward the cognac and toward one another.

In popular advertisements women's sexual fantasies reflect a need to be in control

In the 1980s, many sexual fantasies suggested to the female reader by popular advertisements have stressed the woman's complete control over the sexual affair. While in a "rape fantasy" the woman abandons control over and responsibility for whatever is happening to her. In these particular fantasies she calls all the shots and would be able to end the affair at any moment if she wanted to.

An example of such control fantasies is provided by an advertisement for Nina Ricci's *L'Air du Temps* perfume [© date not given]. The unspeakable suggestions of this ad are obvious. Against the calm and hazy background of a deserted beach, we see the close-up of a young woman. Her eyes are closed and her expression is peaceful and dreamy as she kisses the rounded crystal top of the perfume bottle. The tip of the woman's tongue, barely visible, may be about to caress it. The design of the bottle itself shows two doves whose heads come together as if they were kissing. The advertisement is quiet and peaceful. It contains no threat to the woman's freedom. No other passion is to dominate the woman but her own.

Another naughty young woman in an advertisement for Fendi's perfume [© 1987] is brushing her lips against those of a Roman male statue. Her eyes are closed as if she were kissing a real lover. And the copy reads: *"La passione di Roma."* The ad is loaded with unspeakable content. Are we witnessing a sleeping beauty kind of event where the woman's kiss will actually awaken—even for a few passionate seconds—the ancient lover frozen in the statue? Like the ad for *L'Air du Temps*, this one also stresses the woman's control over the realization of her sexual fantasy.

An ad for Canadian Club Whiskey [© 1984] introduces us to an unlikely couple. The woman is much closer to the camera and is holding a slender glass of a Canadian Club mix. Her expression seems to convey desire, anticipation and perhaps even some doubt. In the background is a boy, much younger than the woman, standing shadowless against an open Mediterranean balcony door, perhaps waiting for her decision. The copy encourages the reader to "be a part of it."

At the level of spoken awareness, we can say that there are two persons in this ad: the woman and the boy. On the other hand, at some deeper level of analysis, there may be only one actual person in the ad—the woman. The whole background seems superimposed and unreal as if it were a theatrical or photographic expedient to depict only an inner fantasy of the woman. She stands in a dark area much closer to the reader. The boy stands farther away in the imaginary outdoor light. To join her, he would have to come into the darkness and she is the only one who can, by the power of her sexual imagination, summon him there. Thus the ad tells us a story of a mature woman who is able to fulfill her sexual fantasies without losing control to a male will.

Yuppies displaced middle-class role models in many popular advertisements of the 1980s

In the 1970s, a lot of popular advertisements kept proposing images of plain, unglamorous, unpretentious, ordinary folks as comfortable role models for the middle-class consumer. In those ads, the promise of happiness was presented together with that of being accepted into the American middle-class community. In the 1980s, on the other hand, such folksy appeals in popular advertisements became less frequent.

An advertisement for the Bell System [© date not given] depicts a typical middle-class family scene. The family is in the kitchen. Dad is talking on the phone to a fellow weekend fisherman and, of course, he is greatly exaggerating his accomplishments. With a mildly reproaching but also forgiving smile, Mom shows us the real size of the fish Dad caught. The daughter also smiles, displaying both disbelief and embarrassment for Dad's outrageous fish story. Then the ad repeats the popular Bell System slogan: "Reach out and touch someone."

At the level of unspoken awareness, the ad promises that anybody may be admitted to share the comfort and closeness of family and friends. We need not be handsome and glamorous to reach out and become part of the Bell System community. The characters in this fish story are very plain and average folks, and the setting is provided by an ordinary middle-class kitchen.

Perhaps the story of Benson & Hedges, a brand of cigarettes which throughout the 1980s, was searching for its true social image, can best illustrate Madison Avenue's difficult and gradual switch from the use of plain middle-class images to hard-core yuppy images.

We all remember that series of folksy ads in the 1970s with the bent cigarette and the funny faces. Then in the very early 1980s, Benson & Hedges launched a series with the slogan "Benson & Hedges & [something like 'Mornings' or 'Weekends'] & Me." These new advertisements continued to appeal to the middle-class reader without using the same funny and folksy characters.

While the folksy ads promised community, friendly people and benevolent acceptance, the new ones stressed tranquility, individualism and intimacy. In a "Benson & Hedges & Mornings & Me" ad [© 1981], a man is fishing with his dog in a small boat in the middle of a golden lake. The man, wearing a weekend fisherman's hat, is lighting his Benson & Hedges cigarette. The ad promises a quiet intimate moment away from the tension of the city or the office.

In 1983, Benson & Hedges cigarettes attempted a radical transformation of their social essence. Instead of the old images of plain middle-class people, the new "Deluxe 100" ads started pushing scenes of high society living. Glamorous socialites were displayed in high society parties, elegant and very expensive restaurants, and fabulous homes and estates. For example, one of these ads [Benson & Hedges, © 1984] shows an elegant young couple finding some time alone on the terrace of a palace during a formal gala party. The ads were meant to appeal to the reader's fantasies of glamour, high society and a touch of chic romance.

Next, in 1985 and 1986, Benson & Hedges cigarettes experimented again with a new image. They dumped the glamorous socialites and started pushing young, handsome, yuppyish—and even amusing—couples. "She likes to read fortune cookies," the copy of one of these ads reads, "He likes to eat them." All the ads in this series, however, assured the readers: "But there's one taste they agree on. Benson & Hedges." Perhaps the ads with the socialites had set the standards too high, thus discouraging the reader from pursuing such impossible fantasies. Reproposing models that were a little bit closer to the middle-class was an attempt to make the higher class appeal seem more attainable.

Finally, toward the end of the Reagan era, Benson & Hedges found its true soul as the yuppies' cigarette. In the new Benson & Hedges advertisements, yuppies replaced the plain middle-class folks and the unreachable socialites. But instead of portraying yuppies in their business suits competing in a dog-eat-dog environment, the new ads showed them relaxed in their safe, comfortable, well-appointed homes.

A typical Benson & Hedges ad of the late 1980s [© 1987] tells us a story of a visit by very close friends. In the larger of the two pictures, we see all the women together in the living room enjoying the intimacy and comfort of their friendship over a glass of wine. In the smaller picture, on the right, is a close-up of the hostess who, perhaps a bit overwhelmed by the good time she and her friends are having, takes a brief time-out from the action to smoke her Benson & Hedges cigarette. "For people who like to smoke...," the copy reads, "Benson & Hedges—because quality matters."

The new Benson & Hedges advertisements seem to repropose a yuppyish version of the old Bell System's "reach out and touch someone" theme. The folksy and plainly middle-class characters are gone, but the promise of happiness, togetherness, security and comfort remains.

Conclusions

The portrayal of the pursuit of happiness in most popular advertisements of the 1980s, it seems to me, reflect the rise of the yuppies as the new upper-middle class.

As yuppies began to displace many of the traditional middle-class role models in popular advertisements, some of the themes that were normally associated with the pursuit of happiness—freedom, success, sex—were reorganized and readjusted by Madison Avenue so that they would better fit with the new yuppy ideal and with some of the changes in women's roles that had been introduced into the American culture in the 1970s.

Freedom has always been associated with the pursuit of happiness both in American culture and in advertising. In the 1980s, the pursuit of happiness and freedom continued to be a major theme in many popular advertisements. The Marlboro cowboys/freedom-fighters continued to ride through the untamed West openly defying the Surgeon General's warnings. At the same time, in part because of the emergence of the yuppies as an ideal consumer force, many advertisements of the 1980s began proposing new concepts of freedom and happiness that were related to social and economic opportunity.

As the women's liberation movement of the 1970s left its mark on some important and also some quite superficial aspects of American culture, the new yuppy ideal of freedom and happiness portrayed in popular advertisements of the 1980s reflected some of these changes. With a few exceptions, however, the images of women portrayed there seem to suggest that Madison Avenue has perhaps embraced only the more mundane and trivial appeals of women's freedom. The Virginia Slims "baby" is now allowed to smoke, or the graduating woman in the Gillette Daisy ad now dares to show off her beautiful legs. In some cases, then, women are depicted as capable of finding their freedom and happiness not in the real world as men would but in an inner personal world of their own. For example, the woman in the Vanderbilt ad can only realize her dream of freedom in a Swan Lake-type of fantasy; the wife in the International Gold Corporation's ad realizes hers in the shadow of her husband's protection.

The concept of success was also revised by Madison Avenue in order to best capture the new yuppy spirit in the readers. As a result, in the 1980s many popular advertisements began to portray success no longer as an end in itself but as a means to finding happiness. In these ads, yuppies appeared in their own homes or in other such non-competitive, secure and comfortable environments where they were finding happiness in the realization of their dreams.

Perhaps to reflect the yuppies' particular style in their pursuit of happiness, the use of sex in popular advertisements of the 1980s became somewhat more discrete but also more pervasive than in the past. Ads like the ones for Barclay, Amaretto di Saronno, Raynal French Brandy, or Remy Martin Cognac do not make any use of overt sexual appeals but leave the reader's imagination free to expand on the many subtle sexual suggestions contained in the pictures.

The portrayal of women's sexual fantasies also changed in some advertisements. On the one hand, exhibitionists fantasies like the one acted out in the Gillette Daisy ad are not really new to the advertising world. Many advertising campaigns (like "The Maidenform Woman" or "Gentlemen prefer Hanes") have exploited them. On the other hand, the ad for Vanderbilt perfume in which the woman dreams of becoming a beautiful swan when she is with her lover is typical of the 1980s newfound interest on the part of Madison Avenue in a woman's inner existence.

Also new is the fact that some popular advertisements of the 1980s portray women maintaining total control over the realization of their sexual fantasies. For example, the women featured in the ads for Remy Martin Cognac, *L'Air du Temps*, Fendi perfume, and Canadian Club Whiskey are never at the mercy of their men's passions and can withdraw from the whole affair at any time they want.

Throughout the 1980s, as the folksy and plainly middle-class role models like the ones shown in the Bell System's "Reach out and touch someone" ad became less frequent, Madison Avenue kept searching for new ones. Eventually the yuppies became, in the eyes of the advertising industry, the best spokespersons for the consumers' spoken, unspoken and unspeakable desires. They rose through the 1980s popular advertisements to become the new and younger upper-middle class that would set trends for all consumers to follow in their pursuit of happiness. Benson & Hedges' experiments with different ideal smoker images seem to reflect the changes in the advertising industry and in American culture.

Notes

[1] In his book, *Captains of Consciousness: Advertising and the Social Roots of Consumer Culture* (New York: McGraw-Hill Book Company, 1976), Stuart Ewen wrote: "Indeed the language of progress and spiritual and physical fulfillment permeates many perspectives on industrialization. It is not

surprising that mass consumption has been conceived of as an apotheosis of human achievement; the wonder of the machine is borne out in the modern infiltration of machine-made goods into the lives and aspirations of people" (5).

Also, in *The Mirror Makers: A History of American Advertising and Its Creators* (New York: William Morrow and Company, 1984), Stephen Fox wrote: "One may build a compelling case that American culture is—beyond redemption— money-mad, hedonistic, superficial, rushing heedlessly down a railroad called Progress. Toqueville and other observers of the young republic described America in these terms in the early 1800s, decades before the development of national advertising. To blame advertising now for the most basic tendencies in American history is to miss the point. It is too obvious, to easy, a matter of killing the messenger instead of dealing with the bad news. The people who have created modern advertising are not hidden persuaders pushing our buttons in the service of some malevolent purpose. They are just producing an especially visible manifestation, good and bad, of the American way of life" (330).

[2] John Burnett and Alan Bush, "Profiling the Yuppies," *Journal of Advertising Research* (April/May 1986): 27-35.

[3] Fox (*op.cit.*) wrote: "In regard to advertising's broader cultural impact—the power to create and shape mass tastes and behavior—outsiders are generally more impressed than those inside the business with the alleged influence of Madison Avenue....In particular, the insiders know that no successful ad can stray very far from where the audience already lives. The ad must be fitted to the audience, not the other way around....Thus the favorite metaphor of the industry: advertising is a mirror that merely reflects society back on itself" (329).

[4] Many advertising scholars have discussed the relationship between advertisers and consumers and the issue of who's responsible for the content and effects of mass communications. Fox (*op.cit.*) wrote: "advertising has become a prime scapegoat for our times: a convenient, obvious target for critics who should be looking at the deeper cultural tendencies that only find reflection in the advertising mirror" (8).

In *The Mechanical Bride: Folklore of Industrial Man* (Boston: Beacon Press, 1967), Marshall McLuhan wrote: "After making his study of the nursery rhyme, 'Where are you going, my pretty maid?' the anthropologist C.B. Lewis pointed out that 'the folk has neither part nor lot in the making of folklore.' That is also true of the folklore of industrial man, so much of which stems from the laboratory, the studio, and the advertising agencies. But amid the diversity of our inventions and abstract techniques of production and distribution there will be found a great degree of cohesion and unity. This consistency is not conscious in origin or effect and seems to arise from a sort of collective dream. For that reason, as well as because of the widespread popularity of these objects and processes, they are referred as 'folklore of industrial man' " (v).

In his *Inventing Reality: The Politics of the Mass Media* (New York: St. Martin's Press, 1986), Michael Parenti wrote:

"If much of our informational and opinion intake is filtered through our previously established mental predilections, these predilections are often not part of our conscious discernment but of our unexamined perceptual conditioning—which brings us back to an earlier point: *Rather than being rational guardians against propaganda, our predispositional sets, having been shaped by prolonged exposure to earlier outputs of the same propaganda, may be active accomplices*" (21).

Trevor Millum wrote in *Images of Women: Advertising in Women's Magazines* (London: Chatto & Windus, 1975): "The communications which this group (advertisers, agencies, etc.) produce are as much the product of the culture as are the communicators; and the people to whom the communications are addressed are equally as much of that same culture, and receiving and interacting with many other stimuli and besides these advertisements. The images and language used are drawn from the culture, and the communications produced are a contributory factor to the body of the culture. The audience understands because it is part of the culture and shares its meanings. The whole process is a complex all-embracing dialectic—but one of the important aspects is that the communications from the 'advertisers' to the 'audience' are stimuli with extra power and deliberation behind them, and may function as transformations and/or reinforcements of particular aspects. In one sense everybody belongs to the culture and is part of its reproducing itself, but in another sense the group of advertisers has much greater power (in terms of thought, money, time, skill—it is after all its job), and although it is *part* of the culture it is one of the groups which helps to give particular meanings a specific emphasis or concretism (e.g., by selection and association), the effect of which is to reinforce certain clusters of meanings and to ignore others" (41).

And finally, Ewen (*op.cit.*) wrote: "The triumph of capitalism in the twentieth century has been its ability to define and contend with the conditions of the social realm. From the period of the 1920s, commercial culture has increasingly provided an idiom within which desires for social change and fantasies of liberation might be articulated and contained. The cultural displacement effected by consumerism has provided a mode of perception that has both confronted the question of human need and at the same time restricted its possibilities. Social change cannot come about in a context where objects are invested with human subjective capacities. It cannot come about where commodities contain the limits of social betterment. It requires that people never concede the issue of who shall define and control the social realm" (219-20).

[5] In *Gender Advertisements* (Cambridge: Harvard UP, 1979), Erwin Goffman wrote: "A further caveat. Advertisements overwhelmingly and candidly present make-believe scenes, the subjects or figures depicted being quite different from the professional models who pose the action. Obviously, then, a statement about, say, how nurses are presented in ads is to be taken as a shorthand way of saying how models dressed like nurses and set in a mock-up of a medical scene are pictured" (25).

Subliminal Seduction: Real or Imagined?

Eric J. Zanot

Introduction

The psychological phenomenon of subliminal perception has been a source of seemingly endless curiosity and interest to both scholarly researchers and the general public. Scientific research on whether subliminal cues could be perceived started over a century ago. Subsequent research attempted to measure whether those cues could affect attitudes and behavior. Most recent research has centered on whether subliminal cues can affect purchase behavior in particular.

General public interest did not arise until the 1950s. Although the public had little knowledge of the continuing and often arid academic research on the psychological phenomenon of subliminal perception, the application of subliminal techniques to marketing and merchandising created public interest. One particular incident precipitated this: James Vicary allegedly increased sales of popcorn and Coca-Cola in a theater through the insertion of subliminal suggestions in a motion picture. A swirl of public interest and debate followed that slackened somewhat in the 1960s and regained momentum in the next two decades.

This re-emergence of interest, in all probability, was primarily due to the work of a former professor. In 1973 Wilson Bryan Key published a book entitled *Subliminal Seduction*. Its popularity led to the publication of three subsequent books in 1976, 1980 and 1989. The author also disseminated his views on radio and TV talk shows and travelled the lecture circuit.

At present a paradox exists. Both popular culture artifacts and opinion research indicate the general public has widespread knowledge and some considerable degree of belief in the phenomenon of subliminal perception—especially in regard to use in advertising. Scholarly research, on the other hand, has cast serious doubt that subliminal cues have any behavioral effects even in highly controlled experimental settings. There is even further doubt of efficacy in mass mediated advertising applications. Advertising tradespeople deny that subliminal advertising exists and less partisan experts concur.

This article examines the public's growing and continuing curiosity and belief in subliminal advertising. It reviews the determinants of awareness and belief and includes an exposition of W.B. Key's thesis and assertions. It follows with a review of scholarly research findings concerning possible effectiveness.

Early Sources of Public Awareness and Belief

As briefly noted, public awareness and interest was first generated by James Vicary's motion picture experiments. During a six week period in 1956 Vicary exposed some 45,000 people to two subliminal inserts in a normal motion picture. When sales results were compared to an earlier period, Vicary alleged that both sales of popcorn and Coca-Cola increased dramatically. Despite the facts that Vicary's results should have been doubted because he was the president of Subliminal Projection Co., Inc. and also that all replications of his experiment failed to produce his results, the mass media widely published his findings (29).

The publication and popularity of Vance Packard's *The Hidden Persuaders* in 1957 reinforced interest and belief in subliminal advertising. Packard's main thesis was that marketers used depth psychology and motivational research techniques to manipulate an unsuspecting public into buying products. Although discussion of subliminal techniques was only a minor part of the book, the major thesis seemed to support public belief in subliminal advertising.

Articles began appearing in the mass media. In *Saturday Review*, Norman Cousins wrote that advertisers "coolly propose to break into the deepest and most private parts of the mind and leave all sort of scratch marks" and stated "an open declaration of war can no longer be delayed against those who view the integrity of the inner self largely in terms of the movement of merchandise" (7). Other articles revealed their contents in their titles: "TV's

Subliminal Seduction

Brainwash Commercials" and "Science Creates New Monster" (23, 24). The concept of subliminal advertising even found its way into a *Morty Meekle* comic strip of the period (6).

A swirl of public debate in the mass media ensued over the use and effects of subliminal advertising that caused both the U.S. Congress and the Federal Communications Commission to discuss the legal and moral implications of the matter. All three major networks incorporated prohibitions of subliminal materials in their advertising clearance documents and the National Association of Broadcasters (NAB) incorporated a prohibition in its Code. Official bodies in Great Britain and Canada made similar responses.

The government hearings produced little or no reliable evidence relating to widespread application of subliminal techniques in advertising. It appears the networks and NAB included prohibitions to prevent potential abuses and to appease both the government and the public. The initial furor of interest and action passed; the public turned its collective mind to the more pressing matters of the 1960s. Subliminal advertising seemed a minor matter in a decade that witnessed the assassination of a president and other political leaders, riots in the cities and on campuses, and a growing and unpopular war in Asia.

Interest Re-Emerges

During the early 1970s a tenured faculty member in the journalism department of the University of Western Ontario found that his class enrollments dramatically increased when he included materials on subliminal advertising. Sensing an interest and a market for his ideas, Wilson Bryan Key prepared a manuscript, found a publisher, and *Subliminal Seduction* appeared late in 1973. Released with an original press run of only 7,500 copies, Key eventually created interest by giving lectures and appearing on radio and TV talk shows.

The media, in their quest for interesting and sensationalistic topics, responded and provided channels for the author to publicize his work. It was a perfect marriage; Key astutely massaged the willing media. Some of his appearances were combative and print reviews were negative. However, the publicity fueled sales of the book. Subsequent editions included back cover teasers that promised "some of the things you should know in order to protect yourself from media rape" and "where the dirty words in an ad for children's dolls can be found" (16).

Colleagues at the university considered the book to be sensationalistic and his ideas of dubious merit. Internecine warfare ensued; charges and counter-charges were traded—including one that Key flunked students who did not agree with his views. Eventually the University of Western Ontario bought out his tenure and contract for $64,000. Key details this battle in a subsequent book (18). The core of Key's ideas can be found in *Subliminal Seduction*. His subsequent books, *Media Sexploitation*, *The Clam-Plate Orgy* and *The Age of Manipulation* serve as expansions and variations on his original themes.

The underpinnings of Key's theories are loosely derived from Freudian psychoanalytic theories that postulate the existence of an unconscious layer of the mind that is not fully comprehended at the conscious level. It is presumed that the unconscious can alter and effect changes in attitudes and behaviors without the individual being aware of this. This school of psychology, approximately 100 years old, was so popular among practicing psychologists in the early decades of the twentieth century that watered-down versions of it became part of American popular culture. Although Neo-Freudian psychologists can still be found, this method of analysis has largely been abandoned in favor of newer and more productive approaches to the study of individual behavior. Behaviorism and gestalt psychology are such examples.

Key couples his belief in psychoanalytic theory with the assertion that advertising practitioners commonly insert hidden symbols in advertisements. The purpose of the "embeds" is to communicate with the mind of the viewer or reader at an unconscious level. It is then hypothesized that this alters attitudes and behaviors so that the individual ends up purchasing the product without ever consciously realizing the true motivations behind the purchase.

The author states that this subliminal seduction occurs from the placement of a wide variety of embedded symbols. Hidden miniaturizations of genitalia seem to be the most common. He also find the letters "S-E-X" evident in his analysis. Faces of skulls and death masks are also somewhat common in his opinion. A typical example is a magazine ad showing a frosty bottle of Gilbey's gin beside a collins drink glass filled with liquid, ice cubes and a slice of lime. The headline says "Break out the frosty bottle" and is followed by a kicker in smaller type "and keep your tonics dry." Within it Key sees sexual parts of three women, two men and a voyeur looking on. In one part of the photo he sees a vagina, in another, a set of vaginal lips, "a drop of water which could represent the clitoris" and "seminal frost all over the bottle." In sum Key sees the ad as an unconscious invitation to "a good old-fashioned sexual orgy." When he tested this ad on over 1000 subjects, none of them saw these symbols until he explained them. Rather than taking this as evidence that the symbols may not be present, he concludes this merely shows the cleverness of those who embedded them (16).

He alleges that ads for Seagram's gin, Chivas Regal scotch, Bacardi rum, Sprite soda, Camel and Kent cigarettes, Tweed perfume, Kanon cologne and myriad other products include embeds surreptitiously placed to induce purchase. Although many of his examples seem outlandish, a few do merit closer scrutiny. Included is an example of a recent Soloflex ad; the abdominal muscles on the model might be construed as a symbolic penis rising out of the jeans (33).

By the time *The Clam-Plate Orgy* was published in 1980, Key had moved from advertising and the mass media into analyses of a very wide variety of phenomena. The title of the book was suggested when he allegedly discovered nine human figures and that of a donkey in a Howard Johnson placemat depicting a clam dish. As he put it: "Who would believe a sexual orgy, oral sex, and bestiality could be so incorporated into an innocent restaurant placemat?" (18).

The world of art has also been placed under Key's subliminal microscope. He alleges that great painters, including Durer, Michelangelo, Titian, Rembrandt, Picasso and even Norman Rockwell, intentionally placed embeds in their work. Before the book has run its course, the credulity of the most credulous is strained. Key has found the letters "S-E-X" imprinted on Ritz crackers and engraved into Abraham Lincoln's beard on the five dollar bill (18).

Although many doubt the veracity of W.B. Key's research and claims, few would doubt that he has made a fortune—literally—by making them. He has appeared on many radio and TV shows and been paid to travel the lecture circuit, making approximately ninety presentations a year by the early 1980s (20). Still active on the lecture circuit, his appearances are arranged and managed by the American Program Bureau of Watertown, Massachusetts (2). He states that there are some 4,500,000 copies of his books in print in four different languages (21). His topic is subliminal; his income is supraliminal.

Scholarly Research

This section provides an overview and summary of scholarly research on subliminal perception and its applications to advertising. It is not exhaustive; literally hundreds of studies have been conducted to ascertain what effects, if any, subliminal cues have on perception, attitudes and behavior. In addition, several excellent summary articles have been written and their conclusions are included.

The earliest studies were conducted more than a century ago (28). This work centered on whether or not subliminal cues could be perceived. Later work sought to measure the effects such stimuli might have on attitude change (22,25,34). More recent work has sought to elicit behavioral change effects and/or behavior related to advertising or purchase behavior response (3,5,8,11,12).

On the whole, work in the area is fraught with methodological difficulties. Trying to find the effects of such minuscule stimuli is akin to trying to find the quark in sub-atomic particle physics. Differing operational definitions of "subliminal" are necessary due to experimental design and the medium in which the stimulus is carried. Differing studies offer contrary results. Despite these problems, enough studies have been aggregated over time to allow for some conclusions.

There seems little doubt that awareness can occur without perception and that the phenomenon of subliminal perception is real and not an experimental artifact. N.F. Dixon's exhaustive review in *Subliminal Perception: The Nature Of A Controversy* concludes it is possible to transmit a stimulus to an individual without the individual being aware of the stimulus. The response to the stimulus can later be measured in dreams, memory and even, in highly controlled experimental situations, in some minimal behavioral reactions (9).

Subliminal stimuli cease to be effective in studies that move more deeply into the hierarchy of behavioral effects—especially those involving conscious choice behaviors. Also, subliminal stimuli cease to have effects in studies that move from highly controlled lab experiments to those that approximate brand choice and product purchase situations (3,5,12,26). Lastly, subliminal stimuli have no effects when forced to compete with stronger supraliminal stimuli in mass media and advertising contexts (8,11,14).

Authors of articles summarizing research on subliminal perception and its applications to marketing and advertising are virtually unanimous in their conclusions. N.F. Dixon concludes "nobody, except perhaps those interested in the

Subliminal Seduction 59

To unlock your body's potential, we proudly offer Soloflex. Twenty-four traditional iron pumping exercises, each correct in form and balance. All on a simple machine that fits in a corner of your home.
For a free Soloflex brochure, call anytime 1-800-453-9000.

BODY BY SOLOFLEX®

Copyright © by Soloflex. Used with permission.

SOLOFLEX,® HILLSBORO, OREGON 97123   ©1983 SOLOFLEX

PEOPLE HAVE BEEN TRYING TO FIND THE BREASTS IN THESE ICE CUBES SINCE 1957.

The advertising industry is sometimes charged with sneaking seductive little pictures into ads.

Supposedly, these pictures can get you to buy a product without your even seeing them.

Consider the photograph above. According to some people, there's a pair of female breasts hidden in the patterns of light refracted by the ice cubes.

Well, if you really searched you probably *could* see the breasts. For that matter, you could also see Millard Fillmore, a stuffed pork chop and a 1946 Dodge.

The point is that so-called "subliminal advertising" simply doesn't exist. Overactive imaginations, however, most certainly do.

So if anyone claims to see breasts in that drink up there, they aren't in the ice cubes.

They're in the eye of the beholder.

ADVERTISING
ANOTHER WORD FOR FREEDOM OF CHOICE.
American Association of Advertising Agencies

commercial exploitation of subliminal stimulation, would maintain that a subliminal stimulus can compete successfully with other more powerful influences" (9).

Another researcher concluded "procedures for the development of commercial exploitation appear so unlikely that subliminal advertising can be said not to constitute a viable mass communications approach" (30). Two other authors conclude "there is no scientific evidence that subliminal stimulation can initiate subsequent action, to say nothing of commercially or politically significant action" (4). Yet another article echoes the same sentiments: "The possibility that subliminal stimulation offers an effective means of controlling consumers or political behavior is highly unlikely. Claims that it does so seem to be based on enthusiasm rather than on hard evidence. Such claims are not supported by published research. The available evidence suggest that subliminal messages have little or no persuasive power" (10). And, at the risk of overkill, the conclusions of another researcher in the area, Timothy Moore: "subliminal directives have not been shown to have the power ascribed to them by advocates of subliminal advertising. In general, the literature on subliminal perception shows that the most clearly documented effects are obtained only in highly contrived and artificial situations. These effects, when present, are brief and of small magnitude.... These processes have no relevance to the goals of advertising" (26).

Do Advertisers Engage In Subliminal Advertising?

The related question of whether or not subliminal advertising is common practice is more difficult to address. Although a number of uses of subliminal perception techniques for varying purposes have been reported (10,31), the major proponent of the theory that advertising applications are commonplace is Wilson Bryan Key. A reading of the few other sources that allege subliminal advertising is commonplace reveals they are heavily grounded in Key's books (15). Unfortunately, Key's methodology is so obscure as to be incapable of replication. Further, serious social scientists fault Key's understanding of psychological processes and how they affect behavior. As a result, Key's allegations remain little more than allegations: serious researchers cannot use them as proof of the existence of subliminal advertising. There is also the question of Key's motives since he is not a disinterested party: his advocacy has proven highly profitable in book royalties and lecture fees.

Advertising practitioners dispute Key. A typical statement comes from Charles F. Adams of the American Association of Advertising Agencies in testimony concerning government regulation: "We are convinced that there is no subliminal advertising in America today. Those who continue to eagerly pursue the search for it are clearly on a witch hunt, and their endeavors have produced no respectable evidence that it does exist.... I suggest we should not take too seriously anyone...for whom a phallic symbol is anything longer than it is wide" (1). A survey of 100 art directors in advertising agencies resulted in 91 percent replying they had never done so themselves (13). But, like Key, advertising spokespeople are not disinterested parties and this is why their disclaimers have had little impact.

One public opinion study queried a population that is both knowledgeable and, in all likelihood, disinterested. One hundred ninety nine professors of advertising from journalism, communication and marketing settings responded to a questionnaire involving subliminal advertising. These academics had an average of 13 years teaching and 9 years of trade experience. Less than three percent felt that subliminal advertising was used "always" or "often." Another eight percent felt it was used "sometimes." Typical comments were "How do you teach something that doesn't exist?" and "My opinion is that the whole thing is a myth" (35). In sum, although it is impossible to completely disprove the existence of the use of subliminal advertising, there is no reliable evidence that the technique is commonly employed.

Conclusions

The psychological phenomenon of subliminal perception has been a topic of serious study for approximately 100 years. Academic research in the last three decades has centered on applications in advertising and marketing contexts. However, the phenomenon did not catch the eye of the general public until the Vicary "popcorn" experiments in the late 1950s. After a flurry of interest on the part of the public, media and government, interest in subliminal advertising waned until the mid-1970s. Wilson Bryan Key published a series of books with wide-ranging claims that re-ignited and expanded public knowledge and interest.

A review of psychological and marketing studies strongly suggests that Key's claims are not supported by the vast majority of serious scholars working in the field. Further, even though a small number of Key's examples appear worthy of further scrutiny, there is little or no evidence from other sources to suggest that advertisers commonly or routinely place embeds in ads.

Works Cited

Adams, C. *Testimony Before the Bureau of Alcohol, Tobacco and Firearms on Its Proposed Regulations for the Advertising of Alcoholic Beverages, with Specific Reference to Subliminal Advertising.* Sept. 9, 1981.

American Program Bureau, Inc., promotion pamphlet for W.B. Key, Watertown, MA: nd.

Beatty, S., and Hawkins, D. "Subliminal Stimulation: Some New Data and Interpretation." *Journal of Advertising* 18 (3: 1989):4-8.

Berelson and Steiner, quoted in Severin, W., and Tankard, J. *Communication Theories.* New York: Hastings House, 1979.

Byrne, D. "The Effect of Subliminal Food Stimulus on Verbal Responses," *Journal of Applied Psychology* 43 (4: 1959): 249-52.

Cavalli, D. "Morty Meekle." *Champaign-Urbana Courier* (May 4, 1958).

Cousins, N. "Smudging The Subconscious." *Saturday Review* (Oct. 5, 1957): 20.

DeFleur, M., and Petranoff, R. "A Televised Test of Subliminal Persuasion." *Public Opinion Quarterly* 23 (1959): 168-80.

Dixon, N.F. *Subliminal Perception: The Nature of A Controversy.* London: McGraw-Hill, 1971.

Dudley, S. "Subliminal Advertising: What is the Controversy About?" *Akron Business and Economic Review* 18 (2: 1987): 6-18.

Gable, M., Wilkens, H., Harris, L., and Feinberg, R. "An Evaluation of Subliminally Embedded Sexual Stimuli in Graphics." *Journal of Advertising* 16 (1: 1987): 26-31.

George, S., and Jennings, L. "Effect of Subliminal Stimuli on Consumer Behavior: Negative Evidence." *Perceptual and Motor Skills* 41 (1975): 847-54.

Haberstroh, J. "Can't Ignore Subliminal Ad Charges." *Advertising Age* (Sept. 17, 1984): 3, 42, 44.

Hart, S., and McDaniel S. "Subliminal Stimulation-Marketing Applications." *Consumer Behavior: Classical and Contemporary Dimensions.* Boston: Little and Brown, 1982. 165-75.

Jervey, E. "Now You See 'Em—Now You Don't: Those Sexy Sublims." *Journal of Popular Culture* 17 (Fall 1983): 161-66.

Key, W.B. *Subliminal Seduction.* New York: Prentice-Hall, 1974.

———. *Media Sexploitation.* New York: Prentice-Hall, 1976.

———. *The Clam-Plate Orgy and Other Subliminal Techniques for Manipulating Your Behavior.* New York: Prentice-Hall, 1980.

———. *The Age of Manipulation.* New York: Henry Holt, 1989.

———. "Subliminal Advertising." Kaleidoscope radio talk show, WAMU-FM, Washington, DC. Oct. 7, 1981.

———. Key, W.B. Personal letter to Susan Malone. April 27, 1990.

Lazarus, R., and McCleary, R. "Automatic Discrimination Without Awareness: A Study of Subception" *Psychological Review* 58 (1951): 113-22.

Lee, T. "TV's Brainwash Commercials." *True or False* (April 1958): 14.

Mabley, J., "Science Creates New Monster." *Chicago Daily News* (Sept. 17, 1957): 3.

McGinnies, E. "Emotionality and Perceptual Defense." *Psychological Review* 56 (1949): 244-51.

Moore, T. "Subliminal Advertising: What You See Is What You Get." *Journal of Marketing* 46 (2: 1982): 37-47.

Packard, V. *The Hidden Persuaders.* New York: McKay, 1957.

Pierce, C., and Jastrow, J. "On Small Differences in Sensation." *Mem. Nat. Acad. Sci.* 3 (1884): 73-83.

Rose, A. "Motivation Research and Subliminal Advertising." *Social Research* (Fall 1958): 275-84.

Saegert, J. "Why Marketing Should Quit Giving Subliminal Advertising the Benefit of the Doubt." *Psychology and Marketing* 42 (2: 1987): 107-20.

Sales brochure. *Psychodynamics Library of Time-Compression Cassettes* nd.

Smirnoff vodka ad. *Adweek* (Nov. 13, 1989): 11.

Soloflex ad. *Gentleman's Quarterly* (Sept. 1986): 247.

Weiner, M., and Schiller, P. "Subliminal Perception or Perception of Partial Cues." *Journal of Abnormal and Social Psychology* 61 (1: 1960): 124-37.

Zanot, E., and Maddox, L. "Subliminal Advertising and Education." *Journal of Marketing Education* (Fall 1983): 13-17.

3
Unusual Advertising Forms and Uses

Since advertising in recent years has become more pervasive than ever, more alternative media such as cable television, billboards, and shopping cart displays are available.

Always of great interest and stimulation are the novel, the unusual and perhaps a bit of the bizarre. Advertising, in recent years, appears to have become even more persuasive than in the past. Print and broadcast media vie for our attention and reach even further and deeper to influence our very motives. Non-conventional advertising arises almost daily. Examples may include pitches on utility poles or even on clothing.

Specifically, the T-shirt craze competes as a viable ad medium. Sayre artfully explores the printed T-shirt as a useful study because it has great capacity for communicating meaning in a relatively simple form. Colorful examples and lively dialogue make this both a fun and instructive essay.

Novel advertising ploys of the past can prove to be enlightening as well as entertaining. Such is the case of Greene's review of nineteenth century trade cards with their commercial and popular culture artistic value.

The use of well-known historical art in modern advertising is becoming more familiar. Strumwasser and Friedman discuss applications of the Mona Lisa masterpiece in numerous ad forms.

Advertising Trade Cards: Nineteenth Century Showcases

Stephen L. W. Greene

There is no telling how Great-Aunt Gussie would have felt about my soaking off the advertising trade cards she had so painstakingly glued into a scrapbook more than a hundred years ago during those long Albany, NY winter evenings.

Gussie shared a passion with other teenagers and women of the 1870s and 80s: collecting the fascinating array of chromalithed pictures that merchants and manufacturers gave away to stimulate interest in their products. Today, these mainly three-by-five and smaller cardboard cards, which many consider the precursors to post cards and trading cards, are collectibles. They are worth up to ten dollars each, an amount that would have astounded Gussie, who, as one of her cards from W.M. Whitney's Dry Goods Store tells us, was used to paying five cents for an all linen lace collar.[1]

Fortunately, money was not that important an issue for Gussie. Her father, my great grandfather—as co-owner of Sherman and Greene, "retailers of fine shoes"—gave her access to many more cards than the average kid. To round out her collection, she would still have to pester her mother to splurge a little on the latest edition of *Demorests Monthly Magazine* or perhaps purchase an unneeded vial of Austen's Forest Flower Cologne. But at least she could be assured a steady supply of cards from the Burt Shoe Manufacturing Company of New York, which advertised itself with such fantasies as cherubs shooting arrows from high heel shoes perched on chariots and propelled by pigeons.

Such whimsey accounts for the continuing charm of these cards, which thanks to printing standards unsurpassed even by today's standards, still retain most of their original luster. Take away the stain of Aunt Gussie's wheat glue and an occasional bent corner or two, and many of them could be back on the counter at Prof. Murray's Private Dancing Parlor or Miss M. Craig's Fashionable Millinery. But no matter how good their condition, there would be no mistaking them for their modern advertising counterparts. Ads have changed considerably since these cards were printed.

Infants of Advertising Media

The nineteenth century trade cards are today viewed as the infants of advertising media.[2] The message was routinely submerged by the art work, often times relegated to the back of the card where it would, in many cases, languish under the glue which affixed its colorful front to the scrapbook page. In these early days of mass consumption, when ad pioneer Albert Lasker was but a boy and Freud had yet to invent the "psycho" to be paired with the "graphics," advertisers worked on the refreshing notion that consumers would have to value something to retain it.

So they spared no expense in reproducing the most eye-appealing art on limited quantities of cards for their mainly youthful and female audiences.[3] Flower bouquets, hirsute organ grinders, chicks hatching from eggs, kids teasing kittens with a mouse on a string—the subject matter was fertile ground for the artist unrestrained by the need to depict the product itself in a suitable context. The advertiser's hope was that the customer would take the card home and retain it; name recognition, not the "hard sell" was the aim.

Post Civil War Developments

Trade cards had been used since at least the early 1800s, but they had developed their bright colors and rising popularity only in the post-Civil War era when printing breakthroughs and socio-economic breakdowns led to the emergence of a more consumption-oriented consumption society.[4] Both the North and the South had multiplied their industrial capacity in order to wage war on each other. When the conflict ended and the South lay in ruins, northern manufacturers tried to maintain their high production in the peaceful post-bellum world. Fortunately for them, massive societal changes were already underway; and upheavals have an insidious way of creating opportunities for those able to take advantage of human disruption.

Farm boys had been torn from their fields to become soldiers, replaced by the ever more sophisticated farm equipment which was revolutionizing agriculture. After the war, many returned to factory jobs, leaving their fields behind. In the cities, their wives sought meaning for lives suddenly wrenched from the rural requisites of consumption. If they lacked enough ashes to make soap, they could now purchase the finished product. If their now small kitchen gardens could not feed the family, they could always buy their produce from the local grocer. Women still commanded the home, but their position vis-a-vis their husband had shifted, from co-producer to consumer of his paycheck.

Many manufacturers were too busy meeting orders to comprehend the consequence of the changing marketplace. Before the war, most products had been made by hand and sold in local communities. Jobbers would handle any minimal distribution outside of that area. In the post-war era, with production at a high level, more and more goods were being shipped outside the home territory. Gradually, power evolved to these middlemen, who were soon to exercise it for their own benefit. As for the retailers and consumers, they were scarcely interested in who produced what since most goods, like the varitable crackers from the cracker barrel, were sold in bulk.

Middlemen were quick to exploit their strategic position position to pit one manufacturer against another and thus lower the wholesale price to themselves. They worked on the assumption that there was no way outside of their own network of personal relationships for manufacturers to communicate directly with either the retailer or the public. But they had not bargained on the power of the printed word or, to be more precise, the power of the pretty picture.[5] Manufacturers used advertising to gain control of the marketplace.

A pair of trade cards from the Rising Sun Stove Polish Company of Canton, Massachusetts shows how far some manufacturers eventually would go to establish their pre-eminence in the marketplace. The cards tell two stories: one about a wise man who went to a "respectable" store to purchase Rising Sun and the other about the foolish man who frequented an "unprincipled" concern where he was led to believe that a costly competing brand was just as good. The first man ended up in Congress while the second was forced to beg on the street because his wife was too busy polishing and re-polishing the stove to feed him.

But such hyperbole was the exception rather than the rule, at least for those cards Aunt Gussie deemed suitable to glue down for posterity. A more frequent approach was the moderate methods of the Burt Shoe people of which, thanks to Gussie's paternal connection, we have a sizeable collection. An 1879 card, featuring a powdered-wigged dandy presenting his "Edwin Burt Fine Shoes" compliments to a curtseying girl, dispenses on the reverse side, beneath a calendar, this simple message: "Caution. Please notice. Genuine Goods of Edwin C. Burt's have his name stamped in full on the lining and sole of each shoe and are warranted."

Two years later, Burt upgraded his trade cards increasing their size, quality of printing and strength of warning. Now, the calendar is gone; the whole back is devoted to telling the customer not only to look for the stamp, but should he not find it, to write the company's New York headquarters for a list of local outlets. By 1885 the card's size has increased again, by twenty percent, and the warning about imitators has changed. The message is smaller, but more positive; Burt uses the increased space to display the many gold medals his shoes have won at fairs around the world. Now, customers are merely informed that the genuine product bears his stamp; they're no longer exhorted to look for it.

Figures assembled by *Advertising Age* magazine show the growth of advertising during this period.[6] Starting at a base of $20 million just before the Civil War, advertisers nationwide were spending $175 million by 1880 and $300 million by 1890. And trade cards were receiving a sizeable share of this outlay. In 1880, other advertising vehicles, such as magazines and newspapers, were still relatively undeveloped. Most did not bother to solicit ads, relying instead on subscriptions. For the few ads they did run, they could accommodate only simple line drawings; inexpensive half-tones were not introduced until 1890. They were mainly local publications with small audiences; *Munsey's* in 1893 was the first magazine to lower its price and seek a wider audience. Adequate public transportation, the rural free delivery system, ad agencies, the telephone, incandescent light and the widespread use of the rotary press would propel newspapers and magazines to the top, burying trade cards in the process, but in 1880 these developments were still at least a decade away.[7]

Gussie's Collection

Great-Aunt Gussie, of course, was blissfully unaware of any of these future developments. For her, 1880 must have seemed strange enough. Factories were flooding the market place with new inexpensive products, exotic goods were streaming in from around the world, European fashions were replacing homespun as the garb of the day. Everywhere she looked, Gussie must have seen change, but nowhere was it more graphically depicted than in the brightly colored pictures of her advertising trade cards. Like the later generation of kids who discovered a universe of commercial constellations on television, Gussie must have viewed trade cards as her window on the world.

She left behind a collection of 340 cards glued into a scrapbook. Each page was a montage of her pride of ownership. On some, for example, cards were carefully pasted over each other to form a fan. On others, she assembled bits and pieces of vines or roses from other cards which she laboriously pasted around the edges to form a border. Gussie, like thousands of other 1880 children, had discovered the multiple delights of collecting and arranging manufactured art work. And manufacturers had discovered that the path to the parent's pocketbook could lead through their offspring. The Cracker Jack prize, cereal premiums, even Bad-breath Seth and all the other Garbage Pail Kids can trace their origins back to the trade cards.

For our purposes, Gussie's collection can be divided into these broad categories: 45 shoe cards, 39 magazines and stationery, 37 dry goods and clothing, 31 food, 28 soap, 15 sewing, 15 drugs, 12 industrial equipment.[8] Some of these categories are obviously inflated by the inclusion of multiple cards from the same establishment. Gussie's paternal shoe connection has already been mentioned; there may have been other friendship ties, some of which are hinted at by romantic or humorous scribblings on the back of some of the cards. But when Gussie's collection is compared to others such as in John Kaduck's *Advertising Trade Cards* or to cards for sale at antique stores, it does seem representative of the major categories of the day.

Dry Goods and Clothing Stores

The dry goods and clothing stores were expanding rapidly in the post-Civil War era. As America moved from an agricultural to industrial nation, the demand for shirts, pants, collars, scarves, cuffs, shirt bosoms, undergarments and everything else swelled. A nation which before the war had been known for its homespun, democratic, rural uniformity was fast maturing into a dandified, European-stylish nation of city dwellers. Second-hand clothes shops gave way to tailors and milliners for the growing number of well-to-dos and to clothing stores for those who could afford only ready-to-wears. By 1880 over one-half of all men's clothes were purchased off the hanger. By the 1890s this steady accretion of clothing would lead some physicians to worry about the health of Victorian women who were expected in winter to don some 37 pounds of garments including nineteen pounds which were slung from the hips.[9]

The stores kept pace with demand by growing ever more spacious. Soon, they would have no choice but to "departmentalize" in order to make order out of the chaos of merchandise. Gussie's collection contains cards from three stores in the Albany area which advertised their wide selection of departments. In New York City, R.H. Macy had made the initial transition from dry goods to department store in 1860, and that edifice was only a short boat ride away down the Hudson River. By 1880 Joseph Wanamaker had set up shop in Philadelphia; Marshall Field had done the same in Chicago.

And so had Frear's Busy Bazaar in Troy where it was advertised "every department replete with novelties." The card goes on to list ten departments ranging from "live silk" to "popular gents' furnishing goods department." Another card reveals Frear's cash home furnishing departments where no good exceeded a set amount ranging from five cents to a dollar. And, as the card proclaims on the front, you will "*Save Money!*" if you buy from Frear's.

Low prices and wide selection were not the only attractions of the new department stores. Many offered features that no "mom and pop" establishment could match: guaranteed satisfaction or your money back, free delivery, exchange of goods, charge accounts, and no haggling. As Daniel Boorstin points out, this last inducement was borne out of necessity. With some stores, such as Stewart's in New York employing more than 2000 people, management could not maintain fiscal controls if a price was established through bargaining, a method which up to then had been the custom of the day.[10]

But the department store's most revolutionary innovation was its open-door, open-shelves policy. Previously, shops were small and presided over by ever watchful owners who would file away their best items until "good customers" came to view them. Now, any member of the public was welcome to enter the department store and browse the many open displays of clothes and home furnishings. What greater inducement is there to mass consumption than mass display of the wares?

Gussie also collected cards from smaller establishments like Sharp's Tailoring Establishment in nearby Troy or R.C. Davis Merchant Tailors who had just been "removed to the marble

Moore's Throat & Lung
Lozenges
The Favorites.
Coughs, Colds & Sore Throat

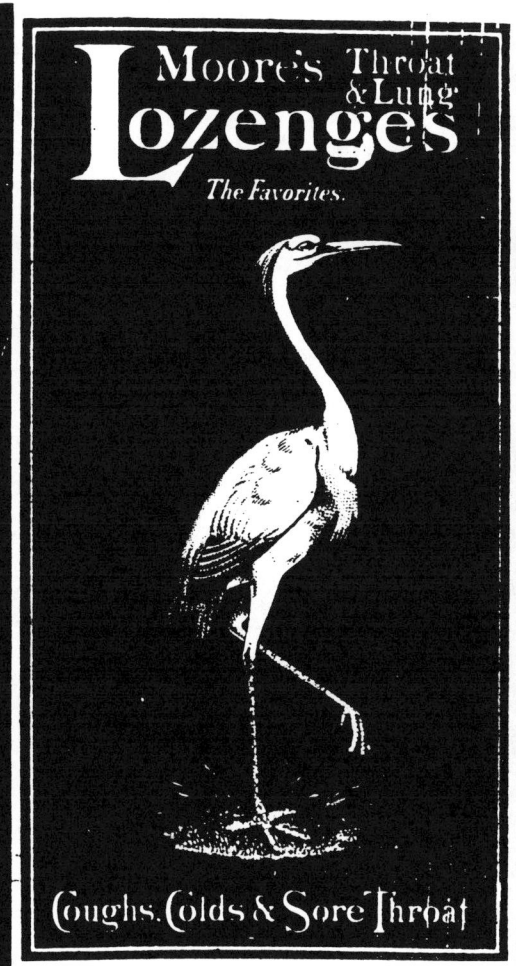

Fig. 1. Card advertising a popular cough drop.

Fig. 2. Reverse side of Moore's Throat and Lung Lozenges card.

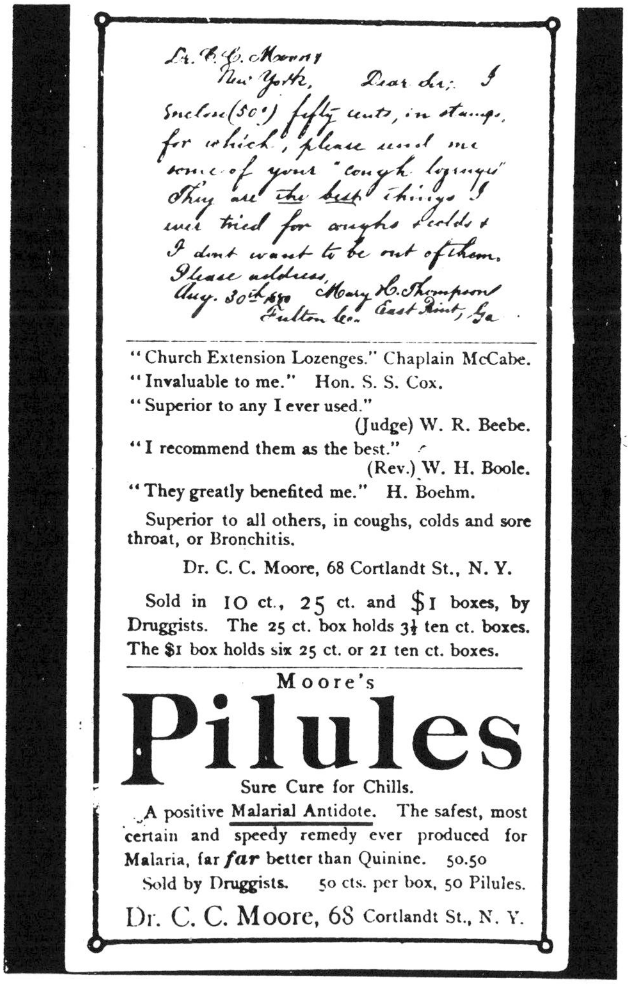

Dr. C. C. Moore, New York, Dear Sir: I Enclose (50¢) fifty cents, in stamps, for which, please send me some of your "cough lozenges" They are the best things I ever tried for coughs & colds & I don't want to be out of them. Please address, Mary L. Thompson Fulton Co. East Point, Ga
"Church Extension Lozenges." Chaplain McCabe.
"Invaluable to me." Hon. S. S. Cox.
"Superior to any I ever used." (Judge) W. R. Beebe.
"I recommend them as the best." (Rev.) W. H. Boole.
"They greatly benefited me." H. Boehm.
Superior to all others, in coughs, colds and sore throat, or Bronchitis.
Dr. C. C. Moore, 68 Cortlandt St., N. Y.
Sold in 10 ct., 25 ct. and $1 boxes, by Druggists. The 25 ct. box holds 3½ ten ct. boxes. The $1 box holds six 25 ct. or 21 ten ct. boxes.
Moore's
Pilules
Sure Cure for Chills.
A positive Malarial Antidote. The safest, most certain and speedy remedy ever produced for Malaria, far *far* better than Quinine. 50.50
Sold by Druggists. 50 cts. per box, 50 Pilules.
Dr. C. C. Moore, 68 Cortlandt St., N. Y.

Fig. 3. "Ever Faithful," is an advertising card for a shoe store.

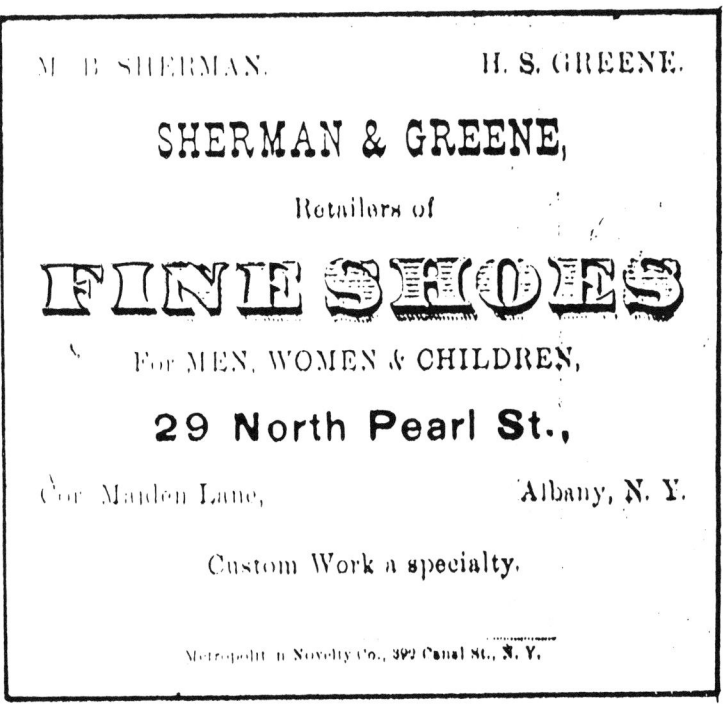

Fig. 4. Reverse side of "Ever Faithful."

Advertising Trade Cards

Fig. 5. "Can't You Talk?" is another advertising card for a cough medicine.

THE very popular picture—"CAN'T YOU TALK?" is the subject of the Album Card herewith presented. The appeal made by the original picture to sympathies as tender as they are universal, will not, we trust, be deemed any the less acceptable in the miniature copy offered for your approval in this, the eighth issue of our series. And now, referring to our remedies:

IF THE HEALTH OF ANY GROWN PERSON is in question, and such symptoms are apparent as low spirits, restlessness, sour stomach, sick headache, a variable appetite, rising of food after eating, oppression of the stomach, low fever, languor, and irregularity of the bowels, rest assured it is a form of Dyspepsia—a complaint tending to break down the general stamina, and thus open the way for many serious physical evils. The remedy needed is: Dr. Jayne's Tonic Vermifuge, not as a Vermifuge, but as a general Tonic. Two teaspoonfuls of this Tonic, mixed with four tablespoonfuls of water, taken after each meal, keeping the bowels gently open when necessary with Dr. Jayne's Sanative Pills, will soon overcome the worst symptoms and remove this distressing disease.

IF THE HEALTH OF YOUR CHILDREN is in question, and such symptoms are noticed as a variable appetite, with strange cravings, picking the nose, excessive thirst, low fever, bad breath, pale, sallow complexion, occasionally flushed cheeks, a wasting away, great nervousness, fitful sleep, grinding of the teeth, accompanied by weakness of the bowels—they indicate that the child is troubled with those dreadful pests, WORMS, which worry its delicate system, and are producing such irritation and debility as will surely break down the constitution, and, if the cause is not removed, may bring on St. Vitus' Dance or Convulsions, and render its after-life a burden. To save your child use Dr. Jayne's Tonic Vermifuge, according to the directions, and you will not only destroy the Worms, but its Tonic properties will rebuild the general health,—no other Worm Medicine possessing such qualities. When Worms are not indicated, and a gentle Tonic is required, the Vermifuge may be given with excellent results after each meal, in much smaller doses than for Worms.

For **Coughs, Colds, Throat and Lung Troubles**, as everybody well knows, DR. JAYNE'S EXPECTORANT is the Standard Family Remedy.

Fig. 6 Reverse side of "Can't You Talk?"

Hall," wherever that was located. Sharp advertises his shop with the picture of a cherub extracting blood from grasshoppers while Davis chooses the more conservative approach of a butterfly unencumbered by attackers. Morris Hein Clothing, however, returns to the adversarial style with a picture of two impish boys delighting in a dog's frenzy as he tries to reach a balloon tied to his tail.

Sewing Machines

The sewing machine had helped many of these smaller shops to stay in business. First invented in the eighteenth century, it was not perfected until Elias Howe added his improvements in 1846. Soon he was embroiled in lawsuits against competitors, including Isaac Merrit Singer, whom he claimed had stolen his invention. By 1871, the case had been settled and factories were turning out hundreds of thousands of commercial machines. And there was no dearth of operators. The machine's widespread industrial application coincided with the arrival of growing numbers of European immigrants, many of them accustomed to work in the needle trades.[11]

By 1880 women were beginning to crave for their own home machine that could sew 250 stitches a minute, seven times faster than by hand, but few families, in a nation with an average income of $500, could afford the $125 price. Manufacturers were not deterred; they offered installment sales, thereby establishing the precedent of financing for an array of major appliances in the home—and creating one of the primary tenets of the modern world: consumer indebtedness.

A sewing machine was probably not yet a fixture in Gussie's house. Her collection contains only one sewing machine card, for the New Home Sewing Machine, whose card proclaims was "The finest and best made Machine in the World!" And it was "warranted for five years!" The bizarre picture on the front may explain Gussie's family's lack of motivation to purchase a sewing machine; it is one of the most inexplicable in the collection. A fat boy with a giant patch on the rear of his pants stands with his back to the viewer watching waves break on a beach. His sister, her face shrouded by a large bonnet, gestures to him and says, "What are the wild waves saying?" He answers, "This patch was put on by The Light Running New Home Sewing Machine."

Gussie's family more than likely still met their clothing repair needs by hand, probably using J & P Coats Best Six Cord Spool Cotton judging from the ten cards in the collection. Lagging behind was Clark's Mile End Spool Cotton with four cards. As a group, these fourteen examples present some of the most imaginative art work in the collection. One of the best cards depicts sailors securing Cleopatra's Needle (pun obviously intended) to their Clipper ship with Clark's thread for the long trip from Alexandria to London with a spool of Coats thread. Another depicts a mustachioed fisherman reeling in a large trout while his female companion, who is sewing, looks on approvingly. The Clark's people tried to go one step further by presenting two unrelated pictures on each card, which, unfortunately for her great-nephew, gave Great-Aunt Gussie license to cut them apart.

These beautiful thread cards demonstrate the advertising sophistication of certain mass producers like J & P Coats. Unlike the new Home Sewing Machine folks, they understood the power of pictures, and were careful not to clutter the front or the back with puzzling dialogue or inflated claims about their product. On most of their cards they presented an eye-catching, colorful picture with a pertinent one-line phrase; on the reverse, they provide a calendar to give the bearer some reason to keep the card around the house.

Drug Sellers

The drug sellers were of a different mind. For them, more words meant more sales. "Promise the public anything" seemed to be the motto in the unregulated days of 1880. Have a chronic liver complaint? Try Jayne's Sanative Pills which will cure "a thousand-and-one disorders." Or how about catarrh, "a known blood disease?" Hood's Sarsaparilla will do the trick. If malaria is your malady, try Moore's Pilules Throat and Lung Lozenges, they are "far better than Quinine," and only cost one cent each.

Stomach disorders seemed to be a major complaint in Gussie's household; upset stomachs had progressed from the "dry belly-ache" of the Puritan days to the "billousness" of the founding fathers to the "dyspepsia" of the 1880s ("acid indigestion" was still fifty years away). Horsford's Acid Phosphate had the solution. It would not only relieve your dyspepsia, but also cure "indigestion, headache, mental and physical exhaustion, nervousness, hysteria, night sweats of consumption, etc." and it was "agreeable to the taste."

Many of the potions, even those which advertised themselves as "Microbe Killers" were primarily water, but some of them contained high doses of drugs which are today subjected to stiff regulations. Cocaine, opium, hashish, chloral and alcohol could work wonders on some minor pain complaints. Women, who would be ostracized for drinking a beer, regularly downed large doses of

Advertising Trade Cards

these drugs at all times of the day. And they didn't neglect the kids. Jayne's Tonic Vermifuge and its high alcohol content not only raised low spirits in adults, but also rooted out worms in children. "The presence of these dreadful pests," the ad warned in one of all-time best examples of advertising by fear, could be shown by such symptoms as "capricious appetite, fitful sleep, craving of strange articles" and yes, even the "picking of the nose."

Prepared Foods

Nowhere was the manufacturers' quest for name recognition more intense than in the prepared food business. Everyone had to eat, and as more rural Americans and Europeans immigrants flocked to the cities, fewer could provide the food for themselves. And technology kept coming up with answers. During the Civil War tinned rations were used extensively thanks to the invention of the can opener in 1858. Afterwards, mechanized farm machinery, refrigerated rail cars, new packaging techniques, and food chemistry discoveries made mass production possible.

But it was not until 1878 that a manufacturer designed a promotion to go along with his product to distinguish it from the growing array of "shelf goods" which were beginning to compete with the traditional hogsheads, crates and barrels of bulk goods in the grocery store. The American Cereal Company designed its distinctive Quaker to feature on the box of oats. Owner Henry Crowell made the choice not out religious conviction, but simply because he wanted a symbol of something that was considered "hard-working."[12] Quite soon, tough new trademark protection laws encouraged other manufacturers to launch their own campaigns. Van Camp, Royal Baking Powder, Jos. Schlitz, Nabisco and a host of other well-known names gained their everlasting national recognition during the 1880s.

Gussie collected five exceptional cards from Libby McNeill & Libby's Cooked Corn Beef. Their colorful artwork and delightful childhood themes warrant them special attention. One depicts Little Red Riding Hood on her way to Grandma's, her basket laden with tinned goods. She is confronted by a leering wolf whose powerful jaws are poised just inches from her seemingly unperturbed smile. "Go away," she exclaims, "This is Libby McNeill & Libby's Cooked Corned Beef for Grandma." In a companion card, we witness Little Red Riding Hood's triumph over the wolf when she arrives at Grandma's door clutching the tins to her breast. On the back of four out of the five cards are ads for local grocers which don't mention Libby McNeill & Libby at all. This must be one of the earliest examples of co-op advertising, in which manufacturers and the local retailer share the costs of advertising.

Other food cards, from Dunham's Concentrated Cocoanut to Magnolia Winter Cured Children's Delight Hams to Napheys Pratt and Co. Choice Family Lard exhibit the same high quality of art. Ridge's Food For Infants and Invalids offers an intriguing recipe for "Blancmange." Simply mix their food—which is "not a medicine," but which is "the cheapest article of the Kind on the Market"— with water and create a concoction which is "invaluable in cases of cholera infantum, dysentery, chronic diarrhea, cholera."

Local merchants had their own cards. H.C. Van Walkenburgh, whose name appears on the back of three Libby McNeill & McNeill ads also had his own with a picture of a grinning Chinaman exploding through a bigger-than-life business card. Chas Miller Jr., "The Grocer," not to be outdone, emblazoned a moronic European face on a card, perhaps his own likeness, and promised a money refund policy and free delivery to "North, West or East Albany" (city records would probably reveal that the overlooked South Albany was one of the poorer sections of town).

Soap Manufacturers

Then, as now, soap manufacturers devoted large sums to advertising. Gussie collected 28 examples which demonstrate a lively competition among nine concerns, the largest number of manufacturers represented in any group in her collection. Jas. S. Kirk of Chicago, Kendall Mfg. Co. of Providence and Rival Soap from nowhere in particular battled each other for Gussie's attention. Kirk and Kendall used gold backgrounds on all of their cards, nine all together. Kendall claims two products, soap and soapine, but does not explain the difference. Both, however, were touted as "Dirt Killers," a fact graphically illustrated by a bustled-bedecked female archer named "Killer" hitting the bullseye on an appropriately entitled target called "Dirt." Kirk took a more devious route in one of his cards by depicting a red, white and blue clad family of anthropomorphic eagles gathered around the family washbin which are supported by the crest of the United States. In another card, Kirk, exploiting what passed for humor in the 1880s, showed a whistling pickaninny skipping down the road with a boll of cotton in one hand while unfolding a regal red bolt of cotton from the other. The Rival Soap would have none of these pretenses.

They advertised their product in five words: "Cheap, Good, Reliable, 5 Cents."

For consumers with higher tastes, they could use H. Thompson's Grand Soap or the Lautz Bros. & Co.'s Acme Soap which prided itself on using "no so-called greases or adulterating materials" in its processes. However, none of the soap companies could match B.T. Babbit for sheer hyperbole. This was no mere product, but a "Soap For All Nations," in which "Cleanliness is the scale of Civilization." The diatribe continues on the back of the card to say this is the finest soap ever produced, a fact borne out by review of the soap as published in the New York *Tribune* newspaper.

Within a decade, manufacturers would be turning more and more to newspapers to distribute their message to the masses, and trade cards would dwindle away as relics of early advertising. But thanks to kids like my Great-Aunt Gussie, modern day archaeologists-of-the attic can delight in their excesses and successes. As ebullient precursors to a more restrained industry, these advertising trade cards demonstrated the eternal appeal of the purity of innocence.

Notes

[1] There are only a few books on trade cards, For instance, see a self-published work by John M. Kaduck, *Advertising Trade Cards*, 1976.

[2] A good work on advertising in the post-Civil War era is Robert Atwan, Donald McQuade, and John Wright, *Edsels, Luckies and Frigidaires* (New York: Delta, 1979).

[3] This is not true for all trade cards. Some of them were used by manufacturers or producers of raw materials to acquaint wholesalers and retailers about their goods.

[4] Besides Atwan, McQuade, Wright above, see also H. Bridges, *Practical Advertising* (New York: Rinehart, 1949) and C.H. Sandage, Vernon Fryburger, and Ken Retzell, *Advertising Theory and Practice* (Homewood: Irwin, 1979).

[5] Trade cards were not the only factors. A few ad agencies, including the pioneering efforts of Volney Palmer and John Hooper in 1841, contributed to this process. Moreover, George Palmer published the first directory of American newspapers in 1869.

[6] Atwan, McQuade, Wright, preface. By 1900 the advertising outlay increased to $500 million.

[7] Stephen Fox in his work *The Mirror Makers* (New York: Morrow, 1984) inexplicably calls the period from 1865 to 1890 the "pre-history of advertising," apparently overlooking the fact that such a term usually refers to a time when no written records are extant. Unhappily, such conceptual problems are far too common in a work which could have provided much information for the neglected field of the history of advertising.

[8] The remainder would fall into a number of miscellaneous groups including a few cards each for tobacco, popular entertainment, washing wringers, watches, diamonds, and a few with no product mentioned. The decision to remove these cards from the scrapbook was not taken lightly. The intact Victorian scrapbook is a valuable source for understanding late nineteenth century domestic life. But the need to examine the ads on the backside outweighed these other considerations. I have entertained thoughts about putting the cards back into a scrapbook of sorts, a computerized HyperCard stack, which would allow an interactive look at the cards' connections to their times.

[9] Atwan, McQuade, Wright, 218.

[10] Daniel Boorstin, *The Americans: The Democratic Experience* (New York: Random, 1973): 105.

[11] Boorstin, 100, estimates more than one-half of the 400,000 early Jewish immigrants would fit this category.

[12] See Sandage, Fryburger, Retzell, 34.

Works Cited

Atwan, Robert, Donald McQuade, and John Wright. *Edsels, Luckies and Frigidaires.* New York: Delta, 1979.

Aunt Gussie's Advertising Trade Cards. Author's Private Collection.

Boorstin, Daniel. *The Americans: The Democratic Experience.* New York: Random House, 1973.

Bridges, H. *Practical Advertising.* New York: Rinehart, 1949.

Fox, Stephen. *The Mirror Makers.* New York: Morrow, 1984.

Kaduck, John. *Advertising Trade Cards.* Cleveland: Privately Published, 1976.

Sandage, C. H., Vernon Fryburger, and Ken Retzell. *Advertising Theory and Practice.* Homewood: Irwin, 1979.

T-Shirt Messages:
Fortune or Folly for Advertisers?

Shay Sayre

Introduction

Printed t-shirts are as much a part of American culture as rock n' roll. T-shirts are found everywhere people congregate. To the delight of advertisers, product t-shirts are coordinated with the fashions, activities and lifestyles of the public. T-shirt advertising can be classified as a human activity in which people become billboards in an effort to communicate their values and lifestyles. For wearers, t-shirts are visual testimony to their identity. Through an association with a product, place, business, event, sport, musical group or social organization, men and women tell each other who they are. They do so with great frequency and delight.

The business of advertising on t-shirts generates *revenue* from sales of advertised products in *metaphorical communication* among special populations. Advertisers may profit or fail because of the symbolic meaning attributed to products by a strong and viable segment of the consumer population—college students.

A walk through any college campus will give testimony to the plethora of t-shirts messages available for communication. The printed t-shirt is an integral part of the collegiate culture, providing a symbolic method of communication among those within that culture. Product symbols, developed by designers and advertisers to promote sales and events, take on meanings specific to the college culture when a symbiotic relationship develops between the product and the t-shirt wearer. That relationship and its significance for advertisers was the focus of a study of t-shirt meanings and messages. Conducted on six college campuses nationwide, the study resulted in findings that are useful for determining the risks involved in placing messages in media which are not controlled by the advertiser.

Form and Function
T-Shirts as Promotion

The sheer number of printed t-shirts currently on the market suggests that their communication potential cannot be ignored for product and sales promotional messages. An historical overview is briefly presented here to provide some perspective on t-shirt proliferation in the Nineties.

The first promotional t-shirt appeared in 1939 at the motion picture debut of *The Wizard of Oz*. The wizard's image was emblazoned on the chests of all who attended the celebration. In 1948, campaigners against Truman developed "Do it with Dewey" shirts for their constituents. In the mid-1960s, rock music promoter Bill Graham's Winterland Productions began producing music group t-shirts for sale at concerts. Today, clients such as the Hard Rock Cafe and Apple Computer distribute their product logos nationwide through Graham's giant t-shirt distribution network.

Fashion histories chronicle the popularity of the t-shirt from its days as an 18th century undergarment to its present fashion function (Berene, Shirt Stuff). T-shirt industry publication *Impressions Magazine* credits some of the growth of t-shirt advertising to advances made by the printing industry which matured from a hot melt rotogravure process in 1902, to the combined process of lithography and plastical transfers currently used to reproduce trademarks and characters on cloth garments (Piazza). Quality resolution, colors and graphically pleasing logos have enabled advertisers to communicate with their publics through t-shirts used for merchandising, sports marketing, product rebuttal advertising, and institutional promotion.

Advertising and Popular Culture

Syndicated research companies are hired to calculate media advertising message exposure and conduct day-after-recall tests for determining reach and retention. Exposure counts for t-shirt messages can also be calculated. However, unlike conventional media, t-shirt message proliferation is controlled by the wearer rather than the advertiser. Even an infusion of free shirts into the marketplace is no guarantee that they will ever be worn in public where other consumers will see them.

Explicitly because of their message exposure potential, t-shirts merit investigation as a method of product communication and advertising promotion. Unfortunately, very little research on t-shirt communication has been published. Advertising message transmission, voluminously treated in academic journals and trade publications, has only recently been linked to cultural artifacts such as the t-shirt. One study correlates t-shirt advertising with consumer behavior patterns of acquisition for personal identification (Cornwell). T-shirts have been studied in conjunction with the popular culture genre under the rubric of "readable objects" which, like other readable objects, may be subject to various traditions of interpretation and criticism (Schudson). The popular culture literature on readables—defined as advertisements, dress, and youth cultural styles—provides a strong case for linking t-shirt messages with meaningful communication. That link, which can be crucial for making decisions about media for promotional purposes, is the subject of this investigation.

Past research provides some justification for such a study. Popular culture in the form of specialty advertising is reported to have been successfully utilized for promotional purposes since the 18th century (McKendrick, et.al.). Positioning promotion as commercial culture eventually led to a study of audiences and the way they modify or resist products created for them by industry. Culture-producing organizations and tactics (such as advertising agencies and media advertising) have been identified by culture students as motivating forces for audience behavior. Scholars examine the relationship which exists between advertising and popular culture by studying the artifacts of our society and their users. Their methods have enabled advertisers to investigate target audiences and their involvement with particular products or brands in the same fashion. A study of t-shirt messages is a natural extension of product image transfer, and contributes to an understanding of how consumers infuse meaning into product communication. Marketers can use this knowledge to evaluate their promotional and media strategies which include t-shirt advertising.

This study, like others which focus on target audiences, begins with the assumption that a method of expression is incomplete until it is received and interpreted by someone else (Bell). If no one sees the ad, no message is received. It also assumes that messages and texts have meanings only when they are interpreted by the audiences.

Advertisers know, from media studies which focus on message form and impact, that a direct relationship exists between the method of communication and the response it brings from its audience. They also know that, within any culture, intentional messages may be received and responded to differently by each of the cultural segments.

An effective method for measuring message reception is to isolate a single consumer market and study how meaning is constructed within the context of that culture. Messages communicated on t-shirts elicit particularly unique meanings when placed within the culture of a college campus. Both stylistic and functional dimensions of the t-shirt produce complex relationships between commodity (a product), cultural form (t-shirt sign) and expression (as self identification and personal declaration for the college students).

The Study

Purpose

Successful advertising must capitalize on trends with timely campaigns, or even create trends with well executed promotional hype. They must be intuitive about reverse trends as well—those which result in negative product image. Such reverses in message association are hard to predict. This prediction may begin by studying trend awareness as manifested in t-shirt messages.

The college campus provides an ideal microcosm for studying the t-shirt phenomenon because college students are the most prolific wearers of t-shirts. By studying college students, we can obtain some sense of the dynamic quality of t-shirt communication. The college market segment gives us clues about how and why t-shirts communicate messages. This is a study of student t-shirt wearing behavior designed to uncover the symbolic meanings attached to t-shirt messages.

Methodology

Because of the complexity of the project, no single methodology could provide the depth of study needed to make definitive statements about t-shirt messages and meanings. Geertz (1973) suggested a form of interpretive anthropology for use in depth studies which is applicable for this research. Utilizing qualitative methods for exploration and discovery, and a survey instrument for validation, this study was conducted during the first six months of 1988 to investigate t-shirts as vehicles of expression within the college culture. Six focus groups of seven students each were conducted at San Jose State University to collect input for survey development and to pre-test the survey instrument. T-shirt wearing diaries were completed by three male junior college students living in Palo Alto, California and three female students attending the University of Colorado at Boulder. In these diaries, students recorded t-shirt inventories and chronicled the wearing activity of their favorite shirt for one month.

Based upon input gathered qualitatively, a survey instrument of 50 questions was developed and sent to instructors for distribution at six universities in five states. Colleges were selected from among states with significant t-shirt sales as reported by clothing industry sales figures for 1987. One hundred students enrolled in introductory level classes at each university were given surveys for a total sample of 600 male and female undergraduate students. Surveys asked students to indicate the number of t-shirts they owned of each of ten different types, describe their favorite t-shirt, and to indicate their level of agreement with statements about t-shirt wearing on a Likert-type scale. Data were tabulated to determine significant gender and campus variables using a Chi Square to the .05 level of probability.

Research Results

Surveys

In March, 1988, 537 surveys were completed by students from one private and five public universities representative of the nation's institutions of higher education as shown in Table 1. The mean age of respondents was 21 years; ages ranged between 17 and 42 years. Sixty-two percent of the respondents were females. Students reported owning a total of 5513 t-shirts in ten categories.

Table 1
Demographics of Survey Respondents

University	Abbreviation	Percent of Sample
University of Colorado, Boulder	UCB	22.3%
San Jose State University	SJSU	21.4%
University of Wisconsin, Madison	UW	20.1%
University of Florida, Gainesville	UF	15.1%
University of Southern California	USC	11.4%
University of Texas, Austin	UTA	9.7%

Respondents were asked to name their favorite t-shirt; Table 2 shows the eight most popular t-shirt types and the school reporting the largest number of each type listed. One hundred forty one students did not respond.

Table 2
Shirts Identified as Favorite by College Students

Type	Number	Percent*	University Reporting Most
Product/Logo	46	11.7	Wisconsin
College	36	9.1	Southern California
Sorority	33	8.3	Florida
Music Event	23	5.8	Texas
Saying	20	5.1	Colorado
Eatery/Store	19	4.8	San Jose
Plain White	16	4.0	Colorado
Foreign Place	13	3.3	Southern California
Other	213	21.6	

*Frequency adjusted to N=396

Table 3 shows student attitudes towards wearing t-shirts. Significant differences were found among colleges in two instances: USC disagreed to a much greater degree with the statement, "T-shirts reflect my lifestyle;" and significantly more males than females reported that they wore shirts given as gifts.

Table 3
Attitudes About T-Shirt Wearing

Attitude	Agree Strongly	Agree Somewhat	Neutral	Disagree Somewhat	Disagree Strongly
T-shirts reflect my lifestyle	20.7	49.9	20.3	6.5*	2.6
I wear t-shirts to send messages to others	7.1	26.4	30.0	18.9	17.3
Wearing the right shirt is important to me	19.6	29.6	31.1	10.4	9.3
I wear t-shirts given to me by others	33.5**	27.6	22.3	9.3	7.1
I don't pay attention to t-shirts	5.2	16.4	22.6	38.1	17.8

N=537 *Significance found using Chi Square with 5 df at .05.
**Significance found using Chi Square with 1 df at .05.

Significant differences in t-shirt preferences were found between all campus cultures and between sexes at most universitites. Regional interests were reflected in t-shirt preferences; environmental concerns were expressed more often on Colorado t-shirts while Midwestern students were most likely to prefer shirts naming beers.

Diaries

Six students submitted inventories totaling 167 shirts. Table 4 shows that product-type t-shirts were selected as favorites by males; two females selected organization-types, and one female chose a personal-message shirt. Gender preferences correspond to those reflected in survey data.

Table 4
Wearing Patterns of "Favorite" T-Shirts

Age	Gender	Total Owned	Favorite Type	Wearings Per Week	Hours	People	Place
19	Male	32	Product	3	6	95	Beach
20	Male	27	Sport Event	2	8	35	Class
19	Male	19	Product	2	5	40	Fraternity
21	Female	29	Organization	1	4	25	Aerobics
22	Female	27	Cartoon	1	5	15	Running
22	Female	33	Eateries	2	5	75	Movies

A review of the wearing patterns for "favorite" shirts indicates three wearings per week for four to five hours each wearing. Males reported that they wore "favorite" shirts to places where an average of 65 people were congregated. Females, however, said that an average of 18 people were present at places they went wearing t-shirts. Calculated in terms of advertising impressions, one male student's normal wearing period for his favorite shirt yields 780 impressions per month for product sponsors. Multiplied by the number of students wearing shirts, this number reveals a plethora of signage opportunities for advertisers.

Discussion

Survey results are presented within a framework which weaves the data on collegiate preferences with a discussion of how meaning is created through t-shirts by their wearers. This is accomplished in three stages. First, t-shirts are categorized to help advertisers attach proper significance to the types of shirts that are purchased or owned by college consumers. Second, a treatment of the symbolic nature of t-shirts in the college culture is provided. Third, a correlation is made between advertising goals, t-shirt symbolism and the management of meaning.

T-Shirt Classification System

In the survey, t-shirts were grouped into categories by message similarity. Results can be understood by discussing t-shirts by message type: Affiliation (belonging), Trophy (achievement), Personal Message (values), and Metaphor (lifestyles).

1. *Shirts With Affiliation Messages*: Club, sorority, fraternity, school and university types of t-shirts are indicative of the need to belong. Students choosing group shirts reflect their need for affiliation; they attain identity through the association with a group. For these students, relationships are expressed as membership messages. Affiliation t-shirts accounted for 23% of those owned and the greatest percentage (33%) of those designated as "favorites" by respondents. Sorority, school and club shirts were preferred by females in focus groups, diaries and surveys.

2. *Shirts With Trophy Orientations*: T-shirts are purchased as souvenirs at a) a travel destination, b) restaurant or shop, and as evidence of c) attendance at a concert or d) participation in a sporting event. Collected by students as trophies, these shirts are testimony to "being in a place" or "taking part in" an activity. Reminiscent of the spoils of war in times past, trophy t-shirts reflect the self-esteem need. As trophies, shirts have value. Their value is dependent upon two factors: exclusivity of the shirt's selective distribution (as opposed to mass distribution in a department store) and distance of the destination t-shirt from the college campus of residency. Purchased at concerts or given as part of the entry fee for marathons, races and events, these shirts often contain the date, location and nature of the event. Travel shirt types are most often purchased as gifts by visitors to ski lodges, tropical islands, or foreign countries. Trophy shirts were the second most popular choice for students listing them as favorites (27%); 55% of total total t-shirts owned by respondents were one of the four types in this category; males sent messages of their participation in sport events, females communicated about their travel with t-shirt trophies, and both genders collected t-shirt souvenirs of eateries and music events. Shirts from Hard Rock Cafe, a 50s theme restaurant with locations in cities worldwide, were named as the "most popular" shirts by more students than another other shirt. That year, Hard Rock Cafe, distributing from eight US and two European locations, had 22 million shirts in circulation (Spindler, 1988). Advertisers who can produce a trophy t-shirt message have an excellent chance of finding favor on campuses which are geographically distant from the restaurant or lodge. However, once they can be obtained in places other than the location designated on the shirt, trophy shirts lose their value to student wearers. This information is useful for advertisers making t-shirt distribution decisions.

3. *T-Shirts With Personal Messages*: Students made declarations about their beliefs, philosophies and causes as well as satirizing current events by way of personal message t-shirts in seven types: a) Belief/Cause/Philosophy, b) Political, c) Satire or Wit, d) Plain White, e) Graphic Design, f) Cartoon Character, and g) Generic Sport. "The Pride is Back" and "Anybody but Bush" are typical of shirts worn as personal expression. Indicative of a Sixties musical group, tie dyed design shirts are worn to communicate appreciation for music written and/or sung by the Grateful Dead. Mickey Mouse shirts were popular with females who said they liked to project the fantasy and playfulness of cartoon characters on themselves. A personal statement can also be made, according to some students, by an *absence* of message. Plain white shirts, worn in one culture, acts as a boycott of the commercial messages worn by other students. In the Rocky Mountain region, many students were seen with plain shirts, and some listed them as favorites on the survey. Generic sport shirts are indicative of participation for its own sake rather than affiliation with a team or accomplishment of a goal, and are therefore considered evidence of self-actualization rather than as a trophy. Personal message shirts were the least popular category (17%), and they accounted for 14% of the total number of shirts owned by participants.

4. *T-Shirts As Metaphorical Expressions*: For many coeds, products, product logos, characters and slogans are signifiers of a life style or an identity preferred by the wearer. Product symbols signify differently between college cultures. On one campus a beer product symbolizes a rite of passage into adulthood; on another, it signifies an addictive vice

Fig. 1. Stanford Rugby as Affiliation and belonging.

Fig. 2. Hard Rock cafe as the most preferred trophy.

T-Shirt Messages

Fig. 3. Mickey as a form of personal expression.

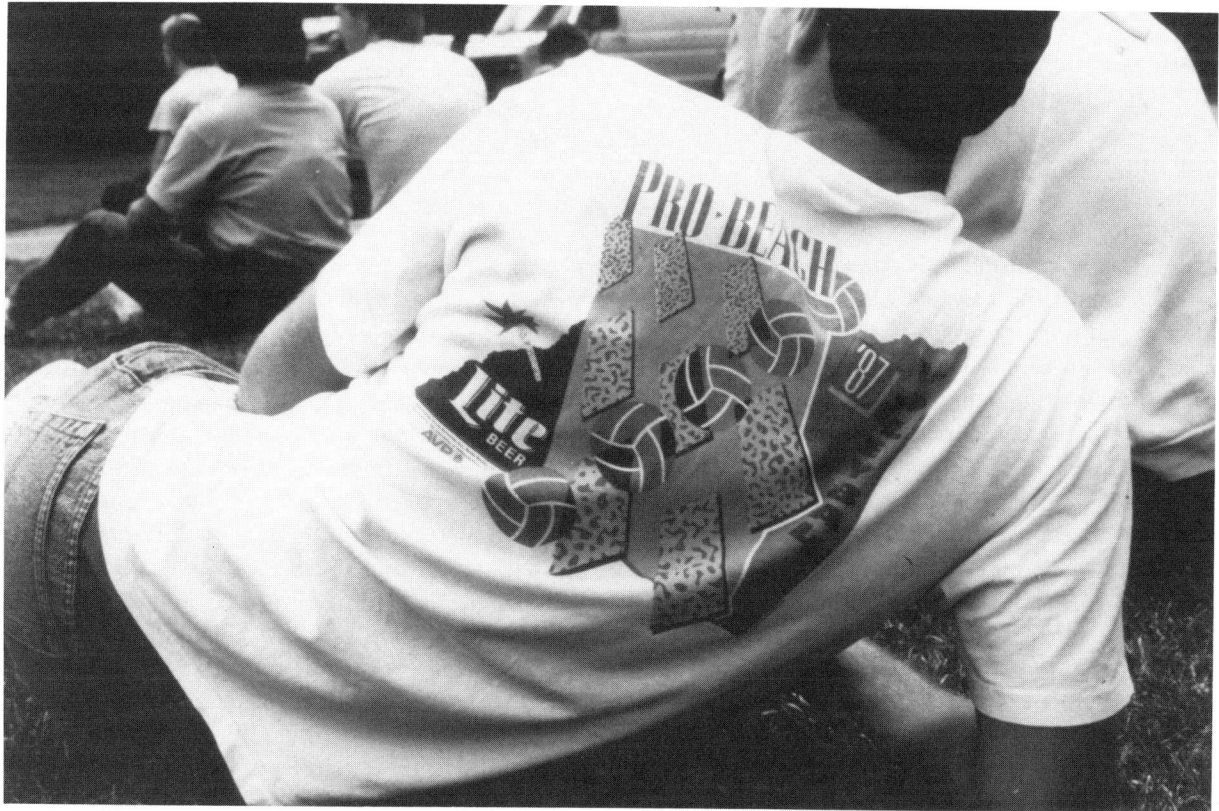

Fig. 4. Lite Beer as a metaphorical expression for lifestyle.

and is negatively connoted. Also included in this category are t-shirts with names and pictures of singers, musical groups and major league teams because they are sold as products through record and ticket sales and are "purchased" as commodities. With these t-shirts, products become a personification of the wearer. Product-oriented t-shirts were designated as one of the most favorite types of t-shirts (23%) by study participants, and they were the most prized shirts according to focus group input. The *Trophy* and *Metaphor* categories account for one half of all the shirts chosen as favorites by college students. Shirts from the trophy and product types are of primary interest to advertisers; therefore, a treatment of the causal relationship which exists between the collegiate consumer and a chosen product or logo as displayed on a t-shirt is warranted. The relationship can be conceptualized through a discussion of the form which products take for presentation on t-shirts—the symbol.

The Nature of Symbols

Advertising often communicates symbolically to consumers. In a similar manner, students use t-shirts to communicate symbolically with one another. Greek letters, for instance, communicate meaning about a group of people who collectively identify themselves with two- or three-letter combinations. Often, products act as symbols for students, one example is the bicycle. Depending upon campus culture, the bicycle conveys several meanings of social status which range from "mountain rider" to "speed racer" to "campus commuter."

The bicycle is an example of how a product functions as a culturally dependent symbol. A complex symbol, the bicycle is an object of envy or of practical purpose; it is also a symbol of skill or of wealth. Students identify with their bicycles and use bicycle brands and logos to communicate social substance, freedom, personal style and sexual maturity. A Specialized Mountain bike prized at San Jose may have a social symbol different from the one it may have at Wisconsin where street riding predominates. The object for advertisers is to imbue products with social status so that they become a symbol to the student based on campus values. Once a symbolic meaning is established for the product, students wear the t-shirts to convey a message about their social status to other students.

Products as Symbols of Self

The facility for products like bicycles to become symbols or personifications of a lifestyle is best accomplished under certain conditions and with certain select groups of individuals. According to Wicklund and Gollwitzer (1982), personifications are a form of "symbolic-self completion" which begins when persons consider themselves somehow "incomplete." They include people who strive for self-definition. According to their definition, a personal state of incompleteness exists for most undergraduate college students for several reasons. First, student commitments, ideals and values are in the process of being formulated; they are in a constant state of change and flux. Student behaviors exhibit a striving toward betterment; classes, lessons and training all occur during the college years. Some students may even overtly "uncommit" themselves from self-defining activities. Second, most students are in constant search for symbols as evidenced by their attachment to Greek organizations, sports skill designations (such as "expert skier"), and clubs. Thus, the quest for social reality by students can be enhanced through symbolic self-definition.

Students may choose products to act as metaphors of self-description and definition. Since students seem to experience a shortcoming of self-definition, they are likely to accept products as symbols to increase their sense of completeness to the extent that these symbols are recognized and accepted by their peers. The meaning of these symbols must be transferred by advertisers within the college culture in order for the significance of the product symbol to enhance self-definition. Corona Beer's campus effort is an example of how a company can successfully infuse the symbolic meaning of "acceptable person as social drinker" into a product for promotional purposes.

Product as Metaphor

As McCracken points out, advertising can serve as a method for meaning transfer when consumers link their identity with a specific product. Sometimes, a product becomes the embodiment of the values and lifestyle of the consumer, acting as a metaphor for the wearer. When the consumer and the product are brought together in a representational t-shirt form, a message is understood by those who share the definition of the product metaphor. As campus-based values become intrinsic to the product, the transfer of meaning from culture to product is made. Wearer and product assume a particular harmony, and the product takes on a meaning which is significant to the identity of the person wearing the t-shirt. Through t-shirt advertising, goods continually shift meaning;

advertising serves as a "lexicon of current cultural meanings" (McCracken 76). In the college culture, product messages cross from their literal meanings to take on a symbolic one. In the case of t-shirts, advertising joins with fashion to act as a manipulator of highly innovative cultural meaning.

Gender Related Difference in the Significance of Products as Symbols

This study validates the notion that men and women have been found to display different patterns of relationships with objects (Csekszenthmihalyi and Rochberg-Halton). Consistent with their findings, collegiate males preferred sports equipment, trophies and objects of action while women in the study mentioned photographics and objects of contemplation. These differences reflect the distinction made by sociologists between *instrumental* male roles and *expressive* female roles. Gilligan points out that women complete their self-definition through relationships, while men tend to link their completion with non-personal objects and have a task rather than relationship orientation. As the French language assigns gender to objects, consumers engender products for their personal associations.

Product Symbols as Campus Rhetoric

This study reveals t-shirts to be icons that are interwoven into important life experiences and expectations. Students' stories illustrate how shirts transcend literal definitions and develop personal and social meanings and complex symbolisms. These meanings are influential in forming attitudes when it comes to thinking about others and themselves. The image surrounding a product transforms wearers and provides them with an emotional experience of association with that product. Perhaps an indication of this phenomenon is connected with Corona Extra, providing a case in point. When students wear Corona beer shirts, they experience a higher level and more adult experience than if they wear Coke shirts—at least they think they do. They believe they are somehow transformed into one of the crowd by wearing Corona shirts, proof that advertising planning may result in significant product impressions generated by t-shirt wearing.

Levy's framework for understanding how product symbols serve a function of representation can be applied to t-shirt wearing. As symbols, t-shirts provide a variety of services for the student wearer. Product symbols as shirt message *economize* by eliminating the need for one person to ask about another. A "Porsche" message provides thousands of words about a person's interests and values without speaking at all. As students experience mind expansion by infusing meaning and association into product signs, they *elaborate*. "Corona Extra" on a shirt can be interpreted to mean that the wearer is playful, adventuresome, fun. The logo enlarges perceptions of the wearer through its implications of sociability. T-shirt metaphors are *expressive*. Product symbols fill a need to project and tell more about one's self. The wearer says, "This is where I stand and how I relate to the world." Shirt messages have the power and ability to influence others. According to students, the right t-shirt message can cultivate a personal relationship.

Students can also use product symbols to *deceive* by sending false messages. "New York Marathon" on a t-shirt connotes athletic endurance; "Club Med" implies vacation traveling. While rules about shirt "lying" are unclear, students indicated that wearing shirts from places one has not visited is permissible, but false declarations about team sport participation or fraternal affiliation is frowned upon. T-shirt metaphors can *clarify*. Products provide an analogy to explain something about one's self or one's life. "Frosted Flakes" says that wearers have a sense of humor, that they relate to Frosted Flakes commercials which parody adult desire. Most importantly, product symbols serve to *gratify* the wearer. People derive pleasure from wearing shirts that elicit a response. "Spring Fucking Break/Palm Springs" delighted collegiate audiences and survey respondents during and long after their spring breaks. T-shirt puns initiate laughter and allow people to fantasize, to indulge themselves.

Management of Meaning

Advertisers understand that the relationship developed between goods and consumers can serve to dramatize social-economic status (BMW connotes membership in an upper economic group while Chevy signals blue collar affiliation). They employ this knowledge for promotion on t-shirts by using product symbols to manifest characteristics of the rich, the healthy, the macho, the elegant and so forth. Advertisers know that goods reflect status, and that college consumers will wear logos of those goods to convey status to others. However, promoters must heed the fickle nature of college consumers who operate in a constantly changing campus culture. On a campus, advertisers cannot assume a fixed standardization of goods. For an adult consumer in a suburban culture, symbols of social class are pervasive and enduring. In the college culture, no such reliability exists, as exemplified by the multiplicity of meanings associated with a single t-shirt sign or message.

And, while advertisers may rely on the fact students create their personal identity through a symbolic association with an advertised product, they cannot always control the meanings transferred onto their products. Nor can they determine when over-distribution renders a shirt out-of-vogue, eliminating the product sign from campus.

T-shirt advertisers are advised to research current campus cultures before attempting t-shirt promotions. Campus promotion requires understanding of collegiate culture on the part of the advertiser. And an acknowledgement that students' upbringing, neighborhood, wealth and culture, otherwise unknown to the world of strangers, are all symbolized through an identification with a product that represents who they are. Or who they want to be. For most students, t-shirts become a form of "ego screaming" (Gusfield & Michalowicz) which ritualizes them in their collegiate social culture. After all, most students' values and experiences are extensions of the commodity marketplace. Through a selection of product oriented shirts, males "scream out" their choices in beverage, athletic gear and sunglasses. The meanings associated with those products are clear—a wearer recognizes quality and correlates the image he has of himself with the specific masculine image developed for that product by advertisers.

In order to be embraced by the collegiate consumer, advertisers must be certain that product associations selected for t-shirt messages reflect acceptable aspirations. This study can act as evidence that products which facilitate a positive personal image association for students are more likely to succeed and are less likely to become victims of non-use on campus than products which imply culture-specific social values. For example, Hard Rock Cafe, a trophy shirt conveying a person's worldliness, has outlived many of the beer shirts which became victims of the changing social mores of alcohol consumption.

Conclusion

College culture rituals are ever-changing. Shirts wane in popularity and advertisers suffer from the fickle affiliation wearers have with their products. As advertisers devise and enhance products' images, the college culture responds by changing the meanings inherent in the products. Like most cultural artifacts, T-shirts arrive with a great wave of acknowledgement and then disappear without a trace. T-shirts have no fixed meaning or permanent status, they simply exist in the context of a culture. When the culture changes, meanings change. Significant only for the moment, symbols become divorced from one product and attached to a new one. Eventually, to the lament of many advertisers, both the t-shirt and the product it bares become testimony to what once was and can never be again.

Works Cited

Bell, M.J. "The Study of Popular Culture." In M. Thomas Inge (Ed.) *A Concise History of American Popular Culture*. Westport, Conn: Glenwood Press, 1982.

Berene, J. "The t-shirt." *Esquire Magazine* 104 (1) (1985): 26.

Cantor, N. & M. Worthham, Eds. *The History of Popular Culture*. New York: McMillan, 1968.

Cornwell, B.T. (1990). "T-shirts as Wearable Diary: An Examination of Artifact Consumption and Garnering Related to Life Events." *Advances in Consumer Research* 17 1-5.

Csekszenthmihalyi, M. and E. Rochberg-Halton, *The Meaning of Things*. NY: Cambridge University Press, 1981.

Gans, H.J. *Popular Culture and High Culture: An Analysis and Evaluation of Taste*. NY: Basic, 1974.

Geertz, C. *The Interpretation of Cultures*. New York: Basic, 1973.

Gilligan, C. *In a Different Voice*. Cambridge, MA: Harvard University Press, 1982.

Gusfield, J.R., and J. Michalowicz, "Secular Symbolism." *Annual Review of Sociology* 10 (1984): 417-35.

Levy, S. *Marketplace Behavior*. Englewood Cliffs, NJ: Prentice Hall, 1972.

Lynes, R. *The Tastemakers*. NY: Harper & Row, 1971.

McKendrick, N., J. Brewer, and J.H. Plumb, *The Birth of a Consumer Society*. Bloomington, IN: Indiana University Press, 1982.

McCracken, Grant. "Culture and Consumption: A Theoretical Account of the Structure and Movement of the Cultural Meaning of Consumer Goods." *Journal of Consumer Research* 13 (1986): 71-84.

Piazza, C. "Consumer Survey '87: T-shirt Buying Habits." *Impressions Magazine*, March (1987): 55-108.

Schudson, M. "The New Validation of Popular Culture: Sense and Sentimentality in Academia." *Critical Studies in Mass Communication* 4: 51 (1987): 68.

"Shirtstuff." *Rolling Stone Magazine*, April 23, 1988, 97.

Spindler, A.M. "Soft Sell at Hard Rock." *Daily News Record*. June 13, 1988.

Wicklund, R.A. & P.M. Gollwitzer. *Symbolic Self Completion*. London: Lawrence Erlbaum, 1982.

Mona Lisa Meets Madison Avenue: Advertising Spoofs of A Cultural Icon

Gina Strumwasser and Monroe Friedman

Almost 500 years ago, Leonardo da Vinci painted the *Mona Lisa* and created an ideal image of a Renaissance noblewoman (Fig. 1). The painting served as a model for the great sixteenth-century Italian portrait artists Raphael and Titian as well as their Northern European counterparts. Now an easily recognizable icon, the Mona Lisa sustains a powerful impact on the modern day viewer. Veneration of the painting for hundreds of years has bred familiarity. But it is only since Marcel Duchamp's metamorphosis of the Mona Lisa in the early years of the twentieth century that the cultural icon has become a major media image employed and exploited by advertisers for the purpose of selling products.

Today, Mona Lisa's compelling attraction depends upon popular imagery. Originally, it was Mona Lisa's smile that was considered universally appealing. We are silently bemused by the original painting of the *Mona Lisa* by Leonardo yet we laugh openly at the image transformed by the advertisers. Different historical and cultural circumstances have engendered diverse reactions to the same image. Although the content remains the same, presentations in advertising and public responses to them have changed throughout the centuries.

This alteration is due, in part, to the use of humor employed to change the relationship between the viewer and the object viewed.* The purpose of this article is to examine the transformation from the original Renaissance image of the *Mona Lisa* to its current status as cultural icon, and to suggest an explanation for the popularity of the painting as a vehicle for advertising.[1]

The Renaissance Origins of the Mona Lisa

For centuries, Leonardo da Vinci's *Mona Lisa* has represented perfection in Renaissance portraiture. For the first time, Mona Lisa's smile invited the viewer to enter the illusionistic realm of the painting. By breaking down the psychological barrier and physical boundaries between art and reality, Leonardo created a unique image.

Prior to the Renaissance, there was no place reserved in the pictorial medieval world for the portrayal of earthly emotions.[2] Life on earth was, after all, only a stepping stone to the hereafter and after a short and brutal experience on earth, death was viewed as an escape from temporal existence, a release from this world. Life was intimately connected to religion and was understood only through symbols that reflected or echoed nature. The symbolic message conveyed through natural objects of this world was celebrated, but not nature herself. Christ and events from his life on earth began to dominate late thirteenth-century literature and art as a response to changing church philosophy. This transformation required a new means of expression in the pictorial arts. The artist could no longer depend solely upon a symbolic imagination for a view of the heavenly realm but was forced to look closely at plants and animals as well as women and men on earth to provide him with stimuli to create appropriate earthly ambiance for Christ. The new exuberance toward life was manifested in the art of the Renaissance.

More than any other artist of the late fifteenth and early sixteenth centuries, Leonardo da Vinci found his primary artistic goal overwhelmed by a passion for the faithful rendering of nature. Even his religious paintings were dominated by a precise rendering of life on earth. He was first in an artistic succession to achieve perfection in the portrayal of the human figure. With renewed confidence in the temporal world and an awakening cognizance of the power to create life, the Renaissance artist possessed a creative potential comparable not only to the ideal prototype of antiquity but to nature as well. In this capacity, the role of the Renaissance artist was considered parallel to that of the divine.

Leonardo was satisfied with neither accepted authority nor conservative observation. Unorthodox in approach to even sacred subjects, he depicted unequaled representations of traditional biblical

Fig. 1 Leonardo da Vinci, *Mona Lisa*, Paris, The Louvre

themes. With *Mona Lisa*, Leonardo designed an exemplary portrait, a courtly woman of the Renaissance and invented a model which would be borrowed by artists throughout the sixteenth century.[3] Earlier Renaissance portraits described mostly surface or physiognomical perceptions of the sitter in profile rather than visually documenting the individual's personality.[4] But to Leonardo and to subsequent High Renaissance painters, it was the "working of the mind" that had to be recorded in paint and revealed to the viewer.[5] Divorced from any religious subject, Leonardo was able to imbue his image with real human emotions exceeding all previous portrayals. To accomplish these representations, he made frequent use of facial expressions including, of course, the smile.

The smile is considered a uniquely human expression of emotion. Both pagan and Christian artists had endowed their images with smiles in order to present a more life-like attitude. Sculptors and painters from Ancient Greece and the Middle Ages had also used the smile to express an animate human spirit in the carved or painted form while they struggled to depict a figure realistically. The smile disappeared as soon as the goal, an anatomically correct appearance, was realized. Even

Florentine artists of the Early Renaissance renewed an interest in this emotion by portraying smiles on the faces of their sculptures. Andrea del Verrocchio, Leonardo's teacher, produced smiling figures of the Virgin Mary and Christ as well as portraits of contemporary Florentine citizens in stone, clay and bronze.[6]

Although previous art historians have argued that Leonardo followed this earlier precedent and even labeled his work as a climax to the sweet Quattrocento tradition, he rarely chose to follow the path of his predecessors. Furthermore, Leonardo employs the smile mostly in his later work after having created an ideal human image.[7]

Mona Lisa's Enigmatic Smile

Art historians and viewers alike have attempted to determine the reason for Mona Lisa's smile. For example, according to Giorgio Vasari, a contemporary of Leonardo and a sixteenth-century art historian and biographer, Elizabeth Giocondo, to whom the smile belonged, was a wistful woman.[8] It was necessary for the painter to hire musicians to keep away the sadness from her expression. The result was a smile.[9]

In his *Lives of the Artists*, Vasari relates Leonardo's wit and jocular behavior through amusing anecdotes. His sense of humor not only led him to play tricks on contemporaries but to experiment with the absurd and extraordinary of human emotion. Interest in the more pervasive realm of emotion is well documented in his paintings and drawings.[10] He responded to each commission with a sense of creative play. The stimulus to create echoed the impulse to give life.

Particularly in drawing, Leonardo explored an extreme range of human emotion which is evidenced in his grotesque heads, fantastic beasts and studies of screaming warriors.[11] In this experimental context, it is important to understand that Mona Lisa's smile went beyond the intent of the ancient Greeks and the artists of the Middle Ages. Leonardo could create a perfect Renaissance man or woman. For this reason, the smile cannot be interpreted as a substitute for realism. Leonardo was interested in penetrating the physical and showing the duality of life of the body and soul. Perhaps Mona Lisa's famous smile is a reflection of the artist's own.[12]

It is also necessary to ask why Mona Lisa is smiling rather than laughing. The depiction of a sitter laughing would not have been appropriate for a woman of noble birth in the Renaissance. Perhaps because a laugh often has a spontaneous eruptive quality to it, laughter suggests someone out of control or lacking in decorum. In this way, the laugh lacks the dignity associated with a smile. We like to be smiled at, not to be laughed at. Also, the negative connotation of a laugh is the butt of a joke.

Mona Lisa's smile makes the painted woman approachable, natural and familiar. We recognize her through her smile. When we think of a smile, we usually think of a momentary or instantaneous response to pleasure. If a smile is fixed over time, it appears as a grimace or smirk, something far less charming which is frozen or smug in affectation.[13]

The smile beckons the viewer to the work of art. As an invitation to participate in the painterly realm, the smile is also evocative of joy or delight, amusement or contentment. Sometimes sensual gratification is implicit in the smiling visage. The smile demands our participation and projects explicit self-confidence. When we meet someone new, we respond in a positive way if the person is smiling. A frown will interfere with the welcome and a grimace will appear unnatural and uncomfortable. The spontaneity of a smile serves to relate more expansively to the world around us. It is a symbol that is universally understood without exception. This may, in part, explain the popularity of the *Mona Lisa* regardless of geographical boundary or historical setting.

The Duchamp Defacement

With each new generation of admirers, Leonardo *Mona Lisa* has been elevated to higher and higher plateaus. The painting has become an object of devotion to be adored and venerated in a manner comparable to Christian deities. It was not until the twentieth century that this potent Renaissance icon was re-examined. In a most brutal manner, the *Mona Lisa* was stripped bare by the great revolutionary painter Marcel Duchamp who attempted to eliminate the barriers that separated the work of art from the viewer. Duchamp's goal was to re-evaluate the work of art without imbuing it with power achieved through centuries of worship. He refused to accept the exalted position of the *Mona Lisa* and was the first to desecrate this sixteenth-century monument and the venerable woman.

As a member of the Dadist movement, Duchamp attacked the traditional and orthodox in art as a "highfalutin pretentious cult."[14] Duchamp developed a means to create art from objects already made. For example, exhibiting a urinal as a piece of sculpture, he was the first to destroy the standard Renaissance ideal of art. His ready-mades were supplemented by adding drawings to the preexisting piece or "aided." By adorning the ready-made with drawing, Duchamp developed the ready-made aided. In 1919, he took a ready made postcard of the *Mona Lisa*, a reproduction of the original painting, and upon it superimposed a moustache and goatee. He identified the postcard by the letters *LHOOQ*, also the title of the painting, which in French sounds like "elle a chaud au cul" or "she has a hot tail" (or "there is a fire down below") and signed the work.[15] In doing this, Duchamp explicitly deflated and boldly devalued the image of adoration and at the same time created an original work of art. He transformed the Renaissance paradigm. Mona Lisa became the "butt" of his joke. Duchamp took away the prestige and dignified status of this sixteenth-century icon and restored the imaginative power to the viewer. Through a process of "osmosis," dependent upon the viewer's "inner" experience, he gave the beholder the creative power to complete the work of art.[16] By doing so, the viewer becomes more than a removed spectator. Similar to the involvement of the artist, the beholder is required to participate in the creative process.

Duchamp stimulated revolutionary thought and turned against established tradition that had evolved since the Renaissance. He evoked humor through a "plastic" or three-dimensional pun (or three-dimensional object) but fundamentally brought down high culture in response.[17] These ready-mades and ready-mades-aided functioned in part to shock and to "exalt scandalous objects."[18] He used the "pun" as a means to achieve this attack and his method of shock. The Mona Lisa is an expression of the ready-made aided which corrects the original product. Duchamp mocked or poked fun at conventional and traditional art. By doing so, he became a trickster. A trickster can be defined as a person engaged in "a crafty procedure or practice [as a means] to deceive or defraud."[19] It involves a complex maneuvering or manipulation of others or objects. In a humorous manner, Duchamp betrayed orthodox artistic ideals and by doing this he freed the imagination to create in a novel way. His attack on tradition was a type of anti-art which would have a significant effect on his own vocation as well as the careers of many other artists working in Europe and the United States.

Mona Lisa as Popular Culture Icon

Marcel Duchamp refused to accept the honored position of the *Mona Lisa* and was the first to violate the sanctity of this Renaissance monument. By humanizing Leonardo's smiling sitter, he transferred the art object from high to low culture. It was only after Duchamp's *LHOOQ* that the *Mona Lisa* could be reinterpreted as human—earthy and ordinary—and was employed in advertising campaigns throughout the Western World. An abundance of Mona Lisa images appear in contemporaneous popular culture. But how do we explain the often humorous employment of the Mona Lisa today? Mona Lisa is, for example, represented in jokes in *Playboy* (Leonardo flashes Mona to get her to smile, or she is represented shooting up heroin); she is portrayed on greeting cards; and she is depicted on cocktail napkins and party invitations. The Renaissance noblewoman is represented with curlers, goggles, braces, eye glasses, or in a graduation cap. She is seen jogging, playing tennis, even masturbating. Mona Lisa has been used to create a contemporary theme for fingernail decoration and T-shirts. There are amusing publications, such as *Leonardo Visits Los Angeles*, depicting Mona Lisa as star and as a member of a sculptural group with George Washington in a bath.[20] In all these instances Mona Lisa is brought down to earth. The already familiar image is transformed into the commonplace and the Renaissance prototype is disguised as an object lacking in nobility and dignity, a victim of a joke. We no longer smile at Mona Lisa but laugh at her metamorphosis.[21]

The synthesis of the familiar smiling woman with the unexpected or incongruous elicits a jovial response, and in this way humor is employed to attract the consumer to the product. Modern day advertisers explicitly juxtapose this classical image with contemporary garb and twentieth-century attributes. Similar to Duchamp's *LHOOQ*, Mona Lisa has been separated from her Renaissance context and cultural setting and removed from her elevated status originally associated with high culture. Although initially exhibited in a sumptuous palace and museum of art (The Louvre, Paris), copies of Leonardo's portrait are displayed in the ambiance of low culture and transferred to the kitchen, bathroom or bar.

Are we updating Mona Lisa to keep her "trendy" or downgrading her in relationship to Leonardo's original painting? Perhaps Alan Dundes' approach to humor might best suit our needs.[22] It is possible to explain the frequency of the representation of the updated Mona Lisa in advertisement through contemporaneous culture. Mona Lisa has been re-examined in the twentieth century to accommodate present needs. More recently, Yuppies have restored popularity to ostentatious consumption. The resurrection of the *Mona Lisa* in the twentieth century through spoof is disguised from the original meaning and is no longer associated with the Renaissance.

Can we measure social change by a study of contemporary portrayals of the *Mona Lisa*?[23] It would be less acceptable to do this with a religious icon such as an image of the Virgin Mary or a representation of an event from the life of Christ such as the Last Supper.[24] A secular or secularized subject, a portrait or familiar theme from ancient literature might serve a similar role as the *Mona Lisa* by attracting and maintaining popular attention aesthetically and socially to a new product.[25]

Mona Lisa is a commonly seen and easily recognizable image. For this reason her smiling countenance has attracted the attention of advertisers. Spoofs continue to prove the potent force of Leonardo's original painting. Miles removed geographically and separated in time by centuries, the classical image of the *Mona Lisa* is infused with modern meaning. Although transformed from a noblewoman of the Renaissance, the impression on the viewer remains a powerful one.

Advertising Spoofs of the Mona Lisa

To understand advertising spoofs of the *Mona Lisa* it is first necessary to provide some background information concerning the use of humor in advertising and the psychological factors which influence its effectiveness.

Humor in Advertising

At the outset it should be noted that the use of humor in advertising has varied over time with relatively few instances in the 1970s and considerably more in the 1980s. While some advertisers have referred to the earlier period as the "serious seventies," the term "serious" would seem out of place in the 1980s with such initiatives as Wendy's "Where's the beef" campaign, IBM's Personal Computer campaign with its Charlie Chaplin character, and the Bud Light campaign featuring a "Bimbleman Lite Beer" competitor with the slogan, "If you want a beer real bad, we've got a real bad beer." Recent changes in radio advertising illustrate the new emphasis on humor. According to Michael Lev, "Comedy radio advertising has become an impressive cottage industry in Hollywood, where several writing and producing teams create more than 1000 funny radio commercials each year."[26] Clio awards winner Dick Orkin believes this new emphasis on humor in commercials is no accident. He notes that major companies, in such fields as automobiles and computers, which had previously declined interest in such advertising are now recognizing the value of humor. Especially attractive to advertisers is its alleged ability to break through the "drone of countless commercials" commonly known as "clutter."

The Research Evidence

While increasing in size and sophistication, the body of behavioral research literature on humor in advertising remains relatively small.[27] On the whole, the literature reveals that the impact of humor in advertisements has been mixed. On the negative side, the addition of humor to an advertising message can have the effect of reducing its comprehension. Other problems are the short life span of gag-type messages and the possibility of negative reactions on the part of some audiences. To illustrate the last-mentioned problem, the Clara Peller character in Wendy's "Where's the beef" campaign was found by some older consumers to be offensive and, indeed, a letter of complaint was sent to the firm by the Michigan Commission on Aging.

On the positive side, there is evidence that humor can attract attention to advertisements but only if they appear in the context of non-humorous programming. Thus humor may be an attention getter for advertisements for documentary or adventure programs but not for situation comedies. Other possible advantages of humor sometimes cited by advertisers are its ability to enhance the credibility of an information source as well as its ability to distract the consumer and, in so doing, to impede the formation of counterarguments.

Psychological Elements in Humor

As a subject area of interest to academics and practitioners, humor is attracting national and international attention. To illustrate, the two-volume *Handbook of Humor Research* appeared in 1983, and *Humor: International Journal of Humor Research* was launched in 1988. In addition, WHIM, an academic association on humor has started meeting each year—and on a most appropriate date, April 1.

In their efforts to understand humor these academics have postulated a significant role for a variety of psychological elements. Three, in particular, which have received attention are 1) incongruity or perceived incongruity, 2) positive affect or pleasant feeling, and 3) aggression and hostility. All three elements are associated with the works of many writers and humor analysts, including Paul McGhee and Arthur Koestler, in the case of incongruity; Mathew Apte and John Morreall, in the case of positive affect; and, following Freud, Alan Dundes and Albert Rapp, in the case of aggression and hostility. The unexpected pie-in-the-face caper illustrates all three elements occurring at the same time in that the action is incongruous and aggressive, if not hostile, and it brings pleasure to audiences which enjoy slapstick comedy.

Analyzing Mona Lisa Ad Depictions

The *Mona Lisa* is a high culture icon, and it seems reasonable to assume that marketers might treat the portrait differently depending upon the nature of the product they are promoting. Indeed, this notion led to the formulation of two hypotheses which are as follows:

1. Advertisements featuring Mona Lisa for low or mass culture products will make use of humorous parody or defacement since the concern here is with stressing pleasant incongruities between the high culture icon and the low or mass culture products.

2. Advertisements featuring Mona Lisa for high culture products will not make use of humorous parody or defacement since the concern here is with seriousness rather than humor and with congruity rather than incongruity between the high culture icon and the high culture products.

A search of popular magazines of the 1980s led to the identification of six advertisements depicting Mona Lisa. Three of the products featured were canned food items which could be considered low or mass culture (9-Lives cat food, Lindsay olives and Prince spaghetti sauce) while the remaining three (Sony Beta video cassettes, Minolta copiers and Richard Ginori chinaware), though not necessarily "high culture," were all luxury or hi-tech items. (The Sony advertisement appeared in 1980, several years before VCRs became a mass-market product.) In addition, the advertisements for all three high culture products appeared in upscale magazines: *Fortune, Money* and *The New Yorker*.

Fig. 2. 9-Lives Cat Food.

Fig. 3. Lindsay Olives.

Mona Lisa Meets Madison Avenue

When we looked next at the treatment of Mona Lisa in the advertisements we found support for our two hypotheses in that all three advertisements for low or mass culture products depicted Mona Lisa as distorted or defaced while all three advertisements for high culture products rendered a true likeness of the portrait. To illustrate the types of distortion introduced, the Lindsay olive advertisement shows a modernized version of Mona Lisa cast as an Italian homemaker offering a platter of meatloaf to the viewing audience. The caption below states "*Presenting Mona Lindsay's Olive Meatloaf*" and also includes a recipe for this dish. In the 9-Lives cat food advertisement, Mona is garbed in a "Morris the Cat" T-shirt. Prince spaghetti sauce has chosen to represent their ad in two parts. The first promotes regular style sauce with an image of Mona Lisa holding up a jar of sauce and the second attempts to sell the "chunky" style by presenting an overweight caricature of Mona Lisa.[28]

While six advertisements are obviously too small a sample upon which to base definitive conclusions, the analysis is suggestive of a selection role for humor in Mona Lisa depictions. It seems to say that to sell mass culture products, marketers sometimes use humor in advertisements by first introducing an incongruous high culture icon, and then proceeding to playfully disfigure it in the hopes of bringing pleasure to a mass culture audience. This notion is hardly a new one as anyone viewing the Marx brothers in the comedy classic "A Night at the Opera" can testify.

Conclusion

The *Mona Lisa* has served as the foundation for portraiture since the Renaissance. Artists of succeeding historical periods employed the painting as a paradigm of ideal womanhood. In creating the *Mona Lisa*, Leonardo da Vinci conceived of an image that was to allow a revelation of what lay beneath the surface of the sitter. It was by means of the smile that Leonardo disclosed a personality, the essence of being and the spark of life.

Fig. 4. Prince Spaghetti Sauce.

The smile also invited the viewer into the realm of art. We recognize the smile as a response to pleasure. In addition, it connotes a positive feeling and connects us to all humanity. The painting has maintained a popularity because of Mona Lisa's bemused appearance, and in this way the *Mona Lisa* has become a household symbol.

In more recent years, advertisers have exploited the familiar icon in order to sell products. The metamorphosis occurred only through the intercession of the revolutionary twentieth-century painter, Marcel Duchamp who was the first to spoil Mona Lisa's reputation by the imposition of a moustache and goatee upon her well known visage. After centuries of adoration, Duchamp transformed Mona Lisa into a butt of a joke.

The dynamic change from extraordinary to commonplace, demonstrates Mona Lisa's sustained popular appeal. The reappearance of the enigmatic smile and the remaking of the Renaissance icon continue to demand public attention. Even today, Mona Lisa's affable smile remains attractive. Freed from its original Renaissance ambiance, Mona Lisa is employed for publicity, as a device for selling commercial products.

To understand advertising spoofs of the *Mona Lisa*, it is first necessary to note that the use of humor in advertising has increased in the 1980s as has the behavioral research literature on humor. Among the psychological factors found to be relevant in humor research are incongruity or perceived incongruity, positive affect or pleasant feeling, and aggression and hostility.

From a psychological perspective it seems reasonable to assume that marketers have treated the *Mona Lisa* differently depending upon the nature of the product they were promoting. This reasoning led us to hypothesize that advertisements featuring Mona Lisa for low or mass culture products—but not for high culture products—will make use of humorous parody or defacement since the concern here is with stressing pleasant

Fig. 5. Sony Beta Video Cassettes.

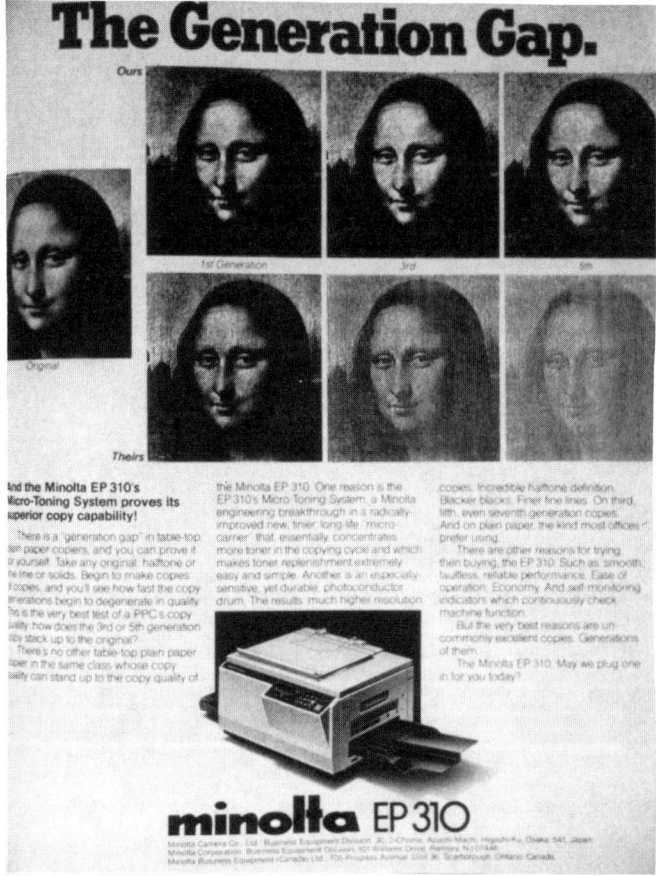

Fig. 6. Minolta Copies.

Fig. 7. Richard Ginori Chinaware.

incongruities between the high culture icon and the low or mass culture products, incongruities which may also exhibit hostile or aggressive impulses directed against the high culture icon. Examination of a small sample of six advertisements (three for high culture products and three for low culture products) lent support to the hypothesis. This finding seems to say that to sell mass culture products, marketers sometimes use humor in advertisements by first introducing an incongruous high culture icon and then proceed to playfully disfigure it in the hopes of bringing pleasure to a mass culture audience.

To conclude in the spirit of this article, if one would return to the title and ask where *Mona Lisa* meets Madison Avenue, the answer suggested is: "It depends." If it's a serious meeting, Rodeo Drive might be the right place. If, on the other hand, it's a fun meeting, the neighborhood supermarket might be as good a place as any.

Notes

*This article is a result of the authors' participation in an NEH Summer Seminar for College Teachers directed by anthropologist Dr. Stanley Brandes, University of California, Berkeley. We are grateful to NEH for providing us with an opportunity to study humor with Professor Brandes who created a conducive atmosphere for the exploration of our initial ideas regarding the Mona Lisa in art and advertising.

[1] At least two books have been written about the *Mona Lisa*. See Roy McMullen's *Mona Lisa* (Boston, 1975) and Mary Rose Storey's *Mona Lisa* (New York, 1980). Neither author has successfully explained how humor is used as a foundation for the popularity of the image. Also not accounted for are the multitude of variants of the Mona Lisa used in advertising and the variety of products, from low to high culture, which employ the image.

[2] See Erwin Panofsky, *Early Netherlandish Painting* vol. 1 (New York, 1971): 21-23 as well as his "Rinascimento delle Antichita: the 15th Century," in *Renaissance and Renascences in Western Art* (New York, 1969): 177.

[3] For a description of an ideal noblewoman see Baldesar Castiglione, *The Book of the Courtier*, trans. Charles S. Singleton (New York, 1959).

[4] The profile portrait is meant to emulate the visage on an ancient Roman coin. See, for example, the two very famous portraits of the *Duke and Duchess of Urbino* by Piero della Francesca (Uffizi, Florence) or Antonio del Pollaiuolo's *Portrait of a Young Woman* (Poldi Pezzoli, Milan).

[5] Leonardo conveys this message in his notebooks. See Carlo Pedretti, *Leonardo da Vinci on Painting: A Lost Book (Libro A)* (Berkeley, 1964): 46, Ill. 33.

[6] See Verrocchio's *Virgin and Child* (Bargello, Florence) or the *Putto with Dolphin* (Palazzo Vecchio, Florence). Verrocchio's Florentine compatriots also depicted smiles on the faces of their sculptures. See Desiderio da Settignano's *Madonna and Child* (Museum of Art, Philadelphia) or Antonio Rossellino's *The Tomb of the Cardinal of Portugal*, especially the smiling Virgin (S. Miniato, Florence).

[7] This idea is discussed in greater detail later in this article. The first creative step of the Renaissance artist was to design a physically perfect human being. The infusion of an animate personality was the second.

[8] We do not know, in fact, the specific identity of the sitter in Leonardo's painting. It has been suggested that the woman may be French instead of Italian. It is also possible that she may represent an allegory. See Carlo Pedretti, *Leonardo* (Berkeley, 1973): 137-39. Also, Vasari, who so vividly described the woman in the painting as the wife of Francesco del Giocondo in his *Lives of the Artists*, probably never saw the painting. It was already in France by the time he was about five years old (Vasari was born in 1516). Leonardo most likely took it with him to France when he left Italy in 1516. See Giorgio Vasari, *The Lives of the Artists*, trans. George Bull (Baltimore, 1965): 266-67.

[9] According to Vasari, Leonardo "employed singers and musicians or jesters to keep her full of merriment and so chase away the melancholy that painters usually give to portraits" (267).

[10] Leonardo's studies for the *Last Supper* or the *Battle of Anghiari* are exemplary of this idea.

[11] See A.E. Popham, *The Drawings of Leonardo da Vinci* (New York, 1945) Ill. 133, 134, 146 (grotesques), 198, 199 (warriors); or Pedretti, *Leonardo*, Ill. 158, 159 (beasts).

[12] A recent computer study indicates that Mona Lisa's facial features are identical to Leonardo's documented, red chalk, self-portrait (Royal Palace, Turin). Leonardo may have used his own features for an image of a woman, inadvertently, as all artists do. We call this style. Ironically, Leonardo warns his students against copying their own features for the representation of figures in their paintings. See Jean Paul Richter, *The*

Notebooks of Leonardo da Vinci, vol. 1 (New York, 1979): 293-94, Ill. 587. Also, Duchamp, who put a moustache on this famous Renaissance lady, may have had an insight into Leonardo's homosexuality. See Calvin Tomkins, *The Bride and the Bachelors* (New York, 1962): 45. In addition, Duchamp can be seen in photographs dressed in female apparel. See Arturo Schwarz, *The Complete Works of Marcel Duchamp* (New York, nd): 93. The first named author, Professor Gina Strumwasser, is presently working on a paper introducing Leonardo as a humorist and a trickster and in this context is exploring further the possibility of the *Mona Lisa* as a self-portrait.

[13] See for example Frans Hals' *Malle Babbe* (Staatliche Museen, Berlin-Dahlem) or Dirck van Baburen's *Procuress* (Museum of fine Arts, Boston).

[14] Meyer Shapiro, *Modern Art* (New York, 1978): 171.

[15] The title, *LHOOQ*, is not only a verbal violation of the *Mona Lisa*, but it contains a deeper meaning for Duchamp. World War I had just been fought and it claimed the lives of the artist's brother Raymond as well as a close friend. See Tomkins, 45. It is also a specific reference to the Dadist view of the "stupidity" of war. See Schwarz, 477. In addition, Leonardo called war a "most beastly madness." See Sir Kenneth Clark, *Leonardo da Vinci* (Cambridge, 1939): 127.

[16] Tomkins, 9.

[17] Schwarz, 45.

[18] Herbert Read, *A Concise History of Modern Painting* (New York, 1974): 120.

[19] *Webster's New Collegiate Dictionary* (1977): 1248.

[20] The piece is by Robert Arneson (Stedelijk Museum, Amsterdam).

[21] We laugh at Mona Lisa because she has become a reflection of ourselves. In jeans or braces, she is made human.

[22] See Alan Dundes, *Cracking Jokes* (1987). Professor Dundes, a folklorist at University of California, Berkeley, has attempted to measure social change through the analysis of jokes.

[23] Botticelli's *Birth of Venus* (Uffizi, Florence) is another image that reappears in pop culture. It would be useful to determine the role of Renaissance art in contemporary advertising.

[24] Contemporary society is not happy to see religious beliefs or moral convictions ridiculed. Religious subjects are also too personal and too controversial to be exploited by advertisers. We thank Cynthia Paden for this helpful information and insight.

[25] The use of an artist's name or work of art adds "class" to the idea of fast food. See Michelangelo's Frozen Gourmet Dinners, Manicotti, for example, with an illustration of the painter's *Creation of Adam* on the box.

[26] Michael Lev, "Advertising," *The New York Times* (July 19, 1989): 31.

[27] For more information, although somewhat dated, see B. Sternthal, and C.S. Craig, "Humor in Advertising," *Journal of Marketing* 37 (1973). For a more up-to-date treatment see the summary in J. Mowen, *Consumer Behavior* (New York, 1987): 257-60.

[28] In another example, more recently discovered, once again a mass culture food product (real dairy cream) is being promoted by using a humorous distortion of the *Mona Lisa*. This time it is found in Britain rather than the United States suggesting support for our hypotheses outside of American culture. The advertisement contains four illustrations in a rectangular shape. In Frame 1, Mona Lisa is accurately depicted; in Frame 2, she is slipping out from under her arms (or pocket) a dairy cream cake; and in Frame 3, the bulge in her cheeks indicates that she is eating the cake. The actual product is portrayed in Frame 4. See Judith Williamson, *Consuming Passions: The Dynamics of Popular Culture* (London, 1986): 72-73.

4
Specialized Advertising Forms and Applications

In its never-ending quest for new and more effective advertising forms and applications, the ad industry leaves "few stones unturned." King's "Senior Boom" surveys one such ploy that is becoming quite popular as well as rewarding.

A major advertising goal is to seek new and unique means of persuasion. Tactics such as Morreale and Buzzard's treatment of a new mini-drama help show that new ideals and challenges can help the advertising community. One of the more unusual and amusing, but still informative, essays in this volume is Zelman's exploration of language and perfume, truly refreshing and informative in its approach.

Humor in advertising, while important and popular in the past, is especially significant today as the vehicle fights through the ad clutter for vital attention. Robitaille's focus on the effective uses of humor in advertising probes some unusual and informative examples. MacGregor discusses with great concern and sensitivity a racially questionable advertising ploy once used in Great Britain.

The Serialized Mini-Drama: A New Trend in Advertising

Joanne Morreale and Karen Buzzard

Modern day television advertising is a cacophony of competing messages: program promotions, news updates, public service announcements, political endorsements, corporate image-building spots, and innumerable product commercials—all urging the viewer to buy or do something. Not surprisingly, this commercial clutter is causing concern in the advertising industry. Advertisers fear that the viewer's ability to recall specific advertisements has decreased as quantity has increased; moreover, they are aware that cable and videocassette technologies have made it possible to "zap," "channel-surf," or fast-forward through advertising messages. Thus advertisers' key problems are to increase visibility and effectiveness. They need to find new ways to break through the clutter of everyday advertising and capture the increasingly elusive viewer. One such strategy, devised by the Cabot Advertising Agency of Boston for New England Telephone (NET), has been to develop a new advertising genre: the serialized mini-drama.

Cabot initially produced two serialized advertising campaigns which appeared on television, radio and in print. Each targeted separate audiences: business and residential phone users. This study focuses on the latter campaign, titled *The Family*, a four-part narrative which gained virtually unprecedented notoriety and acclaim when it was broadcast over a six month period from July to January, 1988, with each episode playing for roughly six weeks. The series chronicled a family conflict between a father and his daughter, Jill. Each episode developed the story, with family members (mother and sister Kathy) using the telephone to attempt to achieve a reconciliation. Though each segment ended with a slight resolution, viewers were kept in suspense about the precise nature of the rift and how the conflict would end until the final episode, which aired during the Christmas season.

Moreover, viewers were given little indication that they were watching an advertisement at all. Viewers were able to associate the mini-drama with a particular company's product only because each episode ended with the NET theme song, "We're the one for you New England, New England Telephone."

The prototype for the NET campaign was a nostalgia-based advertising serial for Pacific Bell, titled *Garland and Me*, which aired in 1987. Though this series lacked the dramatic conflict which structured *The Family*, the advertisements portrayed the evolving relationship of two male friends in thirteen thirty and sixty second installments. The men's lives were depicted from youth to old age, as they endured the Great Depression, World War II, business ventures gone awry, competition to marry the same woman, and finally, a successful business partnership. All of the segments stressed the value of friendship rather than the virtues of the phone company, and the campaign was successful. A tracking survey reported that almost half of all viewers wanted to make a call after seeing the advertisements, and research indicated that as the series progressed, viewers were able to associate the advertisements with Pacific Bell and to identify the intended message (Berry 4).

Although both campaigns emphasized values rather than the product and used dramatic narrative as the primary persuasive tool, *The Family* marked a departure from its predecessor. *Garland and Me* was a series of self-contained narratives, all of which perpetuated the idealized world of relationships typical of advertisements; *The Family* was structured as a soap opera, with a "realistic" depiction of a family conflict which may or may not be resolved. Its form combined elements of a number of different genres: cinema and soap opera, advertisement and public service announcement. It was a dramatic pastiche which did not signal itself as an advertisement, yet all of its episodes centered around the telephone as a vehicle to solve problems. *The Family* related a dramatic narrative about estranged relations, an allegory about contemporary life whose moral—that communication can

The Serialized Mini-Drama

overcome differences—was made concrete by the characters' use of a product, the telephone.

The Family used communication as its subject matter, and it was itself a vehicle of social communication. On one level, it promoted a product and a service. On a deeper, more integral level, it appropriated emotions: anxiety about separation, fear of intimacy, and ambivalence in familial relationships. It reworked these emotions into a narrative whose moral helped to achieve NET's ends. To explore the persuasive power of *The Family*, we use the key dimensions of the communication process as our analytic tools: source, receiver, message, channel, and context. Overall, we aim to increase insight into the serialized mini-drama as a signifying practice which produces a particular mode of subjectivity.

Source

NET spent between five and six million dollars on *The Family* and *The Architects*, a similarly structured series geared to business telephone users (McCabe 77). Although the format of the advertisements posed a risk for the traditionally conservative company, the expenditure for a regional advertising campaign was less so. Pacific Bell spent between ten and twelve million for its residential campaign while the national Reebok *Let You Be You* sneakers campaign cost twenty eight million dollars (Berry 4; Tsiantar and Miller 43).

The Family was a collaborative effort produced by creative personnel at Cabot Advertising under the guidance of NET researchers. NET had three objectives which it wanted to achieve with their advertising campaign: to distinguish NET from AT&T, to create an image of NET as a caring, concerned company, and to increase telephone usage (McCabe 79; Gavalt 20). The breakup of AT&T produced a competitive market which necessitated advertising; however, NET executives were aware that most people who saw advertisements for their telephone company could not remember the content (Ingrassia 25). NET's task was further complicated by the fact that most people don't think of the telephone as a commodity, and thus it was difficult to impress the name of one company on viewers' minds or to secure their allegiance.

To create the advertising campaign, NET and Cabot personnel conducted extensive market research before the commercials were designed. They did focus group research to ask people why they used the telephone and watched them from behind a two-way mirror to gauge their reactions. Researchers found that three reasons predominated:

emotional, functional, and economic (Frieswick 1). After deciding to design the commercials around an emotional issue, they drew up an initial plan and then presented storyboards to 2000 people randomly selected at shopping malls.

Their research led to several conclusions: most people take the phone for granted, they use the phone for highly emotional conversation, and they prefer using the telephone to face-to-face contact to resolve difficult emotional problems. Finally, one last commonality was the prevalence of family conflict which led to some kind of breach in relationships. Daryld Breneman, the creative art director who wrote *The Family*, stated in an interview, "the key to the power of the phone is that breakdowns in communication are universal; everyone identifies with a relationship in trouble."

Breneman developed the idea for the plot of the mini-drama after being introduced to EST, a sensitivity training group led by Werner Erhardt, which he said taught him the importance of communication to resolve problems (McCabe 78). Breneman later summarized the pro-social theme of the mini-drama: "There's a lot of pain that is covered up and then a wall develops and what has to happen is a breakthrough in that wall. Somebody has to give in and say, I'm sorry."

Cabot enlisted the aid of Randa Haines to direct the advertisements; she had previously directed feature films such as *Children of a Lesser God* and *Something for Amelia*. The writer's strike enabled Cabot to secure otherwise unavailable talent: they used actor Bruce Kirby who was already known for his work in television and film, as well as set designer Geoffrey Kirkland and cinematographer John Bailey, both of whom were primarily known for their feature film work. The mini-drama was shot on 35mm film rather than videotape, thus lending it the look of a cinematic film. As a result of its aesthetic and technical qualities, the series has been referred to as "advertising cinema" (McCabe 77).

The Family also broke from advertising conventions because of its portrayal of deeply troubled family relations, and its proponents acclaimed it as a public service announcement that helped people to mend broken relationships. NET representatives cited a father who was prompted to call his daughter after a twelve year hiatus, and two runaway children who were inspired to return home (McCabe 78). Yet, in Breneman's original plan, Jill *was* a teenage runaway. But the results of market research convinced him to change Jill to make her more "universal." A teenage runaway was too anxiety-provoking for the audiences

1988 NEW ENGLAND TELEPHONE ADVERTISING RESIDENCE USAGE CAMPAIGN PART I
PART ONE :30

KATHY: Hi, Mom. Hi, Dad.

MOM: Hi, darling.
DAD: Kathy, how's the apartment?

KATHY: Oh, I love it! Look, I talked to Jill.

(SOUND OF PHONE RECEIVER HANGING UP)
KATHY: Hello?

MOM: I'm here. You know he doesn't like to talk about your sister.

KATHY: It's been two years now.

MOM: I know, but...

KATHY: Mom, we all have to start talking.

SINGERS: WE'RE THE ONE FOR YOU NEW ENGLAND, NEW ENGLAND TELEPHONE

DATE: JUNE 29, 1988

Reprinted with permission of New England Telephone.

The Serialized Mini-Drama

1988 NEW ENGLAND TELEPHONE ADVERTISING RESIDENCE USAGE CAMPAIGN PART II
PART II :30

DAD: Kathy, I want to apologize for hanging up on you

KATHY: That's o.k., Dad.

DAD: I don't like to talk about your sister
KATHY: I know.

DAD: I still can't believe she left like that

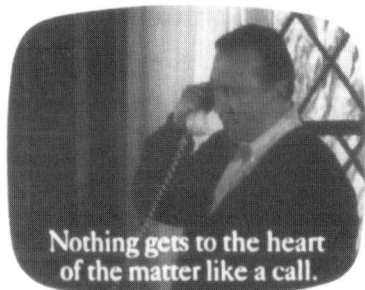

KATHY: Well, you didn't give her much choice. You really miss her, don't you?

Oh, Dad.

SINGERS: WE'RE THE ONE FOR YOU NEW ENGLAND, NEW ENGLAND TELEPHONE

DATE: JUNE 29, 1988

Reprinted with permission of New England Telephone.

NEW ENGLAND TELEPHONE RESIDENCE USAGE CAMPAIGN
PART III :30

KATHY: Jill, you gotta call Dad. I know he was wrong about you and Jeff.

JILL: So he should call.

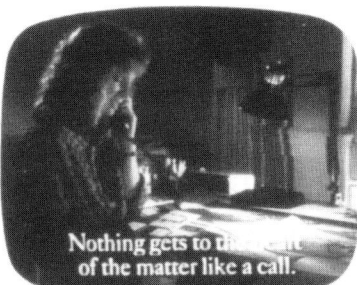
KATHY: You're right. But you know Dad. He can't call. He misses you.

KATHY: Just call him.

JILL: I can't.

KATHY: It's been two years. If one of you isn't big enough to make that call, it's going to be a lifetime.

SINGERS: WE'RE THE ONE FOR YOU NEW ENGLAND. NEW ENGLAND TELEPHONE.

DATE: JUNE 29, 1988

Reprinted with permission of New England Telephone.

The Serialized Mini-Drama

1988 NEW ENGLAND TELEPHONE ADVERTISING RESIDENCE USAGE CAMPAIGN
"FAMILY IV"
:60

(SFX: PHONE RING)
MOM: Can you get that?

DAD: Hello?
JILL: Hi, Dad . . . this is Jill

DAD: Hello
JILL: How are you?

DAD: I'm good

JILL: I'm good too . . . I . . . uh wanted to call you many times. It's been two years now.

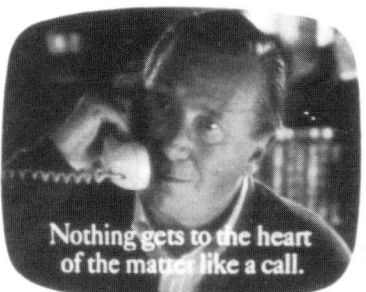

DAD: Jill . . . I was wrong . . . I had no right to interfere in your life like that.
JILL: Oh, Dad
DAD: I'm sorry

JILL: I've missed you so much, Dad

SINGERS: WE'RE THE ONE FOR YOU NEW ENGLAND. NEW ENGLAND TELEPHONE.

DATE: AUGUST 26, 1988

Reprinted with permission of New England Telephone.

surveyed. Thus the advertisements were "realistic," but not too real.

Despite the claims of its proponents, *The Family* was not a public service announcement. NET was not a disinterested party. The telephone, highly visible in each shot, was proposed as the vehicle which enabled people to resolve conflicts. In contrast to the non-partisan aims of a public service announcement, the advertisements suggested that personal problems could be solved by using a commodity, preferably a commodity offered by NET.

Receiver

Response to *The Family* suggested that NET did capture public attention. Both Cabot and NET received an unprecedented barrage of phone calls after airing the first episode of *The Family*. Reaction was mixed—people either protested the negative portrayal of family relationships or wanted to know the resolution. In addition, the actors who played the characters achieved a recognition usually only accorded soap opera stars. While visiting Boston, Bruce Kirby (Dad) was repeatedly admonished by people on the street and told to make up with his daughter. Fans told actress Amy Steele, who played the daughter Kathy, that they approved of her attempt to reconcile her father and sister.

Another extraordinary feature of *The Family* was that it so quickly became inscribed in popular culture. It was parodied by at least two radio stations in the Boston area, and another station even held a contest to determine how the conflict would end. There was talk of turning the series into a TV movie or theatrical film, and a sequel was prepared which further explored the family relationships presented in the series. *Boston* magazine even ran an ad for singles which played on the reader's knowledge of the characters in the series.

Marketing research data also suggested that *The Family* was a successful campaign. NET reported that public awareness of their company doubled and that residential phone use increased 12-14% after the advertisements were first aired (McCabe 79).

Message

A closer examination of the structure of the mini-drama's message may help to account for its receivers' reactions. On first viewing, *The Family* appeared not to be a commercial at all. Rick Ender, associate director at Cabot, confirmed that the series was designed not to look like an advertisement. Its serial format, like that of soap operas, attempted to hook viewers by building dramatic tension and then leaving the ending unresolved, so that viewers would actively look for the next installment.

Like other contemporary advertisements, *The Family* was structured as a moral allegory (Stern 84). It communicated through poetic devices such as metaphor, juxtaposition, association and implication. Its central metaphor—the telephone as instrument which "connects" family members—was developed by the dramatic narrative, which moved from disruption (the family problem) to resolution (the reconciliation via the telephone). The telephone was presented as a commodity which united family members who were otherwise separate, both emotionally and geographically.

The Family provided a simple moral message: communicate to solve problems. The function of allegory, according to Stern, is to convey moral lessons: it does so in part by rendering complex, abstract events into easily understandable terms (85). In *The Family*, visual codes suggested the characters' separation and distance. Vertical boundaries such as doors and windows framed the characters in each shot while the shots themselves were lit with strong contrasts between light and dark. The withdrawn father, who had to be brought back into the family, was portrayed in the first episode with his back to the camera, staring out the window. Similarly, in the third episode, Jill's husband Jeff, the cause of the disagreement between father and daughter, appears for the first time in an almost identical posture.

In each shot, the telephone was central. Family members spoke only over the telephone which united them. Even though the telephone is a technology which is inextricably related to mass society—that is, urbanization, depersonalization, dissolution of the nuclear family (Aronson 303)—and thus it is a technology which is dependent upon boundaries and separation, these advertisements present the telephone solely as a vehicle which facilitates intimacy and brings people together. According to Geraldine O'Brien, director of advertising for Net, "We want to say that NET cares about social and family relationships. Pick up your phone and dial your daughter, father, mother, and tell them you love them. Call them and call them often" (Gavalt 20).

However, NET profits each time someone dials that phone to declare their everlasting love. The telephone is a commodity whose use is purchased, even if indirectly; only face-to-face contact is free.

The Serialized Mini-Drama

Channel

The Family made use of particular communication strategies to convey its message to its audience. Rather than hard-sell commercials which persuade by offering reasons to buy their products or soft-sell commercials which persuade by associating the product with positive feelings or lifestyles, the NET commercials used the "deep-sell" approach outlined by Tony Schwartz in *The Responsive Chord*. They persuaded primarily through the instructive power of allegory which spoke to common fears and anxieties about relationships. Using advertisements which revolved around an ambiguous conflict, having attractive actors and actresses in the leading roles, and resonating with common experiences enabled viewers to identify with the characters portrayed in the advertisements while the dramatic narrative structure intensified their involvement.

Schwartz explains how advertisements draw people in with his explanation of deep-sell advertising. Deep-sell advertisements, he writes, resonate with, or evoke, common feelings and experiences. These can be identified by market research which targets needs, wants and desires of specific groups of consumers. Advertisers, then, design "packages of stimuli" which associate their product with these common experiences. These advertisements "resonate" with viewers who seem to recognize themselves in the characters and situations depicted.

The Family was a paradigmatic example of the deep-sell approach. Market research revealed that most people had a troubled relationship. The mini-drama, then, was a "package of stimuli" which evoked this common experience and offered a resolution. By juxtaposing the telephone with characters in each shot, it became associated with communication and was portrayed as a means to solve emotional problems. The telephone was offered as an allegorical route to personal happiness. In effect, the advertisements induced a psychological attachment to the telephone as a necessary and inextricable part of people's lives.

However, as in all allegories, complex problems become painted in simple black and white terms. This depiction of the telephone also evoked a cultural myth: that more communication is better, that problems can be solved by making a phone call. However, scholars such as George Simmel have pointed to the fact that conflict is endemic to relationships (1325). A conflict-free relationship is not a sign of a good relationship; it is a sign of no relationship at all. Yet advertisements such as *The Family* perpetuate the myth that problems can be solved, immediately and painlessly, simply by picking up the telephone and that it is desirable to do so.

Context

The Family, although a departure from traditional advertising, is characteristic of modern advertisements which have increasingly moved away from providing product identification and information. A recent advertisement for Pepsi Cola, for instance, offered a world premiere of Madonna's new music video. Nissan recently released a series of car advertisements where the product is not pictured at all. These advertisements present themselves as entertainment with the product seemingly only an incidental part of the setting. Rather than characteristics of the commodity itself, it is the symbolic value associated with a commodity that is being sold. In the case of *The Family*, the telephone promises intimacy and the ability to overcome distance. Cabot and NET recognize that harmonious social relations are a cultural ideal, even if problematic relations are the reality.

The Family is indicative of contemporary consumer culture, a culture where advertising has taken over functions previously ascribed to institutions such as the family and religion. Advertisers have become purveyors of values. Whereas in traditional (pre-industrial) societies needs and desires were satisfied by work or spiritual pursuits, in modern society needs and desires are satisfied by products.

Conclusion

Advertisements such as *The Family*, even though their intentions may be honorable, serve only to perpetuate cultural illusions. They depict "realistic" situations but only those which are not too anxiety provoking and those which portray middle class "misunderstandings" amidst an otherwise comfortable lifestyle. Jill, Kathy, and their parents all wear fashionable clothing, live surrounded by luxury items, and have their own houses and apartments. Their problems are not *too* serious, and they are easily resolved by making that phone call and saying "I'm sorry."

Moreover, *The Family* implies that using a commodity can make one's life better. Instead of offering people choices, the advertisements close off possibilities. Jill and her father can only solve their problems through consumption, through the mediation of a product. *The Family* makes use of human emotions and frailties for NET's own ends, and it appears that they have struck a responsive chord. NET followed this initial residential campaign with a second, *The Return*, about the conflict between two brothers which is revealed in six episodes. (They also produced a new eight episode campaign aimed at business users.) Both Nissan and MCI (another phone company) contacted NET because they were interested in running similar campaigns (*Boston Herald* 1988). *The Family* may indeed be a harbinger of a new trend in advertising, one where advertisers appropriate the moral injunctions of allegory in order to make needs and desires into objects of consumption.

Works Cited

Aronson, Sidney H. "The Sociology of the Telephone." *Intermedia: Interpersonal Communication in a Media World.* Ed. Gary Gumpert and Robert Cathcart. New York: Oxford UP, 1986. 300-10.

Berry, Jon. "Tale of Two Friends Pushes Limits of Advertising." *Adweek's Marketing Week* (September 28, 1987): 4, 51.

Breneman, Daryld. Associate Creative Director, Cabot Advertising Agency, Boston, MA. Personal Interview. December 3, 1988.

Carton, Barbara. "Jill...Phone Home." *Boston Globe* (March 9, 1988): 79.

Ender, Rick. Associate Creative Director, Cabot Advertising, Boston MA. Personal Interview. December 3, 1988.

Gavalt, Geoffrey. "Phone Ads have People Talking." *Patriot Ledger* (October 1, 1988): 19-20.

Ingrassia, Lawrence. "Nynex Unit Replaces Schmaltz in Ads with Conflict in Effort to Stand Out." *Wall Street Journal* (July 20, 1988): 25.

"Jill Phones Home for Christmas." *Boston Herald* (December 26, 1988): 47

McCabe, Bruce. "Your Family Crisis is Over." *Boston Globe* (March 9, 1988): 79.

Schwartz, Tony. "Hard Sell, Soft Sell, Deep Sell." *The Commercial Connection.* Ed. John Wright. New York: Dell. 322-24.

———. *The Responsive Chord.* New York: Anchor, 1973.

Simmel, George. "On Conflict." *Theories of Society.* New York: Free P, 1961. 1324-25.

Stern, Barbara. "Medieval Allegory: Roots of Advertising Strategy for the Mass Market." *Journal of Marketing* (July 1988): 88-94.

Tsiantar, Dody, and Annetta Miller. "Tuning Out TV Ads." *Newsweek* (April 17, 1989): 42-43.

Trends for the Twenty-First Century: The Senior Boom

Margaret J. King

> Marketers must now shift from their traditional focus on youth to a focus on older Americans.
> —The Daniel Yankelovich Group
> "The Mature Americans," 1987.

> One of the best kept secrets left in the age of demographic scrutiny.
> —William Lazer, "Inside the Mature Market,"
> *American Demographics*, March 1985.

Quantum theory has proven the futility of trying to separate the observer from the observed. Nowhere is this principle of physics better illustrated than in the complex interplay between advertising and its audiences. As an executive at BBD&O noted about the advertising art, "We [in the profession] are always aware that every time we create a campaign, we are doing more than holding up a mirror to society. We are engaged in changing and leading that society."[1]

In this double role as audience and actor advertising plays a key part in the new humanities—the popular arts and their effects beyond art into nature—into social fact. Advertising has been called the first uniquely American art form. It lies at the very heart of American life with an uncanny talent to sway, lead, and mesmerize as well as inform and enlighten.

In the study of popular culture the "cultural facts" are often considered the generators of "natural" ones. The "humanistic coefficient" identified and tracked by sociologists makes us all social actors, but even more, it makes each of us a creator of the world. These concepts in the social sciences and communications set the stage for a full understanding and appreciation of this rampaging, obtrusive, most persuasive of the arts.

In *Successful Marketing to the 50+ Consumer* (1989), Jeff Ostroff points to telecommunications as the source of myths and misconceptions about aging and the aged:

> Not until recently have the media begun to portray a more realistic, balanced picture of gray America. Unfortunately, the distortions presented over the years have been imprinted in the minds of many, particularly those most influenced by television...the 'baby boom' generation.[2]

To redress the balance, Ostroff's research surveys the new generation of ads breaking those old molds, showing how advertising acts as both conservator and innovator and teaching corporate America how to join the legions of marketers to the mature and maturing. The size and momentum of this unprecedented demographic revolution touches and informs every aspect of popular culture. Advertising is the leading edge of megatrends to come.

The Greying of America

America is poised at the crest of a great and growing aging boom, carrying with its momentum a cultural identity crisis on a monumental scale. For the first time anywhere or anytime in history, people over the age of fifty will be setting the pace of life: financially, socially and politically. The aging of America is a unique, controversial, unprecedented transition from a youth-dominated world to a mature-oriented society. So far, however, very few have considered or planned for their place in this cultural revolution. Still fewer have a positive vision of the future. The universe of far-reaching consequences brought about by the still-building age-quake of the new old is just now starting to be studied, understood and appreciated.

The new old, those already over fifty and the thousands more who join their ranks every day, are increasing to the point where very soon they will enjoy a de facto command of most aspects of American life: the way we shop, dine, travel, and dress; get and make sense of information; build our careers, structure and enjoy our leisure; manage our family and social life; maintain our health and continue our educations; protect ourselves and our investments; and spend, save and invest our time and money.

At this very moment, the leading edge industries and organizations that will be serving this up-and-coming "gerontocracy" are in the ground-floor planning and development stages or just being born. The golden "defining" stage of the late 1980s and early 1990s will be the turning point for this age wave.

Agendas for the perception, anticipation and creation of trends, needs and markets for this new population are being drafted quietly but energetically across the map. Stock in these concepts is still low and the buying time ideal—both for business and for the analyst of social trends and popular culture. Opportunities to redefine and direct American life of the near future by redirecting and repositioning businesses of every type are so far—but not for long—wide open. Those who have the vision to identify and create new markets may have a corner on the 1990s that extends well into the next century. Those who do not will stagnate as they ask themselves how they missed the biggest boat in history. Ken Dychtwald, president of the consulting firm Age Wave and author of the book of the same title,[3] summarizes:

Aging has been the single most dramatic shift in our culture, other than perhaps the invention of computers and the splitting of the atom. Very few changes have this order of magnitude in influencing so many other aspects of our culture.[4]

The Senior Boom: Demographic Destiny

American Demographics declares newly mature America "the demographic discovery of the decade."[5] In fact, the tipping of the age scale from under to over fifty has been in progress for many decades as the result of three major developments: the greying of the baby boom cohort of 1946-63, now migrating into its 30s and 40s; advances in health care that have raised life expectancy from 45 in 1880 to 75 in 1980 to a projected 85 for the year 2000; and the declining birth rate.

Seniors are the fastest-growing segment of the U.S. population, and this growth will accelerate sharply with each coming decade (Fig. 1). From 1985 to 2000, while the adult population at large grows 14%, the over-fifty group will increase by nearly twice that rate at 23%. More and more Americans join the senior ranks each year. People over fifty now make up 26% of the population. By the end of the century, this percentage will increase to 28.4%, nearly one out of every three Americans. Since the early 1980s, for the first time in our history, the over-65 population has outnumbered teenagers. By 2000, 15% of the population will be over 65,

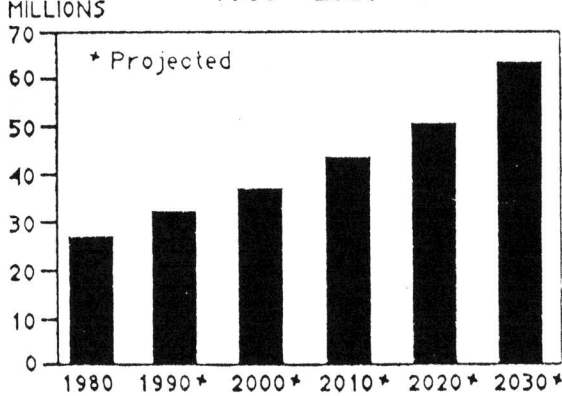

Fig. 1 Source: The Marketing Institute, January 1989.

Senior Shift: The Population Trends

Year	Adults over 50	Percent of total population
1940	27 million	20%
1950	34 million	22%
1960	42 million	23%
1970	50 million	24%
1980	59 million	26%
1990	64 million*	26%
2000	76 million*	28%
2010	95 million*	34%
2020	110 million*	37%

Data from U.S. Census Bureau.
*Estimated

Fig. 2 Mature Market Report, 1:5, September 1987, p. 7.

and by 2050, as many as *one of every four* Americans could be 65 or older (Fig. 2).

Fifty Plus Consumer Power

The biggest buying club in history—a consumer gerontocracy—is quietly amassing hundreds of thousands of members. The upgraded quality of life emerging for the mature American is unique in history. While generations of the past had holdings and investments, their volume and worth cannot compare to the power of the twentieth and twenty-first century senior, either as an individual or as part of a new breed: a well-heeled "ruling class" with very few limits on its ability to enjoy experiences of every kind.

In particular, today's retirees or those somewhere near retirement, have the historical background of the post-World War II boom years at the core of their financial portfolios. It has been

Trends for the Twenty-First Century

an enriching episode; many own their own homes as well as second homes and substantial, even extensive, investments are the rule.

For this age group and those who will follow it shortly into the fifty-plus bracket, there is a steadily evolving outlook on consumerism. Whereas the depression generation was "Save, don't spend" oriented, the interim generation balanced saving with spending. The baby boom generation, especially the younger subgeneration, is almost entirely devoted to a philosophy of deficit spending: liberal credit card use, with little saving to balance the books. The economic psychology that will mark the younger age of the over-fifty market in the coming decade is an emphasis on spending, on self-fulfillment rather than on deferment of gratification, and a dedication to quality over price considerations. All of these factors make the new aged generations superb consumers of goods and services across the board—especially those of the customized industries designed to address their specific expectations.

Hal Margolis, group senior vice president for the Lintas: Campbell-Ewald advertising agency, was quoted in a *Time* article on new images of the aged in television ad campaigns:

For a long time, no one in this business was paying any attention at all to people over 49. Then some of us started looking at the demographics, and we realized these people have got all the money![6]

Already modeling agencies are gearing up to meet the demand for over-fifty models, including the Classic Woman Division of Eileen Ford, and a new agency, Senior Class, opened for business in 1988.

Consumer product corporations, financial institutions and healthcare will see the greatest advances in catering to the mature market. For example, this is the market that is the prime consumer of first-class leisure services and has turned travel from a luxury into a necessity.[7]

In raw numbers, the consumer balance already weighs heavily on the over-fifty side. Half of all discretionary income is concentrated here. A new generation gap has been created by economic cycles: an under-forty population with lower discretionary income, savings, home ownership, and other assets than its over-fifty counterparts (Fig. 3).

In addition to brute financial strength, new-found physical fitness and educational achievements also contribute to making this and future older generations the best consumers on record. It might be said that the fifty-plus market is, in fact, continuing their youth and spending—on an even larger scale in their interest in new products, services, and experiences (Fig. 4). "Today's mature Americans," says a 1987 Yankelovich Report, "have altered many of their assumptions and life goals. Far from being left behind, they are proving to be more vital, vigorous, and committed to living the full, rich life than ever before."[8]

Statistics from the Conference Board profile the

The Incidence of Households with Discretionary Income, 1983
All Householders each age group = 100%

Fig. 3 Source: Conference Board

Fig. 4 *Prevention*, "America's Leading Health Magazine," features an arboreally fit senior. 4 out of 10 spa memberships are sold to people over 50. Photo credit: John Flynn, Jr.

new old as a fully functioning but "forgotten generation."⁹ Of the total financial assets of U.S. households, most (77%) by far are held by older persons. Today's older generation is more stable and holds more promise for business than any before: "The older consumer, so cavalierly ignored by so many marketers, is in fact the prime customer of the up-scale market."¹⁰

The Age Surge:
Age Awareness in Business, Academia, and Government

The maturing of America as a trend of concern, study and action has arrived and is gathering steam. The evolution has been slow but is now at the brink of a cultural watershed. Just 7% of all university level gerontology programs began before 1970; there are now programs on 1100 campuses. Achenbaum's *Old Age in the New Land* came out in 1978. In the same year, mandatory retirement retreated to the age of seventy; 1974 saw the establishment of the National Institute on Aging. Age Wave, Ken Dychtwald's communications and marketing firm, was founded in 1986, and *Age Wave*, his comprehensive "megatrends" study of the greying of America came out in early 1989. On the entertainment front, Walt Disney Studios is running to catch up to the tastes of its aging baby boom audience with Touchstone Films, launched in 1984, and the Disney TV series *Golden Girls* has been a front runner since its debut in 1987. Retirement housing is big business, with projected revenues of $35 billion a year.

Despite these impressive developments, Dychtwald declared in a recent interview in *Inc.*: "It's people who make up the mature market who have the greatest financial capability, and nobody's going after them."¹¹

New Age Images

Traditional stereotypes of seniors as passive, powerless and marginal are on the way out. A new breed of older American is being born every year as two cultural generations—baby boomers and their parents—pass into the over-fifties. Even academic and government-sponsored studies of the aged, based on assumptions of illness and dependency, will change as this group evolves.

Life satisfaction and therefore image are being boosted by higher educational achievement as the society at large becomes more self-conscious and aware. This is a new-born generation of aged whose preoccupation with health maintenance and vitality far into the senior years will be making product line history while it extends the definition of youth into the sixth and seventh decades. Higher standards of style, comfort, and quality will stretch across the generations as the universal consumer chalice.

Donnelley's 1988 "New Age Survey" pointed to the similarities between fifty-plus Americans and their 25-49 year-old counterparts—attitudes, behavior, values and needs that far outweigh differences. With minor deviations, the survey found senior Americans to be *more* physically and mentally active (Fig. 5).¹²

Give high priority to:	39-49	50 & Over
Travel for pleasure	49%	47%
Attending sports events	25	21
Cultural enrichment (concerts, museums)	24	24
Have a strong need to:		
Do things to enrich life such as travel	42	44
Keep up with new technologies	39	38
Keep up with latest trends in home decorating	21	20
Keep up with fashion trends	21	20
Pay more attention to:		
Travel to interesting places	34	34

Fig. 5. Yankelovich study (1988). Comparison of 39-40 age group preferences with those of 50+ group.

In a 1987 story, the Yankelovich Group compared over-fifties to the up-and-coming seniors, aged 39-49, and showed that the older cohort identified "younger"—with the products, pursuits and pastimes of the younger group. The study termed this continuity a "diminishing values gap," emphasizing the youth orientation of the mature market.

Modern Maturity, which goes out to the membership of AARP, has a circulation of nearly thirty million, putting it at the top of all U.S. magazine circulation (Fig. 6). Its press kit invitation to advertisers, "The Beginning of a New Lifetime," begins with the injunction to "Take off 15 years. At least." The copy continues to characterize the new self-image:

They look and act younger than their mothers and fathers did at their maturity.... The lesson to marketers: Talk to a person, not a birthdate. Don't make judgments based on a few gray hairs or wrinkles. Look at the person inside the person. Enjoy their continuing youth with them. How do you cast them in advertising? Looking and acting 10 to 15 years younger than preceding generations at the same age.¹³

Nevertheless, reality has not yet hit home. In a recent report, the Conference Board warned, "the

Trends for the Twenty-First Century

Fig. 6. With 30 million members, AARP's ideology is "Big." Photo credit: John Flynn, Jr.

marketing community persists in a blinkered view of the old—a mindset of past reality."[14]

Marketing Mix

An image that has long ruled the American mind is that older Americans are somehow very much alike and become more so as they age. Once past fifty, personalities, talents and goals that once set individuals apart are supposed to coalesce into one huge grey melting pot. In fact, the reverse is true: age promotes diversity as the characteristics of youth intensify and diverge. Far from blending with age, seniors become more stratified and varied by economic resources, marital status, household configuration, needs, attitudes, capabilities and treatment and view by society. Especially accentuated with age are gender, race, ethnicity, occupation and class differences. Segmentation of these many mini-markets within the New Aged market will be the coming project for business, government and academia[15]

In a report in *The American Consumer*, the senior market is divided into four demographic segments:

The Young Mature (age 55-64)
The Middle Mature (65-74)
The Seniors (75-84)
The Elders (85+)[16]

In a more sophisticated typology, Georgia State University's Center for Mature Consumer Studies has identified four biophysical and psychosocial profiles, based on attitude and affect rather than simple age: hermits, outgoers, recluses and indulgers.[17] Consumer outlook and lifestyle are the lines of distinction. As the senior generation continues to grow and diversify, segmentation will flourish.

Cohort Action and Thinking: Gray Power

The over-fifty cohort has traditionally been at the forefront of the democratic process. Over-fifty voters constitute 40% of all registered voters and, at the 1984 election, cast 41% of the votes—at nearly twice the rate of younger voters.[18] Now, in the era of grassroots political action groups, mature Americans are every day more in evidence in the news, serving on every legislative and public issue front.

Not only is the New Age generation mounting in numbers, raising the average age of the American voter, but their involvement and interest in a wide spectrum of social and political programs is on the rise as well, in greater strength than mere statistics. Seniors have a clear power position. They have the time, the leverage, the connections and the experience to devote to candidates and causes. Senior support or protest increasingly spells the difference between successful and failed campaign. Neal Cutler of the Andrus Gerontology Center at USC sums up by saying, "In 15 years [by 2000] there won't be anybody as powerful as the organized elderly."[19]

A universe of political, lifestyle, cultural, economic pressure and action groups has already begun to form and flex their muscle, and new ones are on the rise. Membership in Gray Panthers, The Older Women's League, National Council of Senior Citizens and AARP exert an unprecedented lobbying and voting influence. One evidence of this clout is the 28% of the federal budget currently devoted to the elderly and their needs—the same percentage devoted to Defense.

The recently founded Gatekeepers to the Future, dedicated to continuity of the generations on issues of environment, national debt, technology-watching, conflict resolution and world peace, recruits the energies of those over sixty as its organizers. This type of association is indicative of the many more to come.

As the new age culture develops, opportunities for the popular culture research will multiply and expand as well. Following the baby boom as it creates still more waves in the ocean of culture should be a fascinating project. It seems that with the Star Trek generation, we are all fulfilling Mr. Spock's imperative to "Live Long and Prosper."

Notes

[1] Telecommunication with Tonese Hayden, BBD&O Chicago, January 17, 1990.

[2] Jeff Ostroff, *Successful Marketing to the 50+ Consumer* (Englewood Cliffs, NJ: Prentice, 1989): 3.

[3] Ken Dychtwald and Joe Flower, *Age Wave: The Challenges and Opportunities of an Aging America* (Los Angeles: Tarcher, 1988).

[4] Margaret J. King, "Catching the Age Wave," Review article, *Age Wave*, *Lehigh University Alumni Bulletin* (February 1990).

[5] Quoted in "Mature America," *Modern Maturity* press kit, 1988.

[6] "Is That You on TV, Grandpa?" *Time* (March 6, 1989): 53.

[7] "The Travel Agent Front Line Report on Leisure Travel," Plog Research, Los Angeles, CA, April 1988.

[8] The Daniel Yankelovich Group, "The Mature Americans," 1987.

[9] "Midlife and Beyond," The Conference Board, Consumer Research Center, 1985.

[10] Ibid., 1.

[11] Ken Dychtwald, "Redesigning America," *Inc.* (June 1988): 58 ff.

[12] "New Age: Perspectives on the Over Fifty Market," Donnelley Marketing, New York, 1988.

[13] *Modern Maturity* press kit, 1988.

[14] "Midlife and Beyond," 1.

[15] For a full discussion, see Chapter 2, "Retiring the Myths of Aging," of *Age Wave*, esp. Myth 6: "All Older People Are Pretty Much the Same," 47.

[16] "The Mature Market," *The American Consumer* (October 3, 1988) 1.

[17] Reported in Rick Christie, "Marketers Err by Treating Elderly as Uniform Group," *Wall Street Journal* (October 31, 1988).

[18] Bureau of the Census, 1988.

[19] Quoted in Ken Dychtwald, "The Aging of America," in *Wellness and Health Promotion for the Elderly* (Rockville, MD: Aspen Systems, 1986): 15.

Language and Perfume: A Study of Symbol-Formation

Tom Zelman

Perfume advertisers in this country have long marketed their scents by tying them to elements of the American dream—macho outdoorsmanship, financial ostentation, gauzy romance, and sexual gratification. In creating such vague but appealing associations for their products, they seem closely akin to advertisers of automobiles ("Heartbeat of America"; "Oh, What a Feeling"), cigarettes (Winston's "winning" taste, Marlboro's cowboy icons), soft drinks (the "Real Thing"), and, of course, presidential candidates. Yet whereas an advertisement for Chevrolets *can* be technically descriptive, and presidential contenders could, if put to the wall, point to their records, there exists no language to describe and distinguish the sensations we smell. In this essay I wish to draw attention to the linguistic shortfall we encounter when attempting to speak about scents and the odd ramifications of this shortfall on perfume advertisements.

Scents and Symbols

In Suzanne Langer's important book on symbol-formation, *Philosophy in a New Key*, the author introduces the concept of presentational, or non-discursive, forms. The presentational symbol, unlike its verbal counterpart, "is non-discursive and untranslatable, does not allow of definitions within its own system, and cannot directly convey generalities.... Their functioning as symbols depends on the fact that they are involved in simultaneous, integral presentation" (97). Words have a "general reference" and are commonly affixed by convention; by contrast, pictures and music, which Langer gives as examples of non-discursive symbols, speak directly to sense and cannot be encompassed by words (97). To this list of presentational forms may be added that of scent, for which there are only the vaguest of descriptive terms. With none of our other senses does there seem to be such an extreme variance in perception. Consequently, it is not unusual that language, a system of commonly-accepted symbols, should be at such pains to cope with the phenomenon of smelling. This essay seeks to investigate the attempts and failures of the perfume industry to find an adequate means of using discursive symbols to define and distinguish individual fragrances and then to survey some of the ways in which advertisers describe and promote their indescribable products.

To the human mind odors can have both signific and symbolic value. Langer notes that signs relate to their objects in a one-to-one correlation, the sign having less interest to the perceiving subject, but greater availability. Where the subject perceives a sign, she can expect the immediate presence of its object (57-58). Where there's smoke, there's fire. The fragrance of hot coffee, the odor of tobacco, the stench of refuse—all indicate that the objects producing them are within our range of perception. Symbols, on the contrary, need not indicate any object near at hand, nor are they proxy for their objects. Here a greater degree of abstraction is required of the subject: "signs *announce* their objects to him [their perceiver], whereas symbols *lead him to conceive* their objects" (61).

The symbolic nature of perfume scents is easy to demonstrate. A chance whiff of a particular fragrance may serve to recreate distant memories, conceptions in the subject's mind which recall an object far in the past. The perfume here cannot be regarded as a sign; there is no rigid one-to-one relationship between perfume scent and object as there is between the coffee odor and the coffee. The subject accepts the fact that the evocative perfume fragrance may be worn by a number of people, not simply by the object he is reminded of. The symbolic value of perfume, and odors in general, has been attested to in the poetry of the French Symbolists and in the novels of Marcel Proust and J.K. Huysmans, where they are used to draw correspondences of various sorts.

Edward Sagarin, a perfumer and organic chemist, suggests that prehistoric humans' sense of smell was essential to their survival, both in locating food and in sensing enemies. However, as the ability to use language and communicate thoughts developed, the signific importance of odors diminished:

> The sense of smell was losing its *raison d'être* and began to carry on an ever-weakening battle for survival in the human being. For nature is ruthless in dealing with an organ without an essential function. In what was probably one stage in the last great evolutionary development of man, the perceptors of odors in the human nose became atrophied. The sharp edges were dulled. The powers of detection became almost extinct, and in place of the protection that it had offered, man turned to his self-created weapons that gave him a distinct advantage over his animal enemies. His nose, unlike that of the other animals that stole through the jungles and roamed the plains, had become almost exclusively a respiratory apparatus.
>
> Almost—but not quite. For as the need for smelling as part of the struggle for existence diminished, it took on a new function. The first man who stopped to stare in admiration at the rainbow forming a myriad of dancing colors in the sky also drew a deep breath of satisfaction at the fragrance of a field of fresh flowers. He had become an aesthete before the perfumes that nature had created[5] (24-25).

(Note: While I have tried to avoid all gender-biased usages in my own text, I have left intact those in the original sources.)

While Sagarin's ideas are hypothetical, they are useful in several respects. They take into account human adaptation, evolving toward increased sophistication. Signific odor is replaced by symbolic words. If, as Sagarin claims, our prehistoric ancestors could appreciate the fragrance of flowers, which held no practical survival-value for them, the pleasure they experienced was aesthetic and derived from subjective associations. With the advent of language, smell, an inferior means of acquiring survival-oriented information, became largely relegated to the end of aesthetic appreciation. Language could be communally shared; smell, by contrast, was incommunicable. Perhaps this is the reason for the large present-day vocabulary we have pertaining to qualities of vision and hearing, both essential to language as we know it, while there is hardly any applicable to qualities of smell.

When we look at a picture, there are any number of ways in which we might apply language to what is seen. We might talk about how colors are used to form symbolic shapes; in non-representational art, where the colors do not form recognizable symbols, we may still consider the relationship of one color to another and the way shapes are arrayed on the canvas. Such terms as texture, balance and harmony can all be applied to a picture even when the art is abstract. Not only is there an ordinary, everyday vocabulary that can be used to refer to what we see; the phenomenon of colors has also been translated into mathematical language whereby each can be denoted and classified according to its wave length. While a picture is a presentational symbol and cannot itself be verbalized, much can be said by way of description.

This is not the case with scents. There is virtually no language, either colloquial or technical, capable of describing what we smell when we consider the scent separately from its source. How can the fragrance of hot coffee be symbolized in language if we ignore the coffee producing the odor? We may say that the odor is pleasant, and perhaps invigorating, but the same might be said of the scents of horsehide or burning leaves or freshly-turned earth. While we can discern the signific meaning of each of these odors, e.g., the smell indicates that hot coffee is on the table, we have no words to distinguish odors from one another aside from such vague generalities as "spicy," "sweet," "pungent," and "sharp." Though an odor may bring to mind associations, the human mind is unable to abstract odors so as to associate them with one another. The problem, it would seem, is one of language. There are no names for odors, only for objects.

Scientific Nomenclature

The language most frequently used by perfumers to denote scents is that of organic chemistry. Sagarin notes that the perfumer "will associate with an odor a name and a mental image of a formula" (94). While a useful form of symbolic notation in some respects, the language of ketones, aldehydes and beta-ionones only relates the *odorants*, not the odors themselves. Moreover, the odorants are related in terms of chemical composition; there is rarely a correlation between compounds of similar atomic structure and their scents. Only experience enables the perfumer to draw the connection from scent to chemical formula. Sagarin remarks with some perplexity, "We state that the chemical known as 'diphenyl oxide' smells like geranium—but what does geranium smell like, unless it is diphenyl oxide?" (137). Chemical terminology thus fails to draw parallels between the odors themselves. Sagarin concludes: "Lacking a satisfactory explanation of the origin and mechanism of odors, and lacking any physical instruments for the measurement of odors, the creation of a scientific nomenclature has not been possible. A trained nose is the last word in passing on a smell" (139-40). To the amateur, odors are not always easily distinguishable and can only be compared with easily recognized scents.

Language and Perfume

The Taxonomies of Perfumes

To a large extent the perfumer is forced to rely on imprecise analogy. Ambergris, for example, has an odor "akin to laudanum. But the description is inadequate. If the comparison, for the perfumer, is poor, it is necessary because no one has suggested a better one" (Sagarin 63). Added to the problem of creating verbal approximations of the experience of smelling is the fact that even amongst perfumers and others interested in the study of odors, there is little agreement. The scent of patchouli oil, for instance, R.W. Moncrieff describes as a "heavy, warm Eastern odor, cinnamon-like;" (20). Steffen Arctander finds it to be "minty, swampy, barnyard-like;" (509), and J.K. Huysmans, in his famous discourse on scents in *A rebours*, claims that it "gives off an odor compounded of wet wood and rusty iron" (Sagarin 119). The object, patchouli oil, sensed by three different noses, is symbolized in words which have little to do with one another. Clearly the highly subjective nature of these associations points to the difficulty in developing a standard descriptive nomenclature.

Over the past eighty years scientists and pseudo-scientists have attempted to devise a symbolic system of relating odors to one another. In 1895 H. Zwaardemaker put forward a systematic classification in which odors were divided into nine categories. Four of these were unpleasant, four pleasant, and the remaining one was generally found unpleasant, but liked when associated with onion and garlic food smells. Each class was divided into sub-classes. Flaws were found, as we might expect, in Zwaardemaker's system, as when such unlikely bedfellows as chloroform and strawberry essence were put in the same class. Another attempt was made by Hans Henning who reduced the number of odor classes to six—ethereal, putrid, spicy, burnt, fruity, and resinous. These six, he claimed, were not separate but rather merged into one another. To depict the way this occurred he constructed a prism, each corner representing a pure odor class (see Fig. 1). (Moncrieff 215). Theoretically every odor could be placed with precision on one of the prism's five planes, its exact location being determined by which of the odor classes it was composed of. While Henning's model received much attention and was given some praise by people who worked with it, the exact assignation of position remained subjective; an odor had to be analyzed into so much fruity, so much resinous, and this was impossible to do with any general agreement. Henning's model also forbade certain combination of "fundamental" odors; an odor which contained some part spicy, some part resinous, and some burnt could not have as a partial

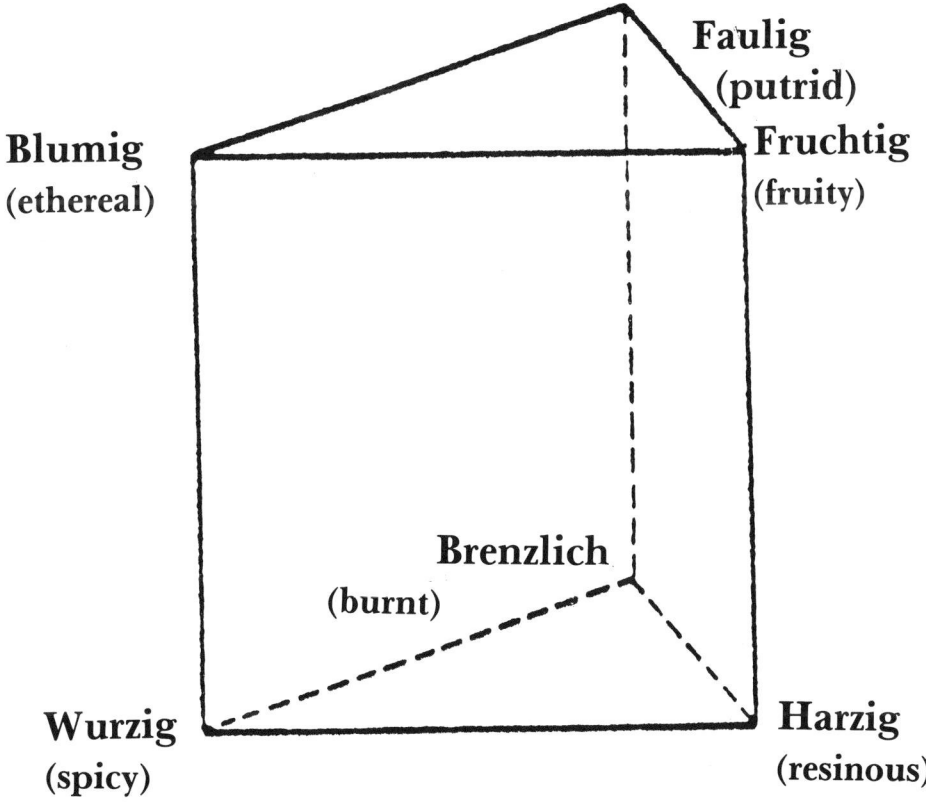

Henning's olfactory prism showing his original descriptions of the type odours.

component fruity, putrid, or ethereal components (Moncrieff 212-15). Crocker and Henderson, successors to Zwaardemaker, reduced his nine categories to four—fragrant, sour, burnt, and goaty—and even managed to develop a means of assigning a numerical coefficient to each odor. Yet as with Henning's system, the final act of placing a number to an odor was reliant on the perfumer's nose, and thus subject to individual opinion. Another contribution, to be considered a little less seriously, perhaps, was that of Septimus Piesse, a noted perfumer and perfume historian. Working from a musical analogy, Piesse created what he called an "odorphone," whereby each odor corresponded to a note on its musical scale (Fig. 2, Sagarin 145). The first, or lowest note, was the "heaviest" odor and the highest note, the sharpest odor. In between was an ascending ladder. Each chord formed a "bouquet," which he considered every finished perfume must be (Sagarin 144-45). The C-chord in the treble clef, for instance, would be composed of rose, acacia, orange flower and camphor.

In his book *Odour Preferences*, R.W. Moncrieff concludes each chapter with some rules drawn from his findings. At the end of the chapter on odor classification, there is only one rule:

> The most successful classification of odours is based on the division of several odour properties into their pleasant and unpleasant aspects. There is, as yet, no classification that provides a reason for the differences between pleasantness and unpleasantness of odours, nor one which provides a clear-cut boundary between them. (221)

Like all other authorities who have commented upon perfume and language, Moncrieff recognizes the limitations of his discipline. Science has not progressed very far toward finding a way to relate odors or even to describe them. For the language of odor character, we must rely on such vagaries as "fragrant" and "pungent" and "barnyard-like." If the scientist throws up his hands in horror, the perfumer can only say that he is at a loss for words.

The Language of Advertising

Scientists and perfumers, we have seen, are in agreement only on the great difficulty of using discursive symbols to distinguish and define odors. As a graphic medium, one of language and images, advertising makes its appeal to our eyes. (I am here excepting the current trend in perfume inserts, "scratch and sniff's," which seem to me a kind of free sample, perhaps the most sensible form of perfume advertising.) Like scientists and perfumers, perfume advertisers encounter the problem of descriptive terminology. How can perfume be marketed if there are no adequate words to describe its individual character? Advertising's solution to these problems is to circumvent them. In most perfume advertisements the entire question of how a perfume smells is ignored.

As we all know, the vast majority of perfume advertisements make no effort to describe the scents that they are promoting. Unable to find discursive symbols to represent a scent, the advertiser instead claims that the scent itself is suggestive of sexuality, wealth, rugged individualism, and so on. Copy-writing then becomes dedicated to the task of creating connotations for a particular indescribable scent to give symbolic import to the fragrance. We need only survey a few advertisements to realize how completely gratuitous the symbol-object relationships are.

A Tweed advertisement features a picture of an attractive young woman. The caption reads: "A $35,000 Ferrari and I'm the first woman he ever let drive it. Tweed succeeds." Wearing this fragrance, we are to believe, has enabled this adventuress to plant herself where her predecessors had never been—the vacated driver's seat. Obviously the Ferrari's owner is at a disadvantage. His olfactory sensors besotted by Tweed vapors, he is disoriented, beside himself in love, and clearly, not in control of his car keys. Such an advertisement typifies the nexus of romantic and financial power, perhaps the two connotations most frequently given to perfume. Moon Drops by Revlon ("Give him something to reach for"), Musk by English Leather ("The missing link between animal and man"), and Givenchy Gentleman ("Think of it as investment spending") are just a few of the many perfumes whose advertisements claim the fragrance symbolic of enhanced sexuality. Advertisements for Joy ("The costliest perfume in the world"), 20 Carats ("Smell rich"), and Je Reviens (estimates of the expense of the materials used to produce it) all imply that scent can symbolize wealth. You can afford to smell like this; your pheromones announce your income bracket. Other advertisements cater to popular conceptions of foreign countries. Rive gauche by Yves Saint Laurent, in a current advertisement, is described as follows: "It has a spirit of a Parisienne cafe, alive with wine, laughter, and love. It's like a smile you wear all over." Not to belabor the obvious, the language of perfume advertisements does not attempt to sell the product but rather a conception of the product created by copy-writers.

In the advertisements where descriptive language *is* used, it is woefully inadequate.

Language and Perfume

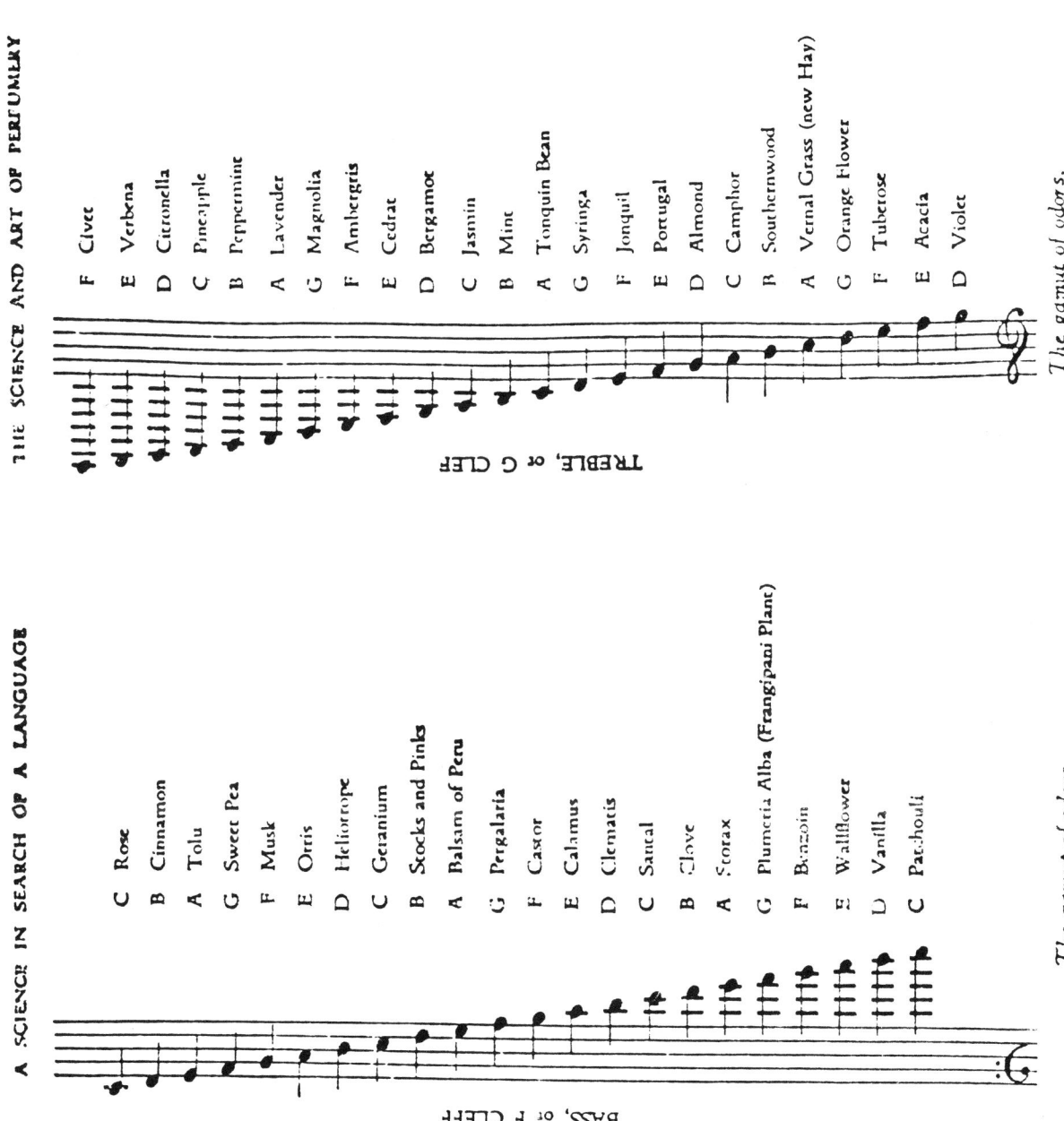

Fig. 2.

According to a recent advertisements, Royal Copenhagen, by B. Altman, is "woodsy, ambery." Timberlane, by English Leather, similarly plays upon the outdoor theme and carries the slogan: "Because who wants to smell like the city?" Yet neither of these would suggest the woods without the accompanying copy; both smell like cologne. The copy-writer here, it would seem, is given a free hand to create a fanciful and attractive conception in the buyer's mind, to stimulate her imagination rather than to summon up associations based upon experience.

Interestingly enough, certain writers capitalize on the difficulty of translating scents into words. Unable to describe an odor, they call it "mysterious" and the inscrutability of a scent that defies language is transferred onto the wearer, or so it is claimed. Infini, for example, simply carries the tag: "Because I like to be mysterious." Jovan Ginseng Perfume not only claims to be "the mysterious fragrance of life and love" (a modest boast derived, I assume, from the legendary aphrodisiac qualities of Ginseng), but goes so far as to print its claims in *Chinese* with an English translation graciously included—an added touch of exoticism. The idea here is to obscure what little descriptive knowledge we have of the fragrance. We translate Chinese to English only to find that the scent is "mysterious." Advertisements of this sort exploit the ineffable nature of scents: the "mysterious" fragrance supposedly becomes a presentational symbol of the wearer's mystery.

At times perfume advertisements even claim that the scents speak for themselves, that the perfume is the subject, capable of using discursive symbols. Perhaps the best-known of these is baseball star Henry Aaron's television endorsement of Brut some years back: "When I'm off the field, I let my Brut do the talking." Altman's Royal Copenhagen, to cite another example of this species of pathetic fallacy, is "the scent that says he's really 'above the crowd.' " Putting the perfume in the position of subject seemingly makes the statement more forceful. The advertiser is no longer making tenuous claims about what the fragrance connotes. Rather it is the fragrance itself doing "the talking." The advertiser, refusing to shoulder the burden of describing his product, turns this refusal to advantage.

Perhaps perfume advertising is destined to turn away from discursive language altogether. Magazines such as *Cosmopolitan* and *Vogue* commonly feature full-page gauzy photographs with only the product's name and its European affiliation identified in prose. A recent advertisement for Obsession by Calvin Klein features shadowy nude figures, faces hidden, a woman limply draped over the shoulder of a man who embraces her: an odd, sexually-charged scene presumably explained by the evocative, obsessive force of the fragrance named on the facing page. In a slightly more verbal ad for Opium by Yves Saint Laurent, an unclothed woman appears to be emerging from a lamé cocoon (her bedsheets?); we seem to be staring down on her as she dreams. This voyeuristic intrusion is hardly explained by the mild caption below: "Opium: The Fragrance Ritual for Body and Bath." Yet what ritual are we seeing reenacted? Rebirth as a sexually appealing woman? Such non-verbal mysteries, with their explicit eroticism, a growing tendency in perfume advertising nowadays, form part of a trend Andrew Sullivan has traced in contemporary advertising of products as dissimilar as Fox Sneakers, Fab laundry detergent and the French Socialist Party (20-21). This "mood advertising" says little about the product but creates numerous tangential associations: nearly any sort of commodity, it intimates, contains sexual implications.

Conclusion

Both scientists and advertisers appear to be aware of the shortage of verbal symbols that can be applied to the sensation of smell. Scientists and perfumers deplore the lack of terminology; advertisers, on the other hand, have found clever ways of exploiting this very lack. Scent, at least for the present time, remains an intangible sensation, a phenomenon that stubbornly resists verbal symbolization; this is attested to by both the admissions of defeat by scientists and by the suggestive and evasive prose of perfume advertisements.

Works Cited

Arctander, Steffen. *Perfume and Flavor Materials of Natural Origin.* Elizabeth, NJ: Gem, 1960.

Langer, Suzanne. *Philosophy in a New Key.* Cambridge: Harvard UP, 1951.

Moncrieff, R.W. *Odour Preferences.* London: Leonard Hill, 1966.

Sagarin, Edward. *The Science and Art of Perfumery.* New York: McGraw-Hill, 1945.

Sullivan, Andrew. "Flogging Underwear." *The New Republic* (18 Jan. 1988): 20-24.

Humor in Advertising: It's Funny Business

Marilyn M. Robitaille

"No doubt our sense of humor grew up along side of our emotions and our language."[1] No doubt about it. Humor has been with us a long time. What is surprising (and perhaps it's not all *that* surprising) is the intensely powerful combination of humor and advertising. The folks on Madison Avenue compliment the general public in realizing we know what is funny and what is not. They give the audience credit for the ability to notice subtle maneuverings of language, to understand lexical quirks, and to see the humor in syntactical variations. Nash points out that "in Britain, the advertising slogan is the new wit-object, to be tested, twisted, turned, much as the Elizabethans manipulated common place puns."[2] The same is true of American advertising. The semantic wizards on Madison Avenue are having a fine time playing with language and selling by appealing to our sense of humor.

It makes perfectly good sense for ads to be funny. No one will argue with the advantages of associating pleasant emotions with a product. Nilsen and Nilsen state: "The best ones [commercials] employ language play to grab the listener's attention and then involve the listener's mental processes in figuring out some kind of pun or an association."[3] The association of humor with a product seems to elevate the level of the consumer from someone who could be duped into making a potentially unwise purchase to someone who has the cunning to see (or hear) subtle word play in action.

Of course, the essence of advertising is in the selling, but when extraordinary care goes into choosing exactly the right word for exactly the right effect, we appreciate the language involved and look beyond the capacity of the ad to sell, transcending consumerism. That, certainly, is the ad designer's nightmare. However, for purposes of semantic analysis, for the most part it doesn't matter whether underwear or an avocado is in the limelight. What counts is the use of sophisticated semantics to create various types of humor; those types create discernible categories. Randomly selected magazine advertisements serve as categorical examples rather than television commercials. This is not to suggest that humor is not rampant in TV commercials. It is, but it is more difficult to pin down, and more of it is dependent on dramatic contexts. All of the ads discussed here are taken from popular magazines, and many of them appear in more than one issue. It does not necessarily follow that the tone of the magazine controls the tone of its advertising, but there were fewer humorous ads in *The Smithsonian* than in more frivolous magazines like *Glamour*.

The categories are not absolute since some of them blend into others, but for purposes of recognizing the semantic techniques at work, categorization is helpful. We should also consider the kinship of humor and wit. Leacock's definition of humor as "the kindly contemplation of the incongruities of life, and the artistic expression thereof" is applicable to what happens in the ads.[4] The reason we can so appreciate the management of the language lies within the ad designer's ability to be witty. Concerning "wit" Leacock says: "And more and more it became possible to derive humorous satisfaction out of the incongruities of speech itself, queer inconsistencies and oddities of speech. So that 'wit' comes into being as the general name for humorous expression, turning upon or accompanied by, verbal effects."[5] Obviously, humor and wit depend on the ability of the audience to take discerning notice of those oddities. Sometimes this is tied to our experience or, on another level, to our state of mind. Some of the ads that were uproariously funny on Wednesday were not all that funny on Thursday. Fresh is best. Like a joke going around for the second time, the printed ads do not lend themselves to repeated performances. Unless, of course, you are looking at the language.

The following categories clarify lexical, syntactical and situational semantic incongruities which occur in the various advertisements discussed here: grammatical violations, overstatement and understatement, parody, lexical overloads, poetic patterns, puns and situational combinations.

Grammatical Violations

Ads in this first category create humor by echoing the kinds of informal folksy statements common people might make in general conversation. Nilsen and Nilsen suggest the use of double negatives causes the audience to consider the message of the ad something a friend might say rather than something a professional writer might include in an ad.[6] Pillsbury's Classic Casserole ad uses the headline: "Pot pies ain't what they used to be."[7] The light humor exists for two reasons: contrast and the folk song resonance. We notice the contrast to language we are accustomed to seeing in magazine ads. The association with folksy speech is further heightened by the slogan's echo of "the old gray mare, she ain't what she used to be." On closer inspection, there is something disturbing about associating an old gray mare with pot pie, but the emotional appeal to common folk sells the product.

Overstatement and Understatement

The effectiveness of both overstatement and understatement is dependent to a large extent on the pictorial layout of the ad. The ad's language can be straightforward, and on the literal level, we understand the ad copy as completely logical. When combined with the ad's pictures (and it is impossible to separate the two when you are confronted by a magazine ad), the copy's tone and the situation pictured contrast sharply. Overstatement and understatement create humor for the same reason: incongruity between words and images. The meaning we interpret from the words is not the meaning we infer from the pictures. Two ads that employ understatement use minimal copy to create the effect. A TV station's (Fig. 1) ad for the evening news pictures a very cluttered desk. Photographs of the nightly news team are strewn haphazardly along with the items we associate with the glamorous business of gathering the news—a microphone, a news notebook, a script and video tape. The copy simply states: "Some desk job...huh?" Another ad uses a long shot to display a magnificent home in what appears to be a posh suburban neighborhood identified in the ad copy as the Livable Forest. Pictured is a woman purchasing lemonade from a little girl who has set up her lemonade stand on the carefully manicured front lawn. The headline states: "One of the nicest things about living in the Livable Forest is shopping there." Understatement occurs when we contrast the shopping she is doing and take note of the splendid brick home in the background.

Three ads which are examples of overstatement all convey a very serious tone. To understand the incongruities and appreciate the humor, the audience must make the interpretative jump from the message communicated in the copy to the contrasting situation pictured—exactly the same effect that occurs in understatement. Bulova's close-up of four teenage boys peering into the hood of a car communicates the excitement teenagers everywhere experience when a friend gets a new car. So immersed are they in the business of looking over the engine, we see only a back-pocket view of them. The copy reads: "On May 5, 1959, Tom Kubiak drove his first car home to show it off to his friends at 9:57 a.m." The humorous perspective of the photograph is in sharp contrast to the weighty tone of the copy. The same contrast of tone and situation occurs in an ad for Manwich. The foreboding fragment "The Five Words a Hard Working Mom Dreads Most..." comes boldly across the top of the page. A photo inset of a child smiling sweetly finishes the shocking fragment by stating "Hi Mom, What's for Dinner?" We can breathe easier knowing the answer but the humor present exists because of the overstated fragment. Another example of overstatement occurs in a Braun Aromaster ad. The copy states: "Life is complicated enough at 7 a.m." There are many things that can complicate life at that early hour: a failed alarm clock, a fire in the kitchen, a sick child. Given the opportunity we can imagine numerous horrible circumstances. However, humor is dependent on the incongruity of the language, the resulting overstatement, and what is pictured—a *glass* of hot coffee and a *cup* of orange juice. Thus, the semantics and the images interact to create the humor.

Parody

For parody to create humor, it must imitate another work and the audience must realize what elements have been ridiculed in the original. Nash refers to the realization as recollection: "Recollection—perhaps one might say *organized* recollection—is fundamental to parody, and the act of recollecting is the act of alluding to actual or typical turns of phrase."[8] An ad for Camp Beverly Hills clothing irreverently parodies the Pledge of Allegiance in its copy and sets up further patriotic spoofing with a picture of a sheepdog and five smiling teenagers hoisting a Camp Beverly Hills flag á la Iwo Jima. The copy is set in stanzas, and it is impossible to miss the allusion: "We pledge allegiance/ to the style/ of Camp Beverly Hills./

Humor in Advertising

Fig. 1. A TV station's ad for the evening news.

And to the principles/ for which it stands./ Always comfortable,/ above trends,/ individuals,/ with colors and sizes/ for all."

Lexical Overloads

One source of humor in many ads is the use of a word in a way that it is not commonly used. Leacock described this situation as "words that are 'made to work overtime.' That is they are forced into a meaning never given to them, but which on examination seems perfectly logical, as a meaning they ought to bear."[9] Often the word's placement in a new syntactical category emphasizes the brand name, as in "I could go for something Gordon's" and "When you live a Cutty above." Though these examples are not as humorous as some, they do create a light tone merely because of the originality of employing "Cutty" as an adjective and placing "Gordon's" in a slot normally occupied by an adjective.

Another kind of lexical overload occurs when ad designers create completely new words. Once again, the originality creates the humor, and we see emphasis on the products as we mentally compare the new words to the familiar ones: "Calciyum" for calcium; "Flopcorn vs. Popcorn"; and "Meow Mix. It's a Meowthful" for mouthful.

Poetic Patterns

Ad designers are frustrated poets. Metaphor, simile, alliteration, meter, rhyme and stanzaic form occur in humorous advertising. Some ads delight us for the same reasons Mother Goose delights children. We enjoy the sounds of the words, the way they play and trip while creating meaning as in "The puffalumps—Lovable lumps of Snuggly stuff." Some of the poetic ads are clever because we have to work a little to see the significance of a metaphor or to appreciate alliteration. We may notice a slogan that stays with us all day because of the meter.

Many ads use a variety of poetic techniques to create humor while others use only alliteration. It is difficult to read some of the alliterative ads aloud without smiling: AT&T's "Friendly Face"; "Liberate a Cuba Libre"; "Stretch to Stravinsky"; "She love Levis, Led Zeppeline and Lenin."

Two ads that employ similes depend on the visual components in the layouts. In the first, Santa is wearing a sweat suit. The copy states "Bassette-Walker Sturdy Sweats Can Make Anybody Look Like a Jock." An ad that plays on the bizarre connects a simile to the product's slogan, "A Unique Breed of Watch" with the line "As Elegant As a Swan." A woman's hand is pictured, a watch on her wrist; but this is no ordinary hand. It is carefully positioned and painted to look like a swan. The simile pinpoints the incongruity which creates the humor.

Budweiser's ad campaign that has made Spuds Mackenzie, Party Animal, a household item lends itself to a kind of metaphorical parody which plays on the familiarity of the figure of speech, party animal, as it relates to humans who like to party. An ad for California avocados pictures a plump avocado complete with party hat and party favor. The copy suggests that avocados should be the main attraction at your next party. The headline in bold print, *"Party Animal"* does two things: it parodies the popular Spuds ad, and it contrasts a pear-shaped fruit to the human party animal.

An ad for Honda is less complicated in its use of metaphor. The headline "Fall in love without paying the price" suggests a comparison between purchasing a Honda Civic and falling in love without the attendant pain. This is extended in the ad's copy with "It makes you happy, without making a lot of demands."

In considering the logic of short sentences in advertising copy, Bolinger notes that "since each [short sentence] has a separate comment and therefore a main accent of its own, the more there are the more accents there will be and the message is made louder and clearer."[10] This notion is applicable in the poetic stanza used in an ad for products in Revlon's Charlie line. Five items are associated with the words "foam," "mist," "splash," "dash" and "spritz." These beauty aids are described as "a little light refreshment" and the sounds of the words create refreshing images. The emphasis of those associations comes through the use of stanzaic form and accented first syllables: "Spritz it on./ Splash it on./ Foam it on./ Mist it on./ Dash it on./ New Charlie Go Lightly." The rhythm and repetition of each line cause associations with the same accented rhythmical patterns of the word "Charlie."

Some ads are not nearly as subtle, and the poetic intentions are immediately obvious. Try "Fine, Dry Lines?/ Minimize the Telltale Signs!" As copy-verse it is a bit disappointing since the product name is not mentioned and the meter is irregular. The ad for Golden Griddle syrup plays on rhythm and rhyme to establish name association: "Can you solve this griddle riddle?/ There's a new pancake syrup we're told,/ That flows out in a stream of gold./ Made with real maple syrup you see/ And thick naturally/ Look deep inside the golden stream/ And the riddle answer can be seen/ New naturally thick,/ With pure maple taste." Though the meter is uneven and we can hardly call this poetry, the phrasing places stress on important associations and makes careful use of inversions: pancake syrup, stream of gold, golden stream, pure maple taste, thick naturally and naturally thick.

Puns

One of the most popular and least respected sources of humor is the pun. Puns are appropriate for ads since they are easily recognizable as humorous, and they are short. Three kinds of puns are most celebrated in ads.

The first one is the phonetic similitude or "mime."[11] We can see this method at work in the following: milk—"Moo and Improved"; diet coke—"Monumental Taste. Mt. Tastemore, South Dacola"; Gund Teddy Bears—"Play it a Gund Sam"; and Roy Blount's book—"Let's be Blount about it."

The second kind of pun is the homophonic pun.[12] Ads using this technique are visually intriguing: "Waist away at our lakeside resort" (Fig. 2); "Haute and Cold—The frozen ice cream dessert that's haute cuisine"; and Jello's "Bring home something special for dinner tonight: Bag a mousse."

The third kind of pun borrows common phrases. Many are trite expressions or clichés. In some ads the play on the cliché is not sufficient to support the meaning, and we must interpret the visuals in the ad. An ad for PAM pictures the remains of a gingerbread boy stuck to a cookie sheet. The headline states "PAM can save you an arm and a leg." Using the similar combination of trite expression, visuals, and ad copy several of the following ads operate on the assumption that the audience will recall the familiar expression and make the contrast to the ad's situation. An ad for LaMansion Hotel (Fig. 3) which features a barge states: "We wouldn't object if you were to barge right in." Magnavox has "the stereo VCR that has everything. Including a cure for the bends." Pictured is a young man awkwardly bending at the waist while reaching for the front-loading VCR beneath his TV. Xerox details the advantages of owning a Memorywriter that makes fast corrections by headlining the ad for it with "how to become a quick change artist." A cartoon character juggles pages of a lengthy business report in an ad for partition folders; the headline states: "How to keep your business from falling apart." A close-up of one Ore-Ida Shoestring potato promises this is a "Shoestring that can't be beat. Or even tied." A close-up of a man's hand as he touches the handle of a car door is accompanied by the headline "The Grandest Slam of Them All." A Range Rover is climbing an impossibly steep hill and the copy reads: "It gives new meaning to the term upward mobility." Shortening the form are "Zap n' Serve" for a microwave sausage ad and "Spot Remover" which emphasizes television viewers' ability to use remote control to change channels and miss the commercials (spots).

Not all ads that use puns on clichés rely so heavily on the visual aspects in the layout. The language carries the force in the following: "Jane Fonda's New Workout is her best ever. It Figures." Two ads with a similar message state: "Life insurance that helps you keep up with the Dow Joneses" and Irving, Texas promises it's "Where to stay when you're going places."

In some situations, word play becomes so enticing the very look of the word on the printed page becomes part of the pun itself. Volkswagen Golf GT's clever visual pun can be missed if you read the headline in a hurry: "*GT Up and Go.*" Dodge Colt is emphasizing its connection with Mitsubishi by including Japanese lettering in the midst of the puns playing on "lap of luxury" and "won't cost you an arm and a leg" with "For those who prefer life in the lap of 贅沢 and "Pure fun that won't cost you an arm and a 健脚."

Situational Combinations

Contrast or incongruity is essential in creating humor; it has to exist in some form. Many ads develop the incongruity through combinations of language and visual components to create situations where neither the message in the copy nor the visual layout itself is inherently funny. The rhetorical questions in ads for Johnnie Walker Scotch and Crown Royal play on juxtaposition. The first "Would Crown Prince Joseph of Austria have given his father a mini-van?" The answer must be a resounding "no!" since an elaborate, gold, highly ornate carriage is pictured. The contrast leads to the ad's message that "Your father should expect only the very best from his heir." Apparently a mini-van will not do. The second ad asks, "Have you ever seen a grown man cry?" The answer to be drawn from the picture is "Yes" because a bottle of expensive Crown Royal has been broken in the street.

An ad for the city of Arlington (Texas) states: "The first folks to visit Arlington didn't make it to Six Flags." Why not? Pictured is a bandit atop a train. In an ad for the Business Committee for the Arts, we see a friendly looking woman standing behind a luncheonette counter holding a priceless masterpiece. The copy states, "Ida's Luncheonette

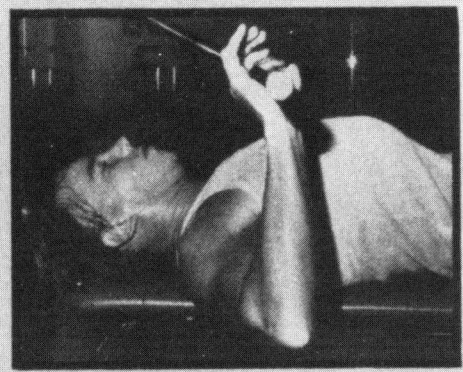

Waist away at our lakeside resort.

WE HAVE AN EXCITING ARRAY OF NEW SPA PACKAGES AT INCREDIBLY LOW RATES!

Enjoy the soothing, serenity of a lakeside setting while waisting away with one of our many special programs for weight loss and self-improvement.

These programs incorporate sixteen daily fitness classes including stretching, toning and aerobics; educational instruction in nutrition and lifestyle enhancement in addition to our complete range of pampering services. And all complimented by our healthy, wholesome cuisine.

So don't waste time and call us today for additional information and reservations. Reservations accepted on a first-come, first-served basis. Call today, as space is limited.

1705 Quinlan Park Rd. • Austin, Tx. 78732 • (512) 266-2444 • Texas TOLL FREE 1-800-252-9324 • Outside Texas TOLL FREE 1-800-847-5637

Fig. 2. Lake Austin Resorts. February 1987, *Texas Monthly*, p. 131. Permission granted 9/10/91; used with permission of Lake Austin Resort.

Fig. 3. LaMansion del Rio Hotel. Used with permission of the hotel.

This Is What You Come To San Antonio For.

Three hundred and thirty-seven luxury rooms.
Located downtown on San Antonio's famed River Walk.
Living history. Legendary hospitality.
A hotel so rare it has been
designated an historical treasure.
La Mansión del Rio Hotel.
What you come to San Antonio for.

La Mansión del Rio Hotel
112 College Street San Antonio Tx. 78205
For reservations call:
(512) 225-2581 *Local*
1-800-292-7300 *Texas*
1-800-531-7208 *U.S., Canada and Mexico*
FAX (512) 226-1365

La Mansión del Rio Hotel
What you come to San Antonio for.

Preferred Hotels Worldwide

is known for fried chicken, apple pie, and Rembrandt." Unlikely combinations create the humor. Another ad for art pictures a wooden Indian. The headline: "He's even better at selling bath towels." This incongruity is explained in light of Bloomingdale's donation to the Museum of American Folk Art.

Sometimes simple incongruities are especially effective. An ad for Diet Coke pictures a close-up of Superman opening his shirt to expose the "S" on his chest. The picture is cropped at the neck to focus on the can of Diet Coke in Superman's hand. The headline states: "Caffeine Free. Kryptonite Free." Most Diet Coke drinkers do not worry about Kryptonite.

Some ads use comic visual effects that are so strong they overpower everything else in the ad. In spite of that, the humor in these ads is still dependent on the copy to supply interpretation. George Washington pictured on a dollar bill wearing sunglasses and a visor, a chicken in tennis shoes, and a tennis shoe the size of a sofa create humor, but the impact of the ad comes through the interpretation of the language. George Washington takes on greater significance with the headline "Southwest Airlines' Weekend Fun Packs. More fun for your money." The chicken offers the line "UHHH...This Week It's Aerobics" while the bold print states: "We're Waiting to Hear your Latest Excuse for Not Giving Blood." 3M Corporation explains the invention of Scotchguard to relate the sofa-sized sneaker to a living room: flurochemicals "spilled onto a tennis shoe and tests showed that part of the shoe just couldn't be easily soiled." The ad's language provides the humor with another dimension the picture alone does not deliver.

Dwight Bolinger calls language "the loaded weapon," and we are all cognizant of its uses and abuses. Advertisers bombard us with images and entice us with words. When the combination makes us laugh, something magical happens. Over and over again, humor in advertising has proven effective.[13] As far as effective use of language in advertising, the old adage applies: "The lighter the touch, sometimes the heavier the wallop."

Summary

It makes perfectly good sense for ads to be funny. No one will argue with the advantages of associating pleasant emotions with a product. Of course, the essence of advertising is in the selling, but when extraordinary care goes into choosing exactly the right word for exactly the right humorous effect, we can appreciate the language involved. We can look beyond the ad's ability to sell. This paper examines a wide variety of humorous magazine ads and classifies the lexical, syntactical, and situational semantic incongruities which produce humor. The approach is systematic although the categories are not absolute. Some of them blend in others, but for purposes of recognizing the semantic techniques at work, the classifications are helpful. The following seven categories provide the paper's framework: 1) Grammatical violations— These ads create humor by echoing the kinds of informal, folksy statements common people might make in general conversation; 2) Overstatement and understatement— Incongruity between words and images provides the source of humor in these ads; 3) Parody—The humor is dependent on the audience's ability to realize what elements have been ridiculed in the original; 4) Lexical overloads—Words are "stretched" and used in a way they are not commonly used. They are forced into a meaning never given to them but which seems logical; 5) Poetic patterns—Many ad designers are frustrated poets and use poetic techniques to produce humor; 6) Puns—Puns are particularly appropriate for funny ads. They are easily recognizable as humorous, and they are short. Puns abound in funny ads; 7) Situational combinations— Juxtaposition between visual components in layout and ad copy often produces surprising outcomes.

Thus, this paper investigates these semantic systems which apply to any humorous ad no matter whether biscuits or beer is being sold. The semantic wizards on Madison Avenue are having a fine time playing with language and enjoying the benefits of designing effective ads that sell. We laugh; we buy. Humor and semantic games play an integral part in the success stories. The old adage obviously applies; "The lighter the touch, sometimes the heavier the wallop."

Notes

[1]Stephen Leacock, *Humor and Humanity* (New York: Henry Holt and Company, 1938), 7.

[2]Walter Nash, *The Language of Humor: Style and Technique in Comic Discourse* (New York: Longman, 1985), 45.

[3]Don L. Nilsen and Alleen Pace Nilsen, *Language Play: An Introduction to Linguistics* (Massachusetts: Newbury House Publishers, 1978), 49.

[4]Leacock, 3.

[5]Leacock, 18.

[6]Nilsen and Nilsen, 50.

[7]Pillsbury Classic Casseroles, *Working Woman* (Nov. 1986), ML5. Bibliographical information for the advertisements cited is not provided in the text of the paper for the sake of textual clarity. The checklist following these notes catalogs advertisement references in the order each appears in the paper.

[8]Nash, 81.

[9]Leacock, 36.

[10]Dwight Bolinger, *Language—The Loaded Weapon: The Use and Abuse of Language Today* (New York: Longman, 1980), 124.

[11]Nash, 139.

[12]Nash, 138.

[13]For further articles establishing the effectiveness of humor in advertising see the following:

Brahma, J. "Larsons Humor Flies for DHL," *Industry Week* (3 April 1989): 33-4.

Fitzgerald, K. "Sprint Campaign goes for Smiles," *Advertising Age* (18 July 1988): 4.

Lawrence, J. "Dr. Pepper Bets on Big Laughs," *Advertising Age* (10 Oct. 1988): 71.

Lippert, B. "Northwest Airline Takes off with Highflying Spot," *Ad Week Marketing Week* (17 Oct. 1988): 46-7.

Woolley, S. "Now, Success is a Laughing Matter," *Business Week* (8 Aug. 1988): 81.

Zurier, S. "Humor Can Be Your Best Sales Tool," *Industrial Distribution* 77 (Feb. 1988): 51.

Works Cited

Bolinger, Dwight. *Language—The Loaded Weapon: The Use and Abuse of Language Today*. New York: Longman, 1980.

Leacock, Stephen. *Humor and Humanity*. New York: Henry Holt and Company, 1939.

Nash, Walter. *The Language of Humor: Style and Technique in Comic Discourse*. New York: Longman, 1985.

Nilsen, Don L. and Alleen Pace Nilsen. *Language Play: An Introduction to Linguistics*. Massachusetts: Newbury House, 1978.

The Golliwog: Innocent Doll to Symbol of Racism

Robert M. MacGregor

I will trace the historical and the present implications of the Golliwog, as a doll in British folklore to a widely used trademark in the British commercial marketplace. Since the early 1980s, the Golliwog has been at the center of social, cultural, economic and political controversy.

The Cultural Meanings of Consumer Goods and Promotions

The idea that products, labels, packages and other facets of promotional processes possess symbolic functions has been well documented. Their social significance extends far beyond the strictly utilitarian values and functional utilities. Products and their extensional properties (e.g., trademarks) possess various levels of denotive and connotative meanings.[1] It is contended in this paper that products and their associated and affiliated stimuli are, in fact, major instruments of meaning and movement of meanings through time and space. It is also believed that these instruments of meanings are not uni-directional and linear but that they are multi-directional and multi-linear. The audiences for trademarks and their products are not only real and potential purchasers but that there are multi-audiences, some of whom are hostile to the trademarks in a non-exchange, commercial process.

A major concern for marketers is to differentiate their products and services from other somewhat similar products and services in the marketplace. Also, it is believed that trademarks and names and symbols can become the most important variable in the exchange process. It is in the context of the clustering of product attributes that the paper will present the doll-like figure, the Golliwog, and how it has evolved from a grotesque-like doll character that appeared in thirteen books for children to a symbol of perceived racism. At the turn of the twentieth century, the Golliwog was widely accepted and adopted by many commercial companies and used as a commercial symbol, tradename and trademark. Its widespread use through seventy-plus years continues today when it is used as the trademark to market a line of jams for James Robertson and Son; Trebor Limited, one of Britain's largest candy makers use it to sell its "Black Jack Chews;" and H & B Ice Cream Company of Dublin, Eire, uses the Golliwog to market its "Golly Bar" throughout the United Kingdom and Eire.

With the major changes in the population composition that has occurred throughout Britain, the new waves of black and Asian immigrants, the innocence of the past times, the acceptance of the Golliwog as only a doll and not an image of the generic Sambo figure has now come under social scrutiny and social boycotts. The long-standing trademark is now the source of major social discontent. If it is true that the racially offensive terminology such as "darkie" and "coon" and "Sambo" are no longer acceptable, then various constituent groups in Britain now want the marketplace to be rid of the symbol and trademark, Golliwog.

The Golliwog: Its Origins

Florence K. Upton (1873-1922) invented the Golliwog in a series of picture books which began to appear in the early 1890s. She was born in the United States of English parents; she went to England when she was twenty and remained there for the rest of her life. The first book in the series "The Adventures of Two Dutch Dolls and a Golliwog" appeared in 1895. The story tells how two wooden dolls on the loose in a toy shop suddenly see "a horrid sight, the blackest gnome."[2] This character was dressed in blue swallow-tailed coat, a red bow tie on a high collared white shirt. To complete his attire he wore bright red trousers. The dress of the Golliwog was, and continues to remain, basically the same clothes as the black-faced minstrels who toured throughout America and Western Europe. The Golliwog, as created by Upton, had two exaggerated wide-white eyes, a coal black face, thick lips and a mass of unruly long black hair. At the beginning of the publications,

The Golliwog

the doll was usually bare-footed, and where it should have had hands and feet, the appendages were usually shown as paws. Overall, the character was quite frightening and grotesque.[3] In all, thirteen books were written between 1895 and 1908. Soon after the publication of the first book and its success, the Golliwog quickly became a commercial symbol appearing on many types of products, toys, postcards, games, novelties and food products. Claude Debussy's Suite "Children's Corner" (1906-1908) included a Golliwog "Cake Walk." In 1908, E. Brockette wrote the "Golliwog-Two Step."

Over the years, the Golliwog continued to be incorporated, or used usually metaphorically, in numerous books. The *Oxford Dictionary* traces some of its uses as shown in the following excerpts:

1904, *Woman's Life*, 7 May 227/1 one of her hobbies is the collecting of those quaint, but unbeautiful dolls known as Gollywogs. 1907 *Westmount Gazette*, 28 May 10/2 a clever golliwog dance received the enthusiastic applause it deserved. 1922 Joyce *Ulysses*, 347 Madcap Ciss with her golliwog curls. 1925 E.F. Norton *Fight for Everest*, 1924 104 Every now and then I was struck afresh with the absurdly golliwog appearance of the party. 1956 G. Durrell *Drunken Forest*, vi., 126 We came to the police-station, . . . shaded by a large, golliwog-headed palm tree. 1969 I. Kemp *Brit. G.I. in Vietnam*, viii. 161 A short, slightly built negro whose appearance reminded me of one of those golliwogs that decorate the labels of Robertson's marmalade jars.[4]

If one looks closely at the general uses of the Golliwog image in the listed literary sources the overall image is less than complimentary. There is an association of the image with the commercial use of the symbol, and here and there the reference is to the ugliness of the Golliwog.

The Golliwog in Cartoons

Occasionally the Golliwog also appeared in other forms of widely read and distributed communications, such as cartoons. Four examples of sightings would include the following cartoons as researched in the well-known satirical English publication, *Punch*. The sightings are dated: January 12, 1921 (33); June 15, 1938 (663); December 15, 1948 (475); and April 6, 1949 (380).[5] During this period, the Golliwog image took on different appearances. Several of the sites show the doll as a doll in the backgrounds of the cartoons. However, this not the case in the other two cartoons. The 1938 cartoon shows very stereotypically drawn blacks as Africans (primitives) with very overly-emphasized features standing agog as two white explorers offer them a jack-in-the-Box with a pop-up Golliwog—a negative-stereotypical reflection "looking glass effect." The most poignant example of how the Golliwog was shown is the 1921 cartoon which shows a mother and child having a conversation as follows: (Fig. 1)

Child: "May I take my best doll to heaven?"
Mother: "No darling."
Child: "May I take my second best doll to heaven?"
Mother: "No darling."
Child: "Well, it looks as if I should have to take my Golliwog and go to hell."

The implication of the conversation between the child and her mother is that the white dolls are alright to go with her to heaven (the upper whiteness and goodness and all that is implied therein) and when that does not seem possible the child will take the black Golliwog and then go to hell (the black place and all that is evil). Here, we can witness an example where now the Golliwog is relegated to the lowest point in the dichotomy, the poles of heaven and hell, just like society's blacks. Is the cartoon telling the readers that whites go to heaven and that blacks to go the darkness of hell?

The Golliwog and Its Commercialization in the Marketplace

As stated previously, the image of the Golliwog appeared on numerous products and services (labels, packages, sales promotions and ways of advertising items). Starting in the early 1900s through 1986, the symbol is basically still the same as it first appeared in 1895. In 1900, the Hamley Brothers used the symbol in one of its advertisements[6] (Fig. 2). In 1925, the Andrews Liver Salts Company used the doll in its advertising. The picture told its viewers that black is bad and white is better, as the complexional coloring of the human. A little white cherubic child is seen patting the Liver Salts onto the black face of the Golliwog saying "Mummy says—it improves the complexion."[7] In 1936, the Bradford Dyers Association used the Golliwog to promote a new cotton finish "Rigmel." When the Golliwog was washed, the doll is made of "Rigmel" and it will not shrink. One interesting aspect of this doll is that the advertisement calls it the Green Golliwog.[8] This was the only example found where the Golliwog was not black. In 1948, Harrod's of London included the Golliwog as an image in a composite picture of a large selection of dolls that could have been purchased in the Harrod's store.[9] In a more recent example of the use of the Golliwog is the crossword book published by Collins of Britain (1975). The page shows a grotesque doll-like Golliwog and the person is to guess the name of the doll and then to insert it—the name

JANUARY 12, 1921.] PUNCH, OR THE LONDON CHARIVARI.

Child. "MAY I TAKE MY BEST DOLL TO HEAVEN?" Mother. "NO, DARLING."
Child. "MAY I TAKE MY SECOND-BEST DOLL TO HEAVEN?" Mother. "NO, DARLING."
Child. "WELL, IT LOOKS AS IF I SHOULD HAVE TO TAKE MY GOLLIWOG AND GO TO HELL."

Fig. 1. From *Punch* 1921.

Fig. 2. Circa 1900 ad for Hamley Bros.

The Golliwog

"Golliwog"—in appropriate place in the crossword.[10]

Three very important examples of the Golliwog that continue to be used commercially include: "The Golly": James Robertson and Son, Jam Maker. "Black Jack": Trebor Limited, Candy Maker. "Golly Bar": H & B Ice Cream Maker. All three makers of the product assortments continue to use and to promote their products throughout the United Kingdom and Eire, and in the case of Robertson and Son, in other countries.

The Trebor "Black Jack" was introduced in the early 1920s (the exact date is not known) when there were few distinctive brand names in use in the British marketplace (Fig. 4). The marketing executive of the firm believed that in its early introduction "the Golliwog was more of an integrated figure in society (Black and White minstrels) or that in those days there was less racial sensitivity. One would probably not choose such a potentially controversial symbol today. But that would be speculation."[11] In the case of "Black Jack," the image is once again dressed as a grinning minstrel-like figure with overly stated features and the "labels of dress," the bow-tie/tail-coat. In correspondence with the author, the senior executive admits that the trademark does have some depth of racial sensitivity with negative stereotypical images. The marketplace/marketing strategy was to introduce a black-chewy candy, differentiate it from other competitive products, and that the grinning, cheerful, lively and appealing trademark would appeal to the candy-buying public. The Step 'n' Fetchit/Sambo (golliwog) figure was believed to be very much part of the music hall and literary sites of the British culture at that time. One must keep in mind though that the trademark is still in use today (even with the statements of the marketing personnel).

Another long-standing Golliwog trademark is the "Golly Bar" (Fig. 5). This image is used to sell ice cream products of the H & B Ice Cream Company, Dublin, Eire. This Golly is very similar to the other Sambo-type images already discussed. The eyes are overly emphasized with a large, thick lipped, grinning mouth. The doll's hands are white gloved, held high as if the image is singing. The overall facial, clothing and body-posturing elements are the standard themes that frequently appeared in much advertising, stage skits, and children's books, for example.[12] When the author tried to contact the Dublin Company there was no reply. The origins of the symbol remain unknown.[13]

Much more is known about the Robertson's Golliwog (Fig. 6). The time of the trademark's introduction was a period in the history of England where Negro immigrants were virtually unknown, and in consequence, its adoption could not have caused any racial unpleasantness which might have rebounded on the brand—so believes one of the senior marketing executives of the firm.[14] The history of the "Golly" began with the visit of the son of James Robertson visiting the "backwoods" of North America and seeing a lot of little children playing with a little black rag doll with white eyes made from their mother's discarded black skirts and white blouses.

The young Robertson was so intrigued by the popularity of the small "Golly" (the name being the children's interpretation of "dolly") that he thought that it would make an appealing mascot and trademark for the Robertson's range of products. The idea of the "Golly" trademark was accepted by the company, and to make him more attractive, he was dressed in a very colorful suit. This was in about 1910. In 1928-30, the first enamel "Golly" brooches were introduced commencing with the "Golly" Golfer. Four years later, a series of fruit badges were made with a "Golly" head superimposed into the berries. Later came the Coronation "Golly" with a Union Jack on his waistcoat and other promotional ideas for the Gollywog.

In 1939, the brooch series was discontinued because of the war effort and the need to conserve metals. In 1946, however, the metal "Golly" was back again. In 1956, the "Golly" pendant chains were introduced and changes were made to the symbol itself. The old-fashioned "Golly" with the "pop-eyes" was changed to the present "Golly" with his eyes looking over his left shoulder. The words "Golden Shred" were removed from his waistcoat, his legs straightened and his smile broadened.

In 1977, to keep up with the changing times, a "Golly" on a skateboard as well as one on a motorbike were introduced. In the same year, fifteen-year woven patches were designed and they have become as popular as the brooches. To date, over twenty million "Gollies" have been sent out to make the sales promotion one of the most successful in the history of that method of promoting products. The "Golly" offer is certainly the longest-running sales promotion in the Western world. The "Golly" is now available on T-shirts, tablecloths, placemats, towels, and children's wear.[15]

More recently, a senior company executive further explained the sales and distribution of the

Fig. 3. Enid Blyton's golliwog, 1960

Fig. 4. Trebor Black Jacks, 1987.

Fig. 5. The Golly Bar, 1987.

Fig. 6. Robertson's Marmalade, 1950-1960s.

The Golliwog

Golly to the author:

We do not, however, utilize the Golly on our export products for two prime reasons. Firstly [sic], in the U.K. Robertson's products are brand leaders appealing to all sectors of the consuming public, including a high proportion of children; the "Golly" symbol is seen as being of prime appeal to children and should thus encourage them to commence eating our products at an early age. On the other hand, our products in most export markets, with prices inflated by ocean freight, insurance, import duty and higher distribution margins, tend to appeal more to the adult rather than to the younger element and we do not feel that the "Golly" is necessarily in keeping with this marketing positioning. At the same time, we do feel that to introduce the "Golly" on to our export packs at such a late date would raise substantial charges of racial prejudice which, whilst unfounded, could well be damaging to our brand name, which is well respected in a large number of overseas markets. For that reason we do not use this symbol overseas.[16]

This statement is not true, however, and further explanation is required. When the author contacted the company in March 1983, another marketing executive said that the trademark is, in fact, registered in 53 countries. However, at that time, as a promotional offer, the "Golly" was distributed as a merchandising item(s) in New Zealand, Japan, Australia and Germany.[17] Later—January 10, 1985—the same executive wrote that the recent consumer protests over the name that were impacting on the company in Britain was now a manifestation of the political "Left." He believed that the movement was instigated by the "politics of the left which seem to abound nowadays in this country."[18] By that time the trademark was not being run in Hong Kong, South Africa and the whole of the Middle East.

Throughout all the correspondence with the company and other concerned parties, there is a consistent ethnocentric bias that appears. Most of the supporters of the symbol publically state that the Golliwog is nothing more, and nothing less, than a doll-like character that is now firmly entrenched in the stories and playthings of British culture and folklore. Starting in the late 1970s and the early 1980s, Britain was witness to many forms of social, economic and political pressures upon the company to stop using the Golliwog as its trademark for its numerous food products.

The Golliwog:
Human Rights and Racial Stereotypes

Lately, there has been a major change in the British marketplace. There are now a large number of recent visible minorities in the United Kingdom. Many of these recent immigrants are found in and around the greater London area. What we see now is various forms of social protests against the use of the Golliwog trademark. Some of the persons involved in the protests are from very different walks of life and with very different ideologies. A radical M.P., Ken Livingstone, has been one of the foremost spokespersons concerning the quest to get the symbol banned from the marketplace. The main reason for his involvement has to do with the numerous complaints that he was receiving from many of his constituents. The essence of all the complaints were that the trademark, the Golliwog symbol, perpetuates a racist stereotypical image of the happy-go-lucky black minstrel performer with fuzzy hair, huge round eyes, thickened lips and a fixed grin.

Other British notables have taken a variety of stances on the Golliwog trademark. Tony Benn, an M.P. in the British House of Commons, "absolutely" agrees about "the offensive nature of the Golliwog." He wanted it removed from the British marketplace. Other British Parliamentarians who supported the withdrawal of the trademark included Shirley Williams and David Owen. Both the National Councils for Civil Liberties and Voluntary Organizations sought immediate cessation of the use of the Golliwog. They believed that the symbol is racist and stood for all the worst elements of a racist society. The Civil Liberties Council "deplores racism and anything which continues to internalize this ugly response in young children."[19]

All of the voices that were raised were not for the banning of the trademark. When a spokesperson for the black community contacted a member of the House of Lords, Lord Scarman said "that since the specific problem...has a very direct effect in the field of commerce...it would be inappropriate for him to make any comment at all."

When the Queen endorsed Robertson's products, Laila Coleman, Principal Advisor (Race), London Borough of Greenwich, wrote to Her Majesty for her views surrounding the controversial trademark. The Queen's Press Secretary replied: "It is not Her Majesty's practice to give her personal views on matters such as the one you raise." J. Enoch Powell, Conservative Party M.P. and a member of the facist group National Front, believed that "...to take exception to the use of the Golliwog doll is an example of the 'hysteria' over race relations which does so much more harm than good."[20] The Advertising Standards Authority of Britain refused to intervene in the debate over the Golliwog trademark. In effect, they saw nothing wrong with the symbol.

While all the written campaigns were underway, other local groups of concerned citizens were busy organizing their own methods to stop the company from continuing using its racist trademark. The Camden Committee for Community Relations mounted a petition for signatures to send to the Robertson Company. The people were also encouraged to start a letter writing campaign and to send to the same firm. Also, the consumers of jam products were told to start a boycott of the line of food products that were marketed by the company. A lapel button and auto bumper sticker campaign were also put into force with a slogan saying "The Racist Golly Has Come To A Sticky End."

At the same time, the National Committee on Racism in Children's Books (NCRCB) mounted a petitioning campaign of its own. The basic point that the NCRCB was making to the general public was that the Golliwog was an element in the company's sales promotion and advertising tools that perpetuated racist images, insulting stereotypes that were derogatory to blacks and in turn to human dignity.[21]

In 1980, while the campaigns had zeroed in on the Robertson Company, another major British merchandiser, Boots the Chemist, the country's largest drug chain, brought out a line of bath sponges that had the Golliwog as a sponge figure. This prompted Silvaine Wiles, Director of the Language Division of the Center for Urban Educational Studies, to write to the director of the company, A.P. Ridley-Thompson. He in turn wrote a most patronizing letter to Wiles basically saying that the use of the Golliwog ("part of our folklore") should not be a cause for distress to "our coloured friends." He cited the long-standing Golliwog used by Robertson, which still enjoyed the honor of "Appointment to the Queen." In the letter, he also admitted that he was totally unrepentant for the Golliwog sponges that his company was selling.[22]

The case was not closed against the Boots Company. Wiles passed on Ridley-Thompson's letter and company reply to the Reverend Basil Manning, Senior Community Worker, North Lewisham Project, London. He immediately became involved. The minister wrote the following letter to Ridley-Thompson. The letter is in the form of a parable and eventually it did the intended trick, so to speak, because the company agreed to stop selling the Golliwog sponges:

Dear Mr. Ridley-Thompson;

As a black person who is deeply concerned about the subtle messages which perpetuate racism in British society, I thought it appropriate to write and share with you the following modern parable.

There once was a director of a large company, a man concerned to please the community and especially thoughtful of the needs of children at Christmas.

One year he designed a product, easy to produce in large quantities, eye-catching and colourful. Children and parents up and down the land bought his "golliwog" sponges. Mothers and fathers taught their young children the word "golliwog," and thousands, maybe millions, of children were happy that Christmas.

Some twenty years later the children who once happily played with their "golliwog" sponges one Christmas were now abusing black people in Deptford and the East End. "Go home Wogs" and "Wogs out" read the slogans on the walls and on the doors of the black families who tried to clear their hallways, hearts and minds of the after-taste of excrement pushed through their letter-boxes. Every one wondered where these young people had learnt these hateful sentiments.

The children who once enjoyed their "golliwog" sponges in their baths, now marched on the streets shouting slogans of hate; "Keep Britain White," "Niggers go home," "Wogs Out."

Then one day they killed an Asian in the East End, another day they beat up black people as they came out of a factory, months later another shot at a black man in Lewisham and still later some killed a man in Southall. A new breed of racists from yesterday's children had been created.

The director was shocked by this state of affairs in his years of retirement and said, "I am to blame. I always saw golliwogs as an innocent part of our folklore, besides James Robertson's used the same image for years on his marmalade labels, the nurseries used 'Little Black Sambo,' people in their thousands went to the 'Black and White Minstrel Show.' The teachers said: 'We are not to blame that the only images of black people we had in reading was that of a 'golliwog,' besides, the image of black people which we were brought up with was that of a caricature with wide eyes, red, thick lips and bright white teeth. We were not to blame for the media's omissions of giving only token reference to black people in positions of authority and responsibility."

Everyone said they are not to blame for the level of racism, the violence and disorder on the streets. Nobody accepted the blame not even the retired director. But the reality was that a new generation of racists was born, worse than their slave-trading and colonialist forebears, more deeply entrenched racism built on that history of exploitation. Some saw the light and made reference to the Nazis and the Germans who claimed they didn't know. And the children, now grown up said: "We have felt support for our ideas and actions—after all we started learning and thinking with products which bore the full stamp of approval...'by appointment to Her Majesty the Queen.' "

And the director said: "Would that I could live my life again." But, alas, it was too late for him, and for Britain. Others have made mistakes, can we learn from them?
Yours Sincerely,
Rev'd. Basil Manning

The letter must have touched the nerve of the actual director of Boots the Chemist because the company agreed to stop selling the sponge Golliwog product.²³

What's Wrong With the Golly?

In many public statements over the years, the James Robertson and Sons Company stated that their trademark was nothing less than an innocent doll that was now firmly entrenched into the folklore of the British society. At the outset of the symbol, this was probably the case. However, the marketplace, the society of Britain has changed dramatically over the past seventy years. Not only was the demographic structure of the countries changing, so too was the ideology of the blacks and other minority groups within the society. More often, and more stridently, they were demanding that their human dignity be respected and their basic desires to rid the marketplace of negative stereotypical images that offended not only them and their children, but also numerous other constituent concerned groups of people.

At the outset of the paper, it was stated that the meanings of words change and that some words have much more of an impact than do others. This has been especially true with the use of numerous ethnoslanderisms that have been used to label and describe the blacks of the Western World. At times, one word was used to damn the whole group and some of the ethnolinguistic labels hurled at blacks would include "coon," "darkie," "Sambo," "chocolate drop," "burr head," and now "golli-wog/wog." It is believed that the use of boundary words used as ethnic/racial terminology marks off groups and the consequences of such boundaries mark group identity, socialization and social control. The sociocultural framework is anchored in group symbols, and their maintenance also acts upon and influences social-group relations, particularly its stability and change.²⁴ Words are identity markers as they are used and imposed upon society by, in this case, the commercial "impression managers" (like Robertson, Trebor and H & B). Words do structure the world and words do differentiate groups one from the other. In the examples that we have discussed the companies have taken, and continue to take, their own particular ethnocentric bias with the chosen trademarks that they selected to market their products.

Within the black communities themselves, we have witnessed how names and their meanings can change, the use of "black" is more appropriate now than the use of "negro." We also see that ethnic labels one group uses towards another group might be viewed as racial/ethnic name calling.²⁵ In the world of commercial trademarks and symbols, we also see that, at times, other folkloric characters have been used as well as words that are sexually laden with connotations that at times go well beyond the marketers original intent.²⁶

It also must be stressed that the flow of communication methods and stimuli are not simply uni-directional as is so often implied. People receive sources of data and information from many sources, from many directions, and this information also bounces back and forth in time and space. What this paper has tried to show is that names were chosen. Names were accepted, in their own time, but times have changed, and change is demanded to get rid of the names that are believed to be derogatory to blacks. Numerous constituent groups were quoted with their replies and the results indicated that not all persons or groups had the same outlook or the same focus of concern. No consensus was reached. However, it must be understood that minority groups as a collective are characterized by the major "impression managers," and at times the minority group is helpless and powerless to do much about it. Such would appear to be the case with the evolution of the name Golliwog. The name is still used to sell the products.

Conclusion

The interrelationships between language and culture are most dynamic. Language is also a mirror of culture as it reflects a group's dominant concerns and interests, in this case commercial (profits, brand differentiation, a stimulating trademark). It is also believed that language is also a molder of culture as it has an effect upon the way people deal with objects and each other in their world.

A name, like Golliwog, which started innocently enough in 1895 now is seen by many as a racially negative epithet. The social significance of the symbol has gone far beyond its original intent. Its significance now rests largely on its ability to carry not only positive images, if there are some, but also negative images laden with negative stereotypical cultural meanings. The socially, culturally constituted world of Britain has changed during the years 1895 to 1986. The perceptions of the commercial trademarks in question as "stations of meaning" have changed.

The original innocence of the Golliwog, as a literary image, as a folkloric image, has now been perceived as a racist symbol by substantial constituent groups of British society.

Notes

¹M.R. Solomon, "The Role of Products as Social Stimuli:

Symbolic Interactionism Perspective," *Journal of Consumer Research* 10 (December 1983): 319-29; and G. MacCracken, "Culture and Consumption: A Theoretical Account of the Structure and Movement of Cultural Meaning of Consumption Goods," *Journal of Consumer Research* 13 (1985): 71-84.

[2]H. Carpenter and M. Prichard, *The Oxford Companion to Children's Literature* (Oxford: Oxford UP, 1984): 554-55.

[3]*I Love My Golliwog* (London: Borough of Greenwich, 1985): 3-4.

[4]R.W. Burchfield, ed., *A Supplement to the Oxford Dictionary*, Vol. 1 (Oxford: Claredon, 1972): 1259.

[5]*Punch* [London] (January 12, 1921): 33; (June 15, 1938): 663; (December 15, 1948): 574; (April 6, 1949): 380.

[6]Advertisement for Hamley Brothers, *The Illustrated London News* (December 29, 1900): 977.

[7]Advertisement for Andrews Liver Salt, *Punch* (June 15, 1925): xi.

[8]Advertisement for "Rigmel" issued by the Bradford Dryers Association, *Punch* (June 15, 1938): 663.

[9]Advertisement for "Alice in Toyland" issued by Harrod's Store, *Punch* (October 6, 1948): viii.

[10]*Pocket Picture Crosswords Book 2* (London: Collins, 1975): 3.

[11]Private correspondence between the author and a senior marketing executive of the Trebor Limited Company, England, October 31, 1984.

[12]J. Boskin, "Sambo: The National Jester in the Popular Culture," *Race and Social Difference*, P. Baxter and B. Sanson, eds. (Harmoundsworth, England: Penguin, 1972): 152-64.

[13]Private correspondence between the author and a senior marketing executive of the Trebor Limited Company, England, October 2, 1984.

[14]Private correspondence between the author and a senior company executive, Robertson Foods International Ltd., December 16, 1981.

[15]*History of Robertson's Golly*, company pamphlet, Robertson Foods International Ltd., Manchester, England, 1981.

[16]Private correspondence between the author and a senior company executive, Robertson Foods International Ltd., January 10, 1985.

[17]Ibid., March 17, 1983.

[18]Ibid., January 10, 1985.

[19]*I Love My Golliwog* (London: Borough of Greenwich, 1985): 3-4.

[20]Ibid., 3-4.

[21]"Campaign Petitions," *Dragon's Teeth* 2 (September 1980): 6.

[22]"You See Them Here, You See Them There, Campaign Report," *Dragon's Teeth* (March 1980): 12.

[23]"Racist 'Gollies' Everywhere," *Dragon's Teeth* (March 13, 1980): 13.

[24]J.A.Ross, "Language and the Mobilization of Ethnic Identity," *Language and Ethnic Relations*, H. Giles and B. Saint-Jacques eds. (London: William Clowes Ltd., 1979): 1-13.

[25]J.E. Williams, "Connotations of Racial Concepts and Color Names," *Journal of Personality and Social Psychology* 3 (5: 1966): 531-40; and P. E. Lampe, "Ethnic Labels: Naming and Name Calling," *Ethnic and Racial Studies* 5 (4: 1982): 542-48.

[26]C.H. Zastrow, and P. Gorski, "Put a Little Cherry in Your Life: The Use of Sexual Words to Sell Products," *Monda Lingvo-Probl.* 6 (1977): 141-48; and T.E. Sullenberger, "Ajax Meets the Jolly Green Giant," *Journal of American Folklore* 87 (1974): 53-65.

5
Gender and Advertising

Gender proved to be a timely and significant advertising topic during the 1980s. While women had been struggling for a generation to obtain a better image in ads, male image problems seemed to arise. Some men's right's groups signal that men have received demeaning treatment in the 1980s via the popular media. This section targets on gender-related advertising.

Leading off this gender area is Whipple's basic, highly revealing study of sexual advertising content.

Hubbard probes the male parenting image, still, a hot topic in the 1990s. The focus is aimed at helping improve the male ad depictions, via magazine advertising examples.

Finally in this volume, Danna's somewhat daring and ground-breaking investigation explores some of the salient aspects of the changing male image in advertising. While this probe obviously emphasizes the male theme, nonetheless, it also presents for women, directly or indirectly, some notable points of interest and concern.

The Existence and Effectiveness of Sexual Content in Advertising

Thomas W. Whipple

Sexual content, in the form of nudity, sexual imagery, innuendo and double entendre, has been employed for decades as an advertising tool. It encompasses sexual appeals made using either male or female models or both to male, female or mixed audiences. Jean Kilbourne's film *Killing Us Softly: Advertising Images of Women* and the *Stale Roles & Tight Buns: Images of Men in Advertising* slide show present many examples of the use of sexual appeals in advertising.[1] Qualitative research has documented the use of symbolic sexual content through visual imagery portrayed by different postures, poses and depictions.[2] Sexual messages, explicit and implicit, in advertising are communicated with both visual and verbal content. With respect to verbal content, ambiguous language and double entendre are common. Visual imagery may include facial expression, setting, body language and clothing. Sexual content can also vary by the degree of nudity, attractiveness, sexiness and suggestiveness of the portrayal; by the level and amount of erotic content; and by the appropriateness of the decorative versus functional roles depicted.

This paper reviews the content analysis research which has documented the use of sex in advertising. The research evidence pertaining to the effectiveness of using sexual appeals in advertising is also examined and the implications of these findings are discussed. Future directions for research are suggested in light of the efforts and findings to date.

Existence of Sexual Content in Advertising
In Consumer Magazines

Based on a review of over twenty content analysis studies, Courtney and Whipple concluded that men and women are shown stereotypically in advertising in general interest magazines.[3] The studies confirmed that both sexes, but particularly females, are likely to be shown in nonactive, decorative roles in consumer magazine print ads. Studies of more specialized consumer magazines provide additional empirical evidence that the most common images are women as alluring, decorative, sex objects and physically attractive.[4] A more recent study by England and Gardner found considerable sex-typing in ad portrayals and little change over a twenty year period.[5] Lysonski's results show that portrayals underwent some metamorphoses during the late 1970s but that stereotypical images of men and women persist in consumer advertisements.[6]

A content analysis, focusing on sexual portrayals in consumer magazine advertising, was conducted by Soley and Kurzbard.[7] Advertisements containing verbal references, depicting male/female contact and portraying suggestively clad, partially-clad, and nude models were coded as containing sexual content. They found that the percentage of ads with sexual content increased from 17.6 percent to 22.8 percent between 1964 and 1984. Although the results indicate a slight increase in the use of sex in advertising over the twenty year period, especially in general-interest magazines, the difference was not statistically significant. The types of sexual portrayals employed, however, did change significantly. There was greater reliance on visual than on verbal sex in 1984 and the sexual illustrations became more overt. The data also indicate that female models were far more likely to be less demurely dressed than male models, even in the same ad, thus supporting complaints that sexism still exists in advertising.

In TV Program Advertising

Both the networks and individual stations attempt to get viewers to tune in their programming by advertising in TV program guides. Solely and Reid studied the link between advertisers and audiences in which the sexual content of television program advertisements brought the audience and station together.[8] They reported the results of a content analysis of the frequency and nature of sex in 806 television program advertisements in *TV Guide*. They found that over 35 percent of print ads for television programs contained sexual elements. Sexual elements were defined as "asserted or implied visual portrayals of and verbal referents to sexual behavior."[9] Also, program ads with sexual content tended to be larger than other program advertisements. They concluded that sex is a predominant feature of television (especially network) program ads and, as a result, reflects the content of the programs advertised.

In Industrial Advertising

Only three published studies have examined the content of sexual portrayals in industrial advertising. McKnight investigated 130 issues of engineering and trade magazines.[10] She recorded the occurrence of advertising she judged to be sexist (women portrayed as passive, silly or incompetent) and concluded that 35 percent of the total magazines examined contained at least one sexist advertisement.

McKnight's view of industrial advertising as sexist was supported by Easton and Toner who examined a random sample of 71 magazine issues taken from a listing of commercial, industrial and business magazines.[11] They concluded that industrial advertising treated women with "reasonable" fairness in the 394 ads which depicted people out of the 2,816 advertisements they examined. Noting that industrial advertising is targeted at a largely male audience and that it is mainly concerned with technical and economic communication, they found it appropriate that men dominated their sample of industrial advertisements. They also found that equal proportions of men and women were portrayed in decorative roles (not involved in using or demonstrating the product). Although both sexes were used to attract attention of the magazines' readers about one-half of the time, the way the attention-getting was applied differed significantly. Men were not shown in sexually explicit ways, but 27 percent of the women were portrayed in either an alluring, provocative, semi-dressed or nude manner.

The most recent study by Reese, Whipple, and Courtney provided a more systematic analysis of the use of sex in industrial advertising.[12] Their investigation sampled U.S. trade advertising, analyzed trends over three decades and included additional content analysis categories to examine sexual portrayals. Those ads that featured at least one identifiable adult were coded for the gender and number of the adults portrayed, their occupations and functional versus decorative portrayals. Decorative tasks were coded as nonsexual or sexual. When sexual portrayals were found, the authors judged whether the individuals featured were dressed appropriately in relation to the advertised product or service.

In the sample of 4,916 advertisements examined, only 1,052 featured at least one identifiable adult. Men were almost five times more likely to be shown than were women. While men were increasingly shown in various decorative portrayals during the three time periods, they were *always* depicted in a nonsexual manner. In contrast, the incidence of decorative portrayals of women declined significantly to 39 percent in the 1980s, after reaching a peak of 67 percent in the 1970s. However, when women were portrayed in decorative activities, almost one-third were still shown in a sexual fashion. To better understand the "manner" of these female sexual depictions, the ad portrayals were coded for appropriateness of the model's attire. For example, a bikini-clad woman was judged as appropriately dressed in an advertisement for a sauna manufacturer. In another ad, a similarly attired model shown decorating power equipment was classified as inappropriately dressed. In the 1970s, when two-thirds of the women appearing in industrial ads were depicted performing decorative activities, over one-half of the sexual portrayals included an inappropriately dressed woman. Although the percentage of inappropriately attired female models, portrayed in a sexual manner, declined somewhat by the 1980s, such depictions of women in trade advertising remained. Approximately forty percent of the sexual portrayals, or about five percent of the total ads showing women, still employed inappropriately clad models in the latest issues of the trade magazines which were content analyzed.

In Broadcast Advertising

The predominant finding of content analyses conducted during the 1970s regarding portrayals of sexuality is that women were more likely than men to be shown in decorative or non-functional roles in TV advertising.[13] Also, women were more likely to be portrayed through exaggerated acting, stereotyped voice tone, and stereotyped body language. Incorporating verbal response mode analysis with continued analysis of 2,736 television commercials, Rak and McMullen's findings suggest that little has changed in the portrayal of the sexes from the late 1970s through the 1980s.[14]

Although some observers claim that the use of sexual portrayals in TV advertising is extensive, the topic has not been addressed in detail by content research. However, Caballero and Solomon did report that women portrayed as sex objects and in fashion roles appear to be occurring increasingly in categories of products targeted specifically to women.[15] Another content analysis of television commercials used a cross-cultural sample of Clio Award-winning television commercials to determine the similarities and differences in the use of sex in American and international television advertisements.[16] The study found that less than 7.7 percent of U.S. television commercials contained anything other than fully-dressed models, and only 0.5 percent depicted partially-clad models. Overall, it was found that nudity was more common in international than in American TV advertising. Content analysis which focuses on the use of sexual messages in radio advertising has not been conducted to date.

In Other Media

Many incidents have been reported in the press regarding the use of sex in newspaper advertising, on billboards, on bus and train cards, on posters and in direct mail pieces. However, this author is not aware of any content analyses that document these reports in a scientific manner.

Effectiveness of Using Sexual Appeals

The first advertising effectiveness study, by Smith and Engel, reported that the presence of a partially-clad female model improved both psychological and functional product ratings of an advertised automobile among male and female respondents.[17] However, it may have been the presence of the model herself, not the partial nudity, which enhanced the product ratings. When the degree of nudity was varied in ads for two products, Peterson and Kerin found that the advertisements containing the nude model were consistently perceived as the least appealing while the associated product and producing company were perceived as possessing the lowest quality and being the least reputable, respectively.[18] Although males were more favorably disposed toward the advertisements, products and producing company than were females, both groups rated the nude model condition the lowest.

Some advertisers try to measure the communication effectiveness of an ad, that is, its potential effect on awareness, knowledge or preference before placing the ad. Communication-effect research seeks to determine whether an ad is communicating effectively. Direct ratings are used to evaluate an ad's attention-getting, cognitive, affective and behavioral strengths. Although this research helps assess the communication effectiveness of an ad, it reveals little about its sales impact. Advertisers might like to assess the sales effect also, but it is generally more difficult to measure. First, a non-artificial advertising environment is needed to assess the sales effect. Then, a controlled experimentally designed study must be implemented.

Measuring Communication Effectiveness

A successful communication requires that a message from a source be communicated through a channel to a receiver who not only receives the message, but also comprehends it and responds to it. In advertising, the communication model can be interpreted as follows: the message is product image and information; words and/or pictures are the source of the message; television, magazines or other media are the communication channels; and the receiver is the consumer. Noise, an interference within the flow of the message, includes competing ads and other distracting elements.

Communication effectiveness research is designed to measure the influence of advertising upon the target audience. However, there has been only limited agreement among researchers about the appropriate measures to use in assessing such impact. A number of studies utilized a response hierarchy model as the framework for assessment, but different cognitive, affective and conative measures were developed. At the cognitive stage, measures of knowledge and comprehension have been used. Affective measures have included interest, liking, preference and favorability. At the behavioral intention stage, conative measures usually include intention to seek out and/or to try the product.

Arousal, attention and information processing all are determining factors on how sexual stimuli affect the communication effectiveness of advertising.[19] The degree of intensity of the stimulus and the context in which it is presented can make a difference in consumer perception of and reaction to sex in advertising. Arousal is a psychological state which results in attention, and quite possibly search, in the consumer decision-making process. When sensory input is presented to the consumer, a disequilibrium state is created. Psychological tension, produced by this disequilibrium, may then cause increased cognitive activity directed toward the product or ad. An affective evaluation of the ad then takes place through this enhanced level of information processing. Product image can therefore be affected by the interaction of the stimulus object, the presentation and the receiver's values. According to self-concept theory, a sexually-oriented stimulus must be appropriate for projection in order for the desired response to occur.[20]

Sexual Content in Advertising

Communication Effectiveness of Sexual Appeals

Gaining product-category and brand attention, recall, recognition, favorable brand attitudes and, eventually, sales are among the reasons cited by advertisers for employing sexual strategies. The lack of available data which would allow direct measurement of the sales effects of sexually-oriented advertisements has forced a reliance on communication measures. Psychological concepts, such as arousal, perception, self-concept, distraction and aggression, have provided a theoretical framework upon which some researchers have based their studies. Others have conducted empirical studies from a strictly pragmatic point of view. Both approaches have provided an interesting and complementary set of findings about the communication effectiveness of decorative, attractive, sexy, suggestive, erotic and nude variations of sexual portrayals.

Recognition and Recall. The presence of a decorative model facilitates the recognition of an advertisement, especially the visual components.[21] However, correct recognition of the illustration does not carry over to recognition of the advertising copy. Even when the model is rated sexy, copy recall is not enhanced.[22] It also appears that the presence of attractive models has no effect upon brand name memory.[23]

Erotic, suggestive and nude female models have a particularly strong attention-getting impact among male consumers, but attractive models are probably as effective in getting the attention of both males and females. The research evidence suggests that it is the presence of an attractive person in the advertisement which accounts for the attention-getting value. When the model is perceived favorably, both the ad and the brand benefit from better recall scores.[24] However, overtly seductive, partially-clad and nude models are likely to produce unfavorable effects. Research studies which have varied the erotic content or degree of nudity in ads have consistently shown that nonsexual advertisements produce better brand recall.[25] In many cases, the attention is focused on the model to the detriment of brand name and copy recall. When brand recall is the objective, Alexander and Judd recommend that a nude female model *not* be used in the ad.[26]

Attitude Measures. In addition to assessing recognition and recall, some researchers have measured consumer attitudes toward advertisements that vary in the level of attractiveness, sexiness and nudity of the models. Specifically, the three dimensions of the hierarchy of effects model (cognitive, affective and conative) have been considered separately. Two studies which investigated the impact of attractive models found that when physically attractive models were used, affective ad measures improved while cognitive evaluations did not.[27] The impact on purchase intention was much more complex. Caballero, Lumpkin, and Madden's results indicated that the physical attractiveness factor was not significant in predicting a willingness to purchase two grocery products.[28] Kahle and Homer, however, found that participants were more likely to intend to purchase after exposure to an attractive endorser while Baker and Churchill found that only to be true when female subjects rated male models.[29] They concluded that an unattractive female model may be more persuasive in creating eventual product purchase when trying to sell unromantically-oriented products to males. The product type, the sex of the model and the subject's sex can all influence the impact of physically attractive models on behavioral intentions.

Of these potential sources of influence, Patzer measured the impact of the respondent's sex in his comparison of sexy and nonsexy ads which featured a female model.[30] His results showed perceived female sexiness to be a determinant to all three dimensions of communication effectiveness for male receivers but not for female receivers. This finding concurs with that of Baker and Churchill who found that communicators who are the opposite sex of the receiver are more effective than same sex communicators.[31]

Two studies which examined the use of sex in advertising defined sex according to two constructs: nudity and suggestiveness.[32] Data from these studies imply that cognitive and affective evaluations of sexual content become generally less positive as nudity increases. The suggestive ads were consistently rated by both males and females as being in poor taste. Again, sex of the receiver had a significant affect on reactions to the use of sex in advertising. The women reacted more negatively to the suggestive ads while both men and women evaluated same-sex nudity poorly and opposite-sex nudity more positively.

Only one study examined the impact of controversial sexual content in TV commercials on the three important dimensions of communication effectiveness. Bello, Pitts, and Etzel chose sexual appeal utilizing innuendo and physical attractiveness, rather than nudity, because it is responsible for the bulk of the controversy in television advertising.[33] Both males and females found the sexually controversial commercial more interesting than the noncontroversial ad. However, apart from merely making the commercial more interesting, the controversial content failed to improve the communication effectiveness of the advertising. In other words, greater interest did not occur with greater communication effectiveness in terms of affect and intended purchase.

The implications for advertisers, of the findings from the communication effectiveness research, are apparent—to elicit more attention to ads, use sexual content. At the same time, however, the reactions may not be favorable. The result may be offensiveness and/or dislike of the advertisement, which may carry over to the product and the sponsoring company. It would appear that those ads targeted at a specific sex should not employ nudes of the same sex. Furthermore, ads employing suggestiveness would not be successful for attracting favorable reactions among females. Opposite-sexed models might, however, be effectively employed if done so with the product and theme of the ad consistent with the use of the model. When using models in ads, attractive models are more likely to be effective than unattractive ones, but there are exceptions. Again, the nature of the product must be considered. However, since raters apparently are unable to discriminate between sexiness and physical attractiveness, care must be taken not to include a model only for decorative purposes.[34] While ad illustration recall may improve, ad copy and brand recall may suffer. In such cases, no model at all may be the preferred condition. One thing is certainly clear from the past twenty years of research findings—using sex in advertising is a very risky business. Its success or failure will depend upon the type of product, the consumer's gender and personal bias towards sex, the sex of the model or presenter, the image of the sponsoring company, and the numerous 'sexy' treatments which are possible to portray in an advertisement.

Sales Effectiveness of Sexual Content in Advertising

Another area of interest is the direct effect that sex in advertising has on sales of the product being advertised. Sales data were unavailable to researchers during the 1970s and early 1980s. A direct result of this unavailability is that researchers had to rely mostly on student samples which judged magazine advertisements in laboratory-type settings. Also, those who use sex in advertising to sell could claim that it still works. Ridge Tool Company has claimed that for over fifty years their Ridgid Pin-Up Calendar, featuring twelve scantily clad beauties holding Ridge hardware, still sells tools.[35] Even a plastic surgeon claimed he traced $60,000 to $120,000 of new business in a few months to one $75,000 ad campaign which featured a sexy model.[36]

In the last few years, two studies have experimentally investigated the effect of model attractiveness on sales. One study was restricted to assessing the effectiveness of an attractive sales representative in a direct mail advertisement for a religious book. Caballero and Pride found that attractiveness was marginally persuasive when associated with a female model.[37] The attractiveness factor alone was not significantly more effective when compared to the "no model" control treatment. The other research study was conducted at point of sale where direct effects on sales could be measured. Caballero and Solomon concluded that physically attractive models did not enhance the sales of beer or facial tissue.[38] In fact, the low attractiveness condition produced more sales of tissue.

Communication and Sales Effectiveness of Sexual Content

Only one study has measured both the sales and communication effectiveness of sex in advertising at point of sale. Their research findings enabled Whipple and Donofrio to draw conclusions in the areas of recall, attitudes and sales effects.[39]

The results regarding recall strongly support past research findings. The model, standing posed in a leotard (sexy treatment), attracted more attention than the same model, sitting dressed in sweatpants and shirt (nonsexy treatment). This heightened model recall for the sexy treatment, however, did not enhance product or message recall for the advertised fruit bowl. On the other hand, the sexy ad did not produce a decrease in product or message recall either, which has been reported in other studies.

Overall, respondents reacted more favorably to the nonsexy ad. Its superior communication effectiveness is apparent in responses to cognitive, affective and conative variables alike. The significant increase in sales when the nonsexy ad was used also supports its effectiveness. Although the sexy ad did produce a higher sales volume than the "no ad" condition, any point-of-sale advertising is possibly more effective at increasing sales than no advertising at all.

The researchers concluded that sex does not appear to be an effective tool in point-of-sale advertising. The effects appear to be quite similar to those found in studies concerning advertising for delayed purchases. A "sexy" ad will draw attention, but what purpose does it really serve if the main objectives are to increase brand recall, brand attitude and eventually sales? Furthermore, the nonsexy ad was rated as more appropriate for the product and the business establishment. These findings suggest that using sex in advertising for a product which has no sexual overtones simply does not work.

Future Research Considerations

Further documentation that sexual content is ever present in advertising should continue to be on the agenda of researchers in the 1990s. The increasing numbers of cases of women portrayed as sex objects and in fashion roles in products targeted specifically to women is a trend worth following. Currently, it appears that these role portrayals are gaining acceptability for advertising products which are designed to enhance appearance, physical attractiveness and sex appeal. While the focus of content research in the past has been on magazine and TV ads, in the future, advertising in other media should be analyzed for the existence of sexual content.

Most of the research on the effectiveness of sexual content in advertising relied on student subjects, usually male, evaluating female models in laboratory settings. Field investigations of nonstudent target audiences must dominate future studies. More emphasis should be placed on women's perceptions of sexy males and females. Instead of testing mock-up ads, more realistic high quality advertisements should be used. Multiple measures of advertising effectiveness, including sales, are essential. Future research should be designed to use criterion measures which are consistent from study to study.

Research which assesses decorative, attractive and sexy models must begin by clearly defining and differentiating the terms. Furthermore, these studies of sexually-oriented advertising communications should be conducted within a theoretical framework. For the most part, past research has not been oriented to theory testing. Also, rather than focus on the presence or absence of a treatment condition, degrees of attractiveness, sexiness and nudity should be measured. Optimal levels may not be at the extremes.

Other limitations of past research including product categories tested, media contexts used and buying situations should be overcome. Most of the products tested so far have been relatively low involvement and low in risk. Results may differ across other product categories. Also, other media contexts, such as billboards, newspapers and cable TV, may produce different results. The findings may also vary for shopping situations which do not involve grocery stores and in-home buying. By improving the realism, reliability and validity of future research, the managerial value of the findings will be enhanced.

Notes

[1] J. Kilbourne, *Killing Us Softly: Advertising Images of Women* (Cambridge, MA: Cambridge Documentary Films, 1979); and OASIS, *Stale Roles & Tight Buns: Images of Men in Advertising* (Brighton, MA: O.A.S.I.S., 1984).

[2] E. Goffman, *Gender Advertisements* (Cambridge, MA: Harvard UP, 1979).

[3] A.E. Courtney and T.W. Whipple, *Sex Stereotyping in Advertising* (Lexington, MA: Heath, 1983).

[4] D.E. Sexton and P. Haberman, "Women in Magazine Advertisements," *Journal of Advertising Research* 14 (1974): 41-46; and M. Venkatesan and J. Losco, "Women in Magazine Ads: 1959-1971," *Journal of Advertising Research* 15 (1975): 49-54.

[5] P. England and T. Gardner, "How Advertisers Portray Men and Women: The Reality Gap and Its Social Consequences," *Current Issues and Research in Advertising*, James H. Leigh and Claude R. Martin, Jr., eds. (Ann Arbor: U of Michigan P, 1983).

[6] S. Lysonski, "Female and Male Portrayals in Magazine Advertising: A Re-examination," *Akron Business and Economic Review* 14 (1983): 45-50.

[7] L.C. Solely and G. Kurzbard, "Sex in Advertising: A Comparison of 1964 and 1984 Magazine Advertisements," *Journal of Advertising* 15 (1986): 46-54, 64.

[8] L.C. Soley and L.N. Reid, "Baiting Viewers: Violence and Sex in Television Program Advertisements," *Journalism Quarterly* 62 (1985): 105-10, 131.

[9] Ibid.

[10] D. McKnight, "Sexism in Advertising: What's a Nice Girl Like You.... *Technology Review* 76 (1974): 20-21.

[11] G. Easton and C. Toner, "Women in Industrial Advertisements," *Industrial Marketing Management* 12 (1983): 145-49.

[12] N.A. Reese, T.W. Whipple, and A.E. Courtney, "Is Industrial Advertising Sexist?" *Industrial Marketing Management* 16 (1987): 231-40.

[13] Courtney and Whipple, *Sex Stereotyping*.

[14] D.S. Rak and L.M. McMullen, "Sex-role Stereotyping in Television Commercials: A Verbal Response Mode and Content Analysis," *Canadian Journal of Behavioral Science* 19 (1987): 25-39.

[15] M.J. Caballero and P.J. Solomon, "A Longitudinal View of Women's Role Portrayal in Television Advertising," *Journal of the Academy of Marketing Science* 12 (1984): 93-108.

[16] L.N. Reid, C. Salmon, and L.C. Soley, "The Nature of Sexual Content in Television Advertising," *Proceedings of the American Marketing Association* (1984).

[17] G.H. Smith and R. Engel, "Influence of a Female Model on Perceived Characteristics of an Automobile," *Proceedings of the Annual Convention of the American Psychological Association* 76 (1968): 681-82.

[18] R.A. Peterson and R.A. Kerin, "The Female Roles in Advertisements: Some Experimental Evidence," *Journal of Marketing* 41 (1977): 59-63.

[19] R.S. Baron, "Sexual Content and Advertising Effectiveness: Comments on Belch et al. (1981) and Caccavale et al. (1981)," *Advances in Consumer Research*, vol. 9, Andrew Mitchell, ed. (Ann Arbor: Association for Consumer Research, 1982).

[20] R.D. Wilson and N.K. Moore, "The Role of Sexually Oriented Stimuli in Advertising: Theory and Literature Review," *Advances in Consumer Research*, vol. 6, William L. Wilkie, ed. (Ann Arbor: Association for Consumer Research, 1979).

[21] R.W. Chestnut, C.C. LaChance, and A. Lubitz, "The 'Decorative' Female Model: Sexual Stimuli and the Recognition of Advertisements," *Journal of Advertising* 6 (1977): 11-14; L.N. Reid and L.C. Soley, "Another Look at the 'Decorative' Female Model: The Recognition of Visual and Verbal Ad Components," *Current Issues and Research in Advertising*, James H. Leigh and Claude R. Martin, Jr., eds. (Ann Arbor: U of Michigan P, 1981).

[22] G.L. Patzer, "A Comparison of Advertisement Effects: Sexy Female Communicator vs. Non-sexy Female Communicator," *Advances in Consumer Research*, vol. 7, Jerry C. Olson, ed. (Ann Arbor: Association for Consumer Research, 1980).

[23] See Chestnut, LaChance and Lubitz, 11-14.

[24] L.R. Kahle and P.M. Homer, "Physical Attractiveness of the Celebrity Endorser: A Social Adaptation Perspective," *Journal of Consumer Research* 11 (1985): 954-61.

[25] M.W. Alexander and B. Judd, Jr., "Do Nudes in Ads Enhance Brand Recall?" *Journal of Advertising Research* 18 (1978): 47-50; M. Steadman, "How Sexy Illustrations Affect Brand Recall," *Journal of Advertising* 9 (1969): 15-19; R.B. Weller, C.R. Roberts, and C.A. Neuhaus, "A Longitudinal Study of the Effect of Erotic Content upon Advertising Brand Recall," *Current Issues and Research in Advertising*, James H. Leigh and Claude R. Martin, Jr., eds. (Ann Arbor: U of Michigan P, 1979).

[26] See Alexander and Judd, 47-50.

[27] M.J. Baker and G.A. Churchill, Jr., "The Impact of Physically Attractive Models on Advertising Evaluations," *Journal of Marketing Research* 14 (1977): 538-55; see Kahle and Homer, 954-61.

[28] M.J. Caballero, J.R. Lumpkin and C.S. Madden, "Using Physical Attractiveness as an Advertising Tool: An Empirical Test of the Attraction Phenomenon," *Journal of Advertising Research* 29 (1989): 16-22.

[29] See Kahle and Homer, 954-61; see Baker and Churchill, 538-55.

[30] See Patzer, "A Comparison of Advertisement Effects."

[31] See Baker and Churchill, 538-55.

[32] D. Sciglimpaglic, M.A. Belch and R.F. Cain, Jr., "Demographic and Cognitive Factors Influencing Viewers Evaluations of 'Sexy' Advertisements," *Advances in Consumer Research*, vol. 6; M.A. Belch, B.E. Holgerson, G.E. Belch and J. Koppman, "Psychophysiological and Cognitive Responses to Sex in Advertising," *Advances in Consumer Research*, vol. 9.

[33] D.C. Bello, R.E. Pitts and M.J. Etzel, "The Communication Effects of Controversial Sexual Content in Television Programs and Commercials," *Journal of Advertising* 12 (1983): 32-42.

[34] G.L. Patzer, *The Physical Attractiveness Phenomena* (New York: Plenum, 1985).

[35] J. Washington, "A Model Sales Approach," *The [Cleveland] Plain Dealer* (December 30, 1984): 21-A, 23-A.

[36] R.L. Cohen, "The Power of One Dramatic Ad," *Healthcare Marketing Report* 6 (1988): 12.

[37] M.J. Caballero and W.M. Pride, "Selected Effects of Salesperson Sex and Attractiveness in Direct Mail Advertisements," *Journal of Marketing* 48 (1984): 94-100.

[38] M.J. Caballero and P.J. Solomon, "Effects of Model Attractiveness on Sales Response," *Journal of Advertising* 13 (1984): 17-23, 33.

[39] T.W. Whipple and J.M. Donofrio, *Communication and Sales Effectiveness of Sex in Point-of-Sale Advertising* (Cleveland, OH: Cleveland State UP, 1990).

Male Parent Images in Advertising

Rita C. Hubbard

Since Erving Goffman's *Gender Advertisements* appeared in 1979, increased attention has been given to both male and female depictions in advertising.[1] His analyses of trivialized and submissive female images and powerful dominant male images were seminal, demonstrating how gender identities are emphasized within the deeply structured cultural meanings communicated through advertising. Goffman focused primarily on females in print ads, women frequently shown with head cocks, pelvic tilts, knee bends and smiling expressions, placed in positions associated with passivity. He found that males in these same print ads were presented as powerful, active, stern and unsmiling.

Most of the subsequent research on sex-role stereotyping in advertising has also given major attention to female depictions with male images examined by way of contrast. This focus has been encouraged by the contemporary feminist movement which has categorized the commercialization of sex as a woman's issue. However, recently several studies have examined male depictions in advertising more closely, with particular focus on how they have changed as a result of the changes in society.

For example, Judith Posner, in 1984, dealt with the objectified male in advertising and noted changes toward eroticization and increased trivialization. She focused on the male as sex object complete with pelvic tilt, maternal hand-to-hip pose, genital bulge, disrobement, self-touching and relaxed postural alignment.[2] In 1988 Diane Barthel's book, *Putting on Appearances: Gender and Advertising*, gave similar attention to the changing depiction of male roles in advertising. She concluded that while complacent female and powerful males images still predominate, there has been a certain feminization of our culture that permits today's male to "operate in both modes: the feminine mode of indulging oneself and being indulged and the masculine mode of exigency and competition."[3]

While both Posner and Barthel described certain androgynous behaviors among males presented in advertising, they did not touch upon male parent images nor upon any demonstrations of male nurturing behaviors. Likewise, no other published research has given attention to such depictions even though the increased number of mothers in the work force appears to promote shared parenting. Therefore, this study was designed to investigate the depictions of male parents in advertising in order to determine their frequency and to investigate the parenting behaviors portrayed, comparing and contrasting these with the behaviors of female parents represented in advertising. All advertisements in three family magazines were examined over a six-month period. The magazines *Children*, *Parenting* and *Parents* were selected because they were judged to be especially sensitive to parental depictions. Issues for the period from July to December 1988 were used in order to provide sufficiently large sets of advertisements for analyses.

Three questions influenced choices affecting the study's development:

1. To what extent are male parent images used?
2. What behaviors of the male parents are depicted?
3. Do male parent images and behaviors differ from female parent images and behaviors?

In order to answer these questions, the 1,264 ads which appeared in the three magazines over a six-month period were separated into six categories:

1. Ads of general interest without child-parent images.
2. Ads showing a child or children with no adults visible.
3. Ads showing a child or children with a non-parent adult or adults.
4. Ads showing a child or children with mother.
5. Ads showing a child or children with father.
6. Ads showing a child or children with both parents.

After separation, those ads which showed a child or children with a parent or parents were analyzed for content reflecting gender behaviors. Specific totals of ads separated into categories for each magazine are given in the following table. (*Children* is published every other month; *Parenting* and *Parents* appear monthly.)

Magazines	Ads with General Interest	Ads with Children Only	Ads Showing Children with Non-parents	Ads Showing Children with Mothers	Ads Showing Children with Fathers	Ads Showing Children with Both Parents	Totals within Magazines
Children	34	72	1	14	6	—	127
Parenting	172	169	11	46	12	4	414
Parents	412	245	4	49	9	4	723
Total across Magazines	618	486	16	109	27	8	1264

Most Ads Unrelated to Parent Images

In the three magazines taken as group, ads of the general interest type were most numerous (618). These were for various products used by the general public such a flooring, appliances, make-up and foods. They did not contain child or parent images. The total was influenced by the preponderance of such ads in *Parents* magazine (412).

Of those ads which presented images of children or parents, most (486) showed a child or children alone, even when in reality the child or children would be in danger if left unattended. A Weebok ad, for example, pictured an unsteady toddler standing on the driver's seat in what looked like an open truck or piece of machinery. Another toddler in a Dreft ad appeared to be alone with three frisky puppies.

Sixteen ads showed a child or children with a non-parent adult who might be a well-known personality (like Bill Cosby), an elderly caretaker, a nurse, teacher, barber, coach or other friendly person. These adults were judged to be non-parents when age, race or professional setting made parenthood unlikely. There were equal numbers of males and females in this category; however, this distribution was influenced by three repetitions of the Bill Cosby image.

Out of the total 1,264 ads, only 144 featured a child or children with a parent or parents. With regard to the "parent" designation, two assumptions were made: a young woman caring for a baby was assumed to be the child's mother, and a young man caring for a baby was assumed to be the child's father.

Mothers Seen as Nurturing Parents

Of the parent-child ads, 75.7% (109) showed a mother with child or children; 18.6% (27) pictured the father, and only 5.5% (8) presented both parents. While having four times more images of the female parent than the male parent made a strong statement about who is considered the major caretaker of children, an analysis of mother and father behaviors in the ads further established the perceived nurturance aspects of mothering. Specifically, mothers were pictured in ads holding, kissing, rocking, cuddling, consoling children; dealing with pain, sadness and illness; correcting constipation, combing out hair tangles; preparing and serving food; driving car pool; teaching and reading aloud; supervising play and slumber; and potty training.

More Fathers Shown in Traditional Male Roles

In the 27 ads featuring fathers, a majority of the men displayed male behaviors considered traditional, e.g. showing a boy how to drive a tractor, teaching a boy how to play carpenter with a toy workshop, or installing playground equipment. A male parent was also seen in one ad posing for a photograph while holding a baby in a cowboy hat on his lap. Additionally, whenever the gender of the child was apparent, the child was male.

There were some notable exceptions which demonstrated nurturing behaviors generally attributed to females. Pure and Natural soap had an ad with a father in a bathtub holding up his naked child and speaking to it gently. The ad accounted for six of the 27 ads featuring fathers. Another ad, appearing twice, was the Oscar Mayer bacon ad showing a little boy and his father, both seeming excited about the bacon. While it implied that Dad prepared food, it also placed the child on the man's shoulders in a typical male roughhouse pose. A gentle pose was struck by the father in a Gerber baby food ad which appeared twice. He was shown with an infant, preparing to introduce a vegetable in the child's diet.

Two Baby Fresh Wipes ads appeared in the magazines, one showing a mother and infant, the other showing a father and infant. They were similar and dissimilar simultaneously. The ad featuring the mother, which appeared twice, had her lying in bed holding a naked infant. Next to

Reprinted with permission.

the bed was a basket of laundry. The ad featuring the father, which also appeared twice, was superficially similar in that the man was reclining holding a naked infant. However, the props and poses in these ads were very different. The man was reclining on a model's stand on which there was placed a jar of paint brushes. The two ads considered together said that the mother did the laundry and the father was a working artist taking time out to hold his child. Another difference was observed: the mother was posed cradling the child with her hands; the father permitted the infant to sit freely on his abdomen without holding it.

No fathers were presented caring for sick children, dealing with constipation and toilet training, consoling or comforting, reading aloud, combing or dressing children or driving in a car pool.

Parent Images Mixed in Family Ads

Only 5.5% (8) of the 144 parent-child ads featured both parents. In two of these ads, male and female parent behaviors varied in nurturing activity. However, the other ads with posing families presented scenarios lacking dramatic parent-child interactions.

In the nurturing category, one ad showed the father nursing. In it a mother stood, and the father sat feeding a baby with two fake terrycloth breasts slung forward over his shoulders. Protruding from one was a bottle. The ad read: "Now nursing can be done by anyone with Dr. Goldson's Baby Bonder. A unique terrycloth and fleece bib designed to simulate the intimacy of breast feeding."

Another ad placed the mother in the caring role. She seemed to be in charge of child care in an ad showing home playground equipment. She sat in a chair reading and monitoring play. The father, standing with golf bag and clubs at his side, appeared to be dropping by for a visit either before or after his game.

Other ads were basically family poses. One showed a family in careful arrangement around a car. Another, a Black and Decker ad, pictured mother, father, son and daughter looking troubled by the need for time spent preparing breakfast and with the implicit promise that Black & Decker products could alleviate the problem. The first full-page ad was followed by several pages showing small appliances.

An ad repeated twice showed two pictures on the page, one of a baby awake in a crib and another of parents eating in the kitchen with the assurance that the Fisher-Price Nursery Monitor will inform them of any crying or other noises in the nursery.

In another twice-used ad, mother, father, son and daughter were enjoying a supper of foods fried in Wesson Oil. A separate picture of Florence Henderson seemed to imply that the meal was female-prepared, but there was no action presented to confirm that.

Conclusion

Advertisements have cultural relevance. They reflect and elaborate upon social tendencies, among them acceptable gender displays. Further, the content of advertising changes, often slowly, in response to societal changes.

While Erving Goffman in 1979 found that male gender displays in print advertising reflected power, strength and rigidity, subsequent researchers in the mid-and-late 1980s noted the gradual introduction of certain softened and androgynous male images. They attributed these new images to social changes, principally the women's movement and a growing feminization of our culture that has led to the male's freedom to operate in less restricted modes.

One of the recent social changes that has had far-reaching effects has been the increased number of mothers in the work place and the consequent growing need for, and discussion of, shared parenting. This study was undertaken to see if print advertising reflects this growing interest in male parenting. It was designed to examine male parent images in print advertising to determine their frequency and to investigate the parenting behaviors portrayed, comparing and contrasting these with the behaviors of female parents represented.

Of the 1,264 advertisements that appeared in three family magazines over a six-month period, only 144 presented parent images. In 109 of these, mothers were seen alone with children and engaged in nurturing behaviors like holding, kissing, rocking, cuddling, bathing, consoling, nursing and teaching the children.

Only 27 ads showed children with fathers, most of them presenting fathers engaged in behaviors considered traditionally male, such as showing a boy how to use or install equipment. Further, whenever the child's gender could be determined, it was male.

There were five exceptional ads showing fathers engaged in nurturing child-care activities, four of these with the father pictured alone with a child, and one with a mother present who was simply an observer. The first of these ads pictured a father bathing a child; it was repeated four times. The second ad, repeated twice, showed a father ready to cook bacon. The third ad, repeated twice, showed a father preparing to feed an infant. The fourth ad, repeated twice, showed a father reclining and holding a naked infant. The last ad depicted a father nursing a baby while using a fake terrycloth breast; in it, the mother watched the activity.

In the other seven ads showing both parents, one pictured the mother supervising children on playground equipment while the father watched. The remaining ads which showed both parents with children were primarily family poses lacking dramatic parent-child interactions.

Several conclusions can be drawn. First, there were a limited number of parent images presented in the advertising of three magazines, designed for parents, over a six-month period. Of the 1,264 ads examined, 11.4% showed a parent or parents with children. Mothers alone with children were depicted in 75.5% of these 144 ads, fathers in 18.6%, both parents in 5.5% of the ads.

Second, mothers were pictured routinely as care-givers while most fathers were cast in traditional male roles. Only five constructed ads showed fathers in roles generally considered care-giving. Four of these five ads were repeated in different issues, making a total of twelve.

Even if we use the number twelve, indicating all repetitions of the five ads picturing fathers in care-giving roles, they represent only 8.4% of the total number of parent images appearing in three family magazines over a six-month period.

Since advertising images contain implied narratives that reflect acceptable social roles, the advertisements discussed here have a structured cultural meaning related to gender behavior. The stories they tell about parenting behavior revolve around mothers who still care for the basic physical and emotional needs of children, train and teach them, read to them and drive them in car pools.

Fathers in these advertising scenarios are lesser participants in the day-to-day care of infants and children. These narratives embedded in the images of the print advertising discussed may or may not reflect the realities of current family life, but they do appear to work within the edges and boundaries of society to reflect traditionally acceptable and prescribed gender behavior.

Additional research is needed in two areas. First, studies need to determine if shared parenting is a social reality involving all aspects of child care or if it is an unfulfilled proposition. Only then can we determine if print advertising has failed to keep pace with social changes or if it is simply reflecting the basic maintenance of traditional male and female parenting roles. Second, a longitudinal study is needed using a substantial representative number of magazines of various types for purposes of comparison within types.

Viewers construct gender meanings from advertising's abstract representations of acceptable gender displays and ritual actions. With regard to advertising's representation of male parenting, the major question to be resolved is whether advertising is representing the present repertoires of daily life or is perpetuating regressive forms of social relations.

Notes

[1] Erving Goffman, *Gender Advertisements* (New York: Harper, 1979).

[2] Judith Posner, "The Objectified Male: The New Male Image in Advertising," *Atkinson Review* 1 (Spring 1984): 17-22.

[3] Diane Barthel, *Putting on Appearances: Gender and Advertising* (Philadelphia: Temple UP, 1988): 183.

Changing Male Image in Advertising: An Investigation

Sammy R. Danna

Considerable Image Change:
Advocates' General Agreement

When the notion of writing this paper came to mind, probably the main reference contributing to its impetus was an article in *Newsweek* by Jennifer Foote: "Ad World's New Bimbos." The piece begins with the provocative subheadlined remark: "After years of portraying women as half-wits and sex-objects, it's [advertising] turning those stereotypes on men." This new image, "reverse-sexism," is not limited solely to advertising. It is becoming a source of big business in publishing (*No Good Men* and *Men Who Can't Love*) and in films (*Three Men and a Baby*, a story about a trio of lady-killers inheriting and attempting to rear a baby). But Foote says "the most conspicuous examples of the new sexism are in advertising."[1]

The article seems to advance the notion of a trend-setting male turnabout. Although it is not quite clear when the "tables turned," consumer surveys show some female amusement with the "goofy men" in some ads, says Judith Langer, market researcher. Langer relates that men may be getting a "little touchy" about these barbs in commercials, notably the so-called "kitchen klutz syndrome." Psychologist Warren Farrell states in the Foote article that many women increasingly view men as either "success-objects" or "jerk-objects." The new sexism may also show men in sexier contexts, ranging from fully or partially clothed to even more provocative nude poses. All in all, this new sexism may reflect nothing more than "the ad world's never-ending search for novelty." The article concludes with this quip: "Men, 'naked and foolish,' make customers wake up and notice. They make people laugh."[2]

In *USA Today*, June 7, 1989, a companion article to the Foote piece appeared: "Men in Ads Play Dumb: Bimbo-Boys Sell," by Martha T. Moore. Most ads are pitched to women who "don't like being depicted as buffoons," the piece notes. Ann Simonton of Media Watch, the women's portrayals monitoring medium, says "bimbo-boy ads 'appeal to our worst instinct.'" In the same article, Lawrence Deitch, management representative for Frusen Gladje (ice cream) at McCann Erickson, remarks: "I don't believe that this advertising is chauvinist in either way, male or female," for it is really "a tongue-in-cheek look at contemporary life."[3] Nevertheless, "when the new bimbo ads aren't putting down men's brains, they're leering at their bodies," the article notes. Women used to be "swooning over whiter than white laundry," but "now it seems to be trendy that men should be on the chopping block," asserts Don Chavez, President of the National Congress for Men, a men's advocacy group. Fred Hayward of Men's Rights, Inc. (Sacramento) says in ads the man "ultimately ends up as a jerk."[4]

Turning to Dr. Farrell's *Why Men Are The Way They Are*, numerous men's problems surface. Early on, the author explores the DeBeers diamond ad campaign of the early 1980s. He notes that ads for diamonds readily appear in women's magazines. In *MS.*, April 1982, a small diamond appears on a woman's finger. However, in a later DeBeers ad (March 1984), the woman's finger contains a larger diamond than seen in the earlier pitch.[5] While the man buys the woman the diamond and the woman takes him to the jeweler, she nevertheless transfers the credit to herself. This idea is part one of the two-part "DeBeers Transfer." Part two is summarized as follows: "Experience has taught the DeBeers Company that if a man is to spend money on a woman, the woman should be sold—she decides, he pays!"[6] Diamond pitches to men do not stop here. For instance, with an excess of smaller diamonds in 1981, DeBeers attempted to interest men as well as women in these gems.[7] The firm initiated in 1980 the ad campaign dubbed "Diamonds for Men."[8]

Diamonds certainly are not men's only product problem. Recent articles on male image stereotypes suggest that ads tend to show males as aloof, distant, cold, and in many instances, not interacting well with women. In Aramis fragrance ads, man had been "alone" for about a decade, but finally by 1985 AC&R Advertising (New York) created a blurb featuring him as looking at the Aramis woman.[9]

On March 27, 1989, a *Media Marketing* article by editorial assistant Mary Jung relayed some of Hayward's other views. Once more he noted grave concerns about demeaning male ads depictions pointing out that when a jerk is depicted in a male-female relationship, it is always the man who is the fall-guy. "Advertisers are willing to say anything" to sell their products. They are "just listening to the loudest voices, and those voices are yelling, 'Men are Jerks!' " However, Sheila Gibbons, editor of *Media Report to Women* (Silver Springs, Md.), claims that advertisers at times "make both sexes look foolish." She relates that one of women's major quarrels is with advertisers who use the female body to sell products which often have nothing to do with her body, e.g. ads for cars or tires.[10]

Hayward continues his male image comments, saying that sexism exists in ads although advertisers were beginning somewhat to respect men more by 1989. However, Gibbons notes that women are made to look "less effective" than men in ads. Her newsletter reports on a study which found that in men's and women's magazines, the women in ads were shown in some way "subordinate" 27% of the time while men were subordinate only 3.8% of the time.[11]

Hayward says that the more advertisers try to appeal to women, the more negatively they are likely to depict men. "Dumping on a male" is hardly a very acceptable means to cater to women, relates the MR, Inc. director. The Jung article offers a more encouraging view from John Muhlfeld, account supervisor at Carrafiello Diehl Advertising (Irvington), stating that fathers are truly a "part of the parenting process today more than ever." Placing fathers in such ad pitches as Liquiprin, a children's cough remedy, makes "practical sense."[12]

Hayward during 1988-1989, began to feel more strongly that what was happening in advertising overall was tantamount to "male-bashing," inflicting non-physical but nevertheless severe psychological lashing out at males in advertising.[13] In *Media & Values* "Male Bashing on the Rise," the MR, Inc. director continues: "By far, 'male bashing' is the most popular topic in my current [1989] talk-shows and interviews." While Hayward notes the practice occurs especially in advertising, he claims that "male bashing" is not much better in entertainment. He reports that

> "male-bashing" even appeals to the male mentality. Forced to compete with each other...men enjoy "male-bashing" (as long as the "bashee" is another male). Males have long had negative self-images, and every man has a deep fantasy that he can be better than all other men...the hero will earn woman's love by rescuing her from all the other "rotten men."[14]

Further comments on male image advertising come from another strong men's rights advocate. In one of his talks relating to male stereotypic images, Boston-based OASIS (Organized Against Sexism and Institutionalized Stereotypes) spokesman Michael Weisskoff (a management consultant) said that ads try to shock us and prey on our emotions; they are deliberate, and no coincidences and no accidents occur. One of OASIS' goals is to help people sort out ad propaganda and thus become aware of the real message in male advertising images. OASIS believes that stereotyped images may reflect the socialization that men undergo in our society: "Like women, men must endure impossible comparison, in ads, to the 'ideal body.' " For example, ads showing excessive physical power or great adventure often put men in such impossible situations.[15]

Promoting further the ideals of OASIS, another newspaper piece, "Men Losing Their Appetites for 'Roles,' " suggests that unrealistic macho-like stereotypes can severely limit the male image. It is important to be aware of the crippling effect of gender stereotyping. Weisskoff specifically refers to the commercial notion of success which means to climb a "ladder on others' backs, to a level where diamonds replace words of love." Furthering this point is a pitch on a Chicago billboard for Oro International Jewelers dominated by a gold gem with the words: "Tell Her in Gold."[16]

Besides detailing men's rights in meetings throughout various areas of the nation during the 1980s, OASIS tries to warn about male stereotypes. Jean Kilbourne, a well-known feminist, associated with the film relating to women's images in ads, "Killing Us Softly," says that the "true image of men is distorted, but not to the same extent as women's. Women are paying a higher price for their image. While I think women and men are both damaged by sexism, it's much more real for women. It's subtler for men." She asserts that if men are truly dissatisfied with their poor ad image depictions, they have the power to change them because men still run the ad industry.[18]

Weisskoff and OASIS take a similar position: "Our group is striving to see more 'real-looking' male images in the mass media and that includes advertising as a major focus." For instance, in the late 1980s, ads latched onto men as "fathers." Unfortunately, however, more often males are depicted with oversized muscles as stereotypes, like Superman and Tarzan. To live up to such portrayals is virtually impossible for the real man. On the other hand, to present males in media as the inept klutz, boob and fall-guy is equally disconcerting. These depictions hardly bring out authentic spiritual, sensitive and interpersonal qualities which should contribute to the "real male image," relates the OASIS spokesman.[19]

Weisskoff feels that the 1980s brought about numerous male depiction changes. Some were good, but many proved damaging. The male stereotypic image includes aloofness, silence and insensitivity. OASIS is dedicated to helping eliminate such harmful stereotypes. It believes that such depictions are destructive to both genders. Both men and women are hurt in relationship to themselves and to each other.[20]

OASIS has learned over the years that helping people to become more aware of male stereotypes is a major task. For instance, during the mid-1980s the Better Business Bureau's national guidelines of "Dos and Don'ts" for racial, ethnic and gender groups listed "guidelines" for properly depicting these groups in the media. "All major ones were covered *except* men," asserted Weisskoff. OASIS presented a set of guidelines which the BBB accepted and put into effect. Among them is included the depiction of men in a balanced fashion, showing males with other men, enjoying each other's company without competing, fighting, or one-upmanship. OASIS also wishes to see relationships between men and women portrayed as more normal and the showing of men in ads as a natural, integral and respected component of a family, and in general, with children.[21]

"Stale Roles and Tight Buns" is the media piece OASIS has developed and distributed. An example of a stereotypic image includes the Marlboro man cowboy figure, a person cold, aloof and detached. This figure has become the epitome of machoism in advertising, supposedly depicting the independent spirit, the rugged individualist image of the American male. Despite serious image problems and overall declining sales of cigarettes, the Marlboro man's long-running campaign was still going strong in 1990.[22]

OASIS claims that even boys are not immune to the negative image problems, for they are often depicted as overly tough, rough and "man-like." A Levi blue jeans commercial reveals the following scenario: "He's 50 pounds of raw courage, held together by Levi's jeans. He's tough, alright, and he's only six-years old. In a few years, he might trade in his football for a cigar, his helmet for a briefcase, his tire for a suite on the 39th floor." Other ads in the "Stale Roles" series depict the familiar male stereotypes which are over-adventurous, macho, supermen and lady-killers, the men who are always winners. Additional related negative image qualities which OASIS points out include men as violent and women oglers, people devoid of compassion and sympathy.[23]

OASIS wants males to be depicted not as if they were immune to physical and emotional pain and, above all, not depicted as "expendable." The latter, in particular, refers to any encouragement to men to risk their lives to prove that they are truly "real men." OASIS emphasizes that it believes men's and women's rights organizations should work closely together as a united front, fighting sexism for the sake of the whole human race.[24]

Additional views cultivate various rationales for apparent sexism. Barbara Lippert, *Adweek* columnist, in late 1988 said that women are not generally out to get even with men for past advertising discrimination toward females: "These unfortunate portrayals do not help anyone, but unfortunately it appears to be a sort of 'rule-of-thumb' that if you are going to do sexist ads, it is 'safer' to do them with a 'man's skin.' " Men's advertising changed especially in 1988 to include frequent examples of gratuitous nudity.[25]

Furthering her commentary on male treatment in advertising Lippert turns to another phase. In an early 1989 interview, she refers to bimbo and fall-guy type ads: "It naturally falls upon men, for the present, since women are 'quite sensitive' about discrimination toward their gender." However, the relatively new male bodily displays have something for everyone, assuming that they are not debasing or tasteless. For women, this is in the form of an appealing sex object, and for men they present a new and more flattering masculine image.[26]

Lippert notes two particular nude-like ads during 1987 involving Fab and Drano. In the Fab commercial, the male does a "reverse strip." He begins nude and puts on clothes to "striptease" music while seemingly having a good time.[27] Drano features a handsome male also having a good time, taking a bath. He gets out of the tub, clad only with a towel around him, moves about and ultimately ends up pouring Drano into a clogged bathtub drain. Lippert remarks in a 1989 telephone interview that this is a reversal of the traditional ploy "in advertising of using women's bodies gratuitously...I wouldn't quite call it progress that men seem to be shouldering the burden of nudity."[28]

In "Advertising's New Hunks: A Post-Feminist 'Tat for a Tit,'" Lippert supports her male sex symbol comments with some historical data. The beefcake barrage of the late 1980s began in 1982 with the Calvin Klein ad which featured a young male hunk photographed by Bruce Weber from the thighs up and placed against a white sculptural form. Klein followed this ad and similar pitches with comparable ones using women. The blending of conventional gender roles began. Actually, the issue was less about sex and more about the beauty of the human form as Klein's print ads became filled with scantily clad bodies.[29] Lippert admits that, "indeed, reaction to feminism is no small part of the increasing use of men's flesh in ads." A fashion ad for Italian designer Miguel Cruz shows a man completely naked, standing next to a woman richly attired in a full-length evening gown. Lippert points out that "she seems to be leaving him at home, barefoot, as the saying goes, if not pregnant." Many suggestions were made about the flesh-type ads, pro and con, but everything is getting more competitive. Advertising seems to be getting rough because it is difficult to get attention.[30]

The year 1988 proved to be a high-point for male nudity and other sexy bodily displays in advertising. Lippert continued her attack on potential excesses: "advertising with its long tradition of depicting half-naked, half-witted women to push its message across, has come up with a new stereotype—man in all his unglory, the hunk as bimbo, the he-man as wimp and preferably as undressed as possible." Martha Farnsworth Riche, senior editor of *American Demographics*, attributes the "'male-bashing' in advertising" to the fact that "economically, men have been demystified" in society. Screenwriter and actor Marshall Efron reviews the wimpy male image that had become another issue as it began to appear in numerous commercials during 1988. He says that advertising often relies on the device of making a dumb person become much smarter "with the help of the right product." Lippert implies that the macho man was losing out to the wimp: "Take the previously innocuous category of cereal advertising, where rugged individuals/hickory-nut heroes used to reign. These days [1988] we see men getting knocked on the head by tennis balls or being told that they're not kissable or marriage-material, even being humiliated by their own kids, and all because they're eating the wrong breakfast."[31]

Several trends in male ad image treatment since 1988 are obvious. According to Lippert, male stripping had "slowed down" from the 1988 activity high-mark. Men holding babies is a positive sign of progress, "but still, when fall-guys are needed, men are usually the 'chosen victims.'"[32] In a more recent interview, Lippert reveals that not too much had changed for the male image in advertising from 1989, but a somewhat "alarming problem" for women in advertising is developing. The *Adweek* critic feels that some unfortunate ads depict women in the old sexist ways, e.g. "bikini-babes" or "sex-kittens," simply tasteless or exploitative.[33]

Hayward observed earlier events that while some of these ad types can often be negative, some may be conversely complimentary. Some individuals viewing ads may feel that women, like men, who show off their bodies can present a pleasing positive statement. This is especially true if more substantial images for women such as executives, authorities on numerous subjects, leaders, educators, critics, athletes, politicians are presented. The feminist agenda of usually condemning such "flesh depictions" should instead take these positive points into account as well, notes the MR. Inc. director.[34]

Hayward further amplifies the point: "Such bodily displays can be a positive statement for either gender, appealing to the values of some of the ad viewers. Feminists seem to state the 'powerlessness' of women, but seldom relate the positive side of their 'actual power.' Power in feminine sexuality, unexploited or otherwise cheapened would be the same as in the case for males." He says that if such sexy portrayals appear to be the "only gender asset," then the result is obviously unfair, causing the old female/male stereotypes to reappear.[35] Farrell concurs (and says Hayward agrees) that certainly nothing demeaning exists in either gender's display of its physical attractiveness so long as such is not cheapened or presented as if it were virtually the only asset.[36]

Valerie Mackie, *Advertising Age* managing editor, agrees that while in at least a few recent ads, men seem more caring and sensitive, a problem still persists. For instance, when the "heavy fall-guy types" are demanded, men almost always are chosen to fill the dubious roles.[37] Mackie feels that the picture has improved recently for the male, but admittedly not too much, for a more enhanced image is still slowly emerging (1990).[38]

Jennifer Pendleton, former editor-at-large for *Advertising Age*, agrees that some negative male ad image depiction is still taking place in the media.

Reprinted with permission.

Changing Male Image in Advertising

In a telephone interview, Pendleton said that prior to her introduction to the negative male ad image topic, she had not really thought much about the problem. She did indicate that she saw more and more negative male image ads, many of which "would not be tolerated by women." Pendleton further related: "Although many feel men can take it better than women, since they're still dominant in business, still it is not a good practice." She denounced unfavorable ad image portrayal toward either gender. Pendleton concludes: "All discrimination is bad and such should not be encouraged."[39]

Degrees of Image Change: Advocates Differ

Comments in numerous interviews with *Advertising Age* critics, writers and editors, reveal little male ad image change occurred during the 1980s. Compared to gender rights groups such as MR. Inc. and OASIS, these critics' remarks and opinions appear to be more impartial and even more objective. The following is a condensation of remarks and comments from selected *Advertising Age* staff members. Also included in this section is a Popular Culture professor's companion views on the subject.

In early 1988, the editor of *Advertising Age*, Fred Danzig, said that "it is not so much that men are being ridiculed more, but that women have simply stopped being ridiculed." The fall-guy image is a carryover from the old radio and TV sitcoms, from movie and comics equivalents: "Advertising does not set the agenda for popular culture but always lags and follows what is accepted in society." However, even more encouraging is the trend toward showing older men in a more positive manner. Danzig is emphatically quick to relate the "boobism (demeaning depiction as a buffoon) in men hasn't taken the same 'reverse-discrimination path' as that of females in the years past." Men's positions have been far different from those of women. Women's groups such as NOW (National Organization of Women) began fighting in earnest to eliminate pervasive female discrimination, and even more significantly, to obtain equal rights. In short, Danzig feels that the attacks on men generally have been relatively mild and that men have "not been too badly hurt in advertising of the latter 1980s."[40]

When asked in an early 1989 interview what changes in the male ad image fray had taken place during the past year, Danzig responded: "It is really not the 'image' but the 'lack of image' that we should likely focus upon." Men simply were appearing "less in ads," and their places were being assumed more by children, cartoon characters, animals and the like. Males, however, were still being seen in more traditional ads such as beer drinking, footwear, clothing and cosmetics. Older males, even the grandfatherly images, were appearing more frequently from 1988-1989, because they were considered "safer to depict than those of younger men."[41]

Danzig, in early 1990, indicated that a somewhat improved male ad image depiction was presented during much of 1989, specifically less "wimpy male characterization" and more "down-to-earth male portrayals especially in family settings." While the traditional beer-drinking macho-type ads continued, more "male hunk" ads were appearing, but unfortunately so were at least some "klutzy-type" pitches. Most of the latter were not considered offensive but rather humorous. Overall, men were still somewhat scarce in advertising by 1990 compared to the early or even mid-1980s. While older men were filling the gaps in the male image ranks, few ads used them. Nevertheless, even these were a welcome relief.[42]

Danzig concludes: "It is not entirely realistic to eliminate men in family authority settings—with only women present in such ad depictions. By-and-large, the male image did not seem to deteriorate much by the start of the 1990s. Its improvements showed that less demeaning and less slurring ads were becoming more common, but that some remedy should be sought for the lack of younger male ad images."[43]

Larry Doherty, deputy editor of *Advertising Age* in Chicago, supplements Danzig's views in three interviews from 1988 to 1990. According to Doherty, in 1988, men can now appear more attractive and appealing, not only showing off their bodies nude but also partially or completely clothed. While indicating that the male ad image was not too negative in the latter 1980s, he also recalls that "men have always been subjects of certain amounts of 'sexist barbing' in ads. Take for instance, the old Noxzema Shave Cream commercial, featuring the 'Stripper' song. The sexy female voice is coaxing the male who is shaving with a fully lathered face: 'Take it off—take it all off!' "[44] Bare-chested and other sexy male poses continued to be even more popular during 1989. Gillette's "Men of Success" singled out notable men of achievement for praise.[45] Doherty feels that the male advertising depiction plight was essentially unchanged by 1990.[46]

Larry Edwards, Chicago-based *Advertising Age* senior associate editor, presents a different aspect of the gender image problem. Interviewed in early

1989, he noted that for women in business, and especially in advertising, discrimination had been so significant in the past that some of the applied remedies needed to be somewhat drastic. A specific area highlights that women have been slighted in TV commercial "voiceovers" which to date are still overwhelmingly male. Research shows, he says, that women's voices are just as effective as those of men for this type of ad.[47]

Amplifying Edwards' comments is a *Television/Radio Age* article which highlights the Screen Actor's Guild Women's Voice-over Committee work on this topic. Actress Barbara Feldon related her dismay in trying to find voice-over work. She was told to forget about it, since 90% of such jobs are performed by males because their voices "have historically been considered more authoritative." In monitoring thousands of hours of TV commercials, New York and Chicago SAG members found that of 71 ads for cleaning products, 92% used male voices and of 441 food and beverage pitches, 93% tapped male voices. The advertising industry seems to think that "male voices carry the ring of authority."[48]

Advertising Age special projects director Bob Goldsborough sees a more balanced gender treatment in ads today. He indicates that some "klutz and boobism" male types in ads are evident, but they usually seem to be non-malicious and actually in good humor. However, women are still depicted as dumb, awkward individuals—but certainly not as much as in the past. In reality, extremely negative image treatment in ads has leveled off for both sexes with "equal opportunity digs." Goldsborough indicates that he and other *Advertising Age* judges, when reviewing their annual "Best TV Commercials of the Year," tend to reject advertising which features bumbling stupid people. He states: "Unfortunately, there are as many of these negative depiction pieces produced at present as in the past." Referring to the apparent scarcity of younger men in TV ads, Goldsborough remarks: "It is not so much that male authority roles have decreased, but that women and other minorities are now taking a more 'rightful place' in advertising." Better use of older men in ads with such personalities as Art Carney appeared more frequently during the latter 1980s.[49]

A somewhat different but certainly complementary set of views and remarks on the alleged increase in negative male advertising depictions is held by Jack Nachbar, Professor of Popular Culture at Bowling Green State University in Ohio. He admits that substantial differences exist between the way men and women experience discrimination. Women have a stronger and more immediate history of not only negative advertising image portrayal, but also of unfair treatment in business and politics. For men the opposite is true. But now when women are offered promotions, men have to "move over" a bit to make room for the relative newcomers. Men come into this problem area with the advantage of strength, dominance and success: "In reality, they can take some heat, so long as it does not become too inequitable or demeaning."[50]

Nachbar also focuses on the issue of sexism toward both men and women. Generally, sexism is not really as dangerous to men as it is to women, considering the long history of discrimination against females. While nudity is but one aspect of sexism, "the rise of men who are nude in ads may parallel, deliberately or otherwise, the rise of the male stripper in show business. It has become acceptable for women to view men under such conditions and express their amusement at such antics. Males in underwear ads are relatively new, but the male has expressed his masculinity in varying degrees of nude poses from the earliest of times." Advertising's perchant for a "quick image" often omits the data required for a balanced and credible image. Nachbar cautions that when ad depictions of men or women get "tasteless, start belittling, offending basic dignity, give unbalanced views of an entire gender," then they are truly unacceptable and signal a need for some notable change.[51]

In addition, Nachbar feels that the male image had not worsened between 1988-1990. Macho-type ads continue, especially for beer commercials and athletic gear. Most of these pitches are aimed at selling to men, for whom the stereotypic overly masculine images are not really too offensive.[52]

Clashing Views:
Male Ad Image Discussion Heats Up

Two views which appear to be extreme are chosen for inclusion. Fred Hayward represents the strong men's rights position of MR. Inc. in his extensive work on male advertising image problems of the 1980s. Bob Garfield, critic for *Advertising Age* in Washington, chose to summarize more briefly his views that the male ad image has not changed during the 1980s. Both were asked to respond to the other's comments. Hayward consented to a special interview and to a request for a lengthy formal letter further detailing his overall male image views and his special rebuttal to Garfield. Both were asked to respond to the other's comments. Hayward consented to a special interview and to a request for a lengthy formal letter

Changing Male Image in Advertising

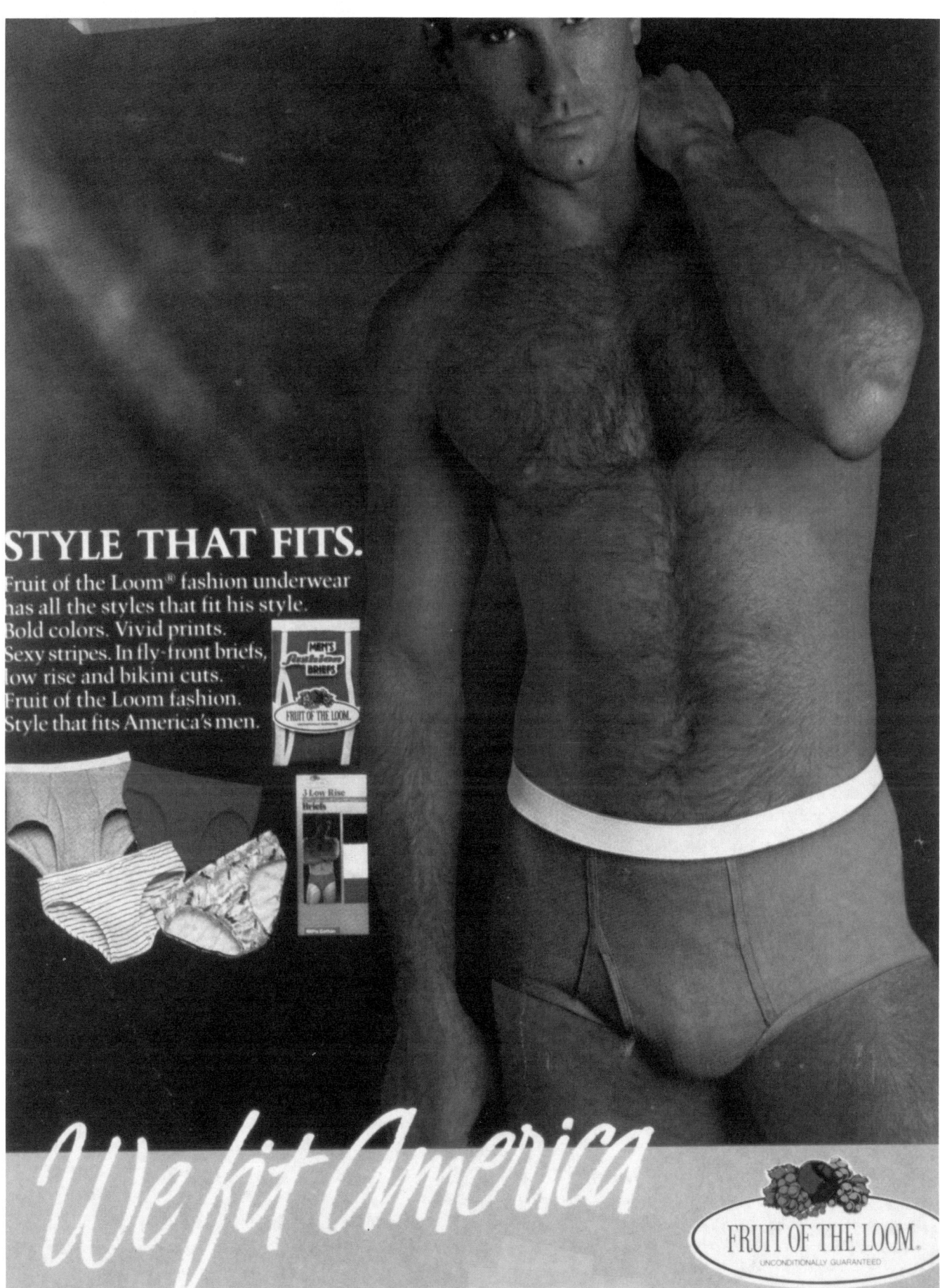

Reprinted with permission.

Reprinted with permission.
Soloflex Muscle-Machines Company.

further detailing his overall male image views and his specific rebuttal to Garfield.

Whereas Garfield contends that no particular discrimination or negative image such as "bimbo" or "klutz" had been aimed toward men in advertising in recent or in past years, Hayward feels differently. Even though his group has not delved into the distant past history of male ad images, its work during the 1980s does, indeed, reveal a decidedly prejudiced image against men. Hayward claims that it is undeniable that men have been discriminated against in ads, especially where a woman appears in the same ad with the man.[53]

According to a 1990 letter from the MR head: "For several years, we have been studying 1,000 random ads per year, focusing only at ads for products consumable by both men and women." In ads directed to the general audience and national campaigns (women's products and daytime television are even worse), the group analyzed the male-female relationship (such as husband-wife or boyfriend-girlfriend). The general pattern seems to be that whenever one is singled out to look worse than the other, the male is the one singled out:[54]

When one panicked and the other remained in control, the one who panicked was the male. When one was incompetent and the other was capable, the incompetent one was the male. When one was ignorant and the other knowledgeable, the ignorant one was the male. When one was sleazy and the other had integrity, the sleazy one was the male. When they engaged in a physical competition and one lost, the loser was the male. When they engaged in a mental competition, the loser was the male. When one smelled bad or got dirty, it was the male. All objects of anger were male. All objects of violence were male. All objects of rejection were male.[55]

Furthermore, Hayward's letter notes that the pattern is clear; very rare exceptions were found in a random ad sample of 1000: "Anyone who disputes that pattern, reveals more about that person's agenda than about reality. After several years of these surveys, it is still amazing to find such rare exceptions to the rule. The main exception is that we have now found a few instances where the female was the less knowledgeable or the less competent one. On the other hand, we have yet to find a single instance where a father is shown as more competent than a mother."[56]

Hayward's letter also relates that he concentrates on ads primarily because they can be used more practically. A single TV sitcom takes thirty minutes to survey while an ad takes only fifteen to thirty seconds to present. Actually, the male image pattern pervades all formats: movies, sitcoms, talk shows, popular literature, news coverage and the like. It may very well be true that nothing is new in this pattern. Certainly the era of feminist assertiveness appeared to be a lot more abusive toward males and seemed to contain more negative messages to and stereotypes of males than feminists have asserted. The problem is that analysis of feminine issues did not separate the private male-female relationships from other forms of relationships. "MR, Inc.," Hayward emphasizes, "is dedicated to fighting sexism in general, and in a special way it recognizes the social, psychological, physical but also legal and economic problems of men."[57]

To this end, MR. Inc. feels that men have not always been fairly depicted in advertising. Hayward in a late 1989 interview, cites an example as one of his favorite "pet peeves." The long-running Folger's Instant Decaf ad touts a "darker cup of instant crystals" and initially features the woman as the competent one—the expert on better coffee. At the end of the commercial, the "dumb man really appears to be put-down." However, in the reverse role, he is portrayed as the competent one concerning the merits of darker Folger's, but he does *not* "put down his lady-friend." An encouraging note is that by the start of the 1990s, although this commercial still portrays the lady-friend as more knowledgeable, the husband is depicted as an average, even somewhat sensitive guy and not as a "boob."[58]

Hayward laments that "where there are rejection, violence, humiliation or sexism aimed at individuals in ads, in 100% of the cases the male is still the 'victim.' In addition, where anger is vented, it is always 100% toward the male; and in situations dealing with children, it is still the mother who is the competent one. The father is usually not even in the scene, much less consulted." The MR Inc. director cautions: "These 'put-downs' are especially harmful to young males from eight to twelve years of age. 'Male-bashing' seems to be acceptable in the media and can become a form of 'child abuse.' The youth has no other context from other experiences to help present a balance to such destructive images. Older males have experienced times when the male image was certainly much more favorable than at the end of the 1980s."[59]

Bob Garfield, in response to Hayward, believes that the dominance of men in society is a crucial point in this discussion: "A pie in the face is only funny if somebody powerful is hit. If the weak or defenseless get hit, the act is viewed as mean or offensive. Thus it is men's very empowerment that makes negative portrayals of zero consequences to anyone." Garfield poses the question: "Since when are advertisers, movie-makers or novelists responsible for depicting a demographically perfect cross-section of America?" Their job is to entertain or to sell, and they may do so with whatever methods they see fit. A lot has to do with glamour and fantasy, and not with social science. Advocates like Hayward are making a career on a basically groundless premise.[60]

As for discrimination, Garfield asks the reader to remember that the business of marketing is about discrimination—determining who your prospective customer is and using the appropriate message, imagery and icons for appeals. He states that Hayward's complaints are both groundless and trivial in the extreme. "There is *plenty* that is wrong with today's advertising but, except to the degree that most of the oafish portrayals of men are insipid cliches, male-bashing is not one of them."[61]

Best and Worst in Male Ads: MR's 1989 Selections

MR. Inc. has noted in the national media some of the "Best and Worst" in male-related advertisements since 1986, the first year for its "awards." Hayward and his group's purpose has been to make the public aware of these negative male ad depictions and alert advertisers of their objections. The following are a few samples from the 1989 selections which were *not* released by January 1990, as had been the case in past years. Published here for the first time, these include:

Positive Image Ads:

Pioneer Electronics: for its print ads depicting a wholesome family togetherness setting (with the father prominently included).

Miller Beer: for two video commercials showing men as everyday heroes. One was especially commended for integrating three necessary themes for improving the lives of men: supportive relationships between males who do not know each other; supportive relationships between males of different generations; and supportive relationships between males of different races.

Negative Ad Images

Robitussin: for its video campaign of "Dr. Mom" commercials. Especially offensive was the one where a child comes to her sick mother to tattle on her "incompetent father" who has burned the laundry, messed up the house, and is now helplessly watching TV.

Diamond Industry: for its escalating "harassment of men." It now urges women to act cold to a man until he buys a diamond for her. "Let him know there's a perfect way to melt your heart;" deny him "pleasure" until he buys a diamond; "remind him that you cannot play until he has the proper attire;" and be unsympathetic to his financial situation: "If he flinches, tell him love hurts."

Hallmark Cards: for bashing the entire male population with a commercial promoting a card which says: "Men are only good for one thing...and how important is parallel parking, anyway?" Hayward comments: "A similar insult aimed at women would never air—(nor should it ever air)."[62]

Male Ad Image Depiction In Early 1990: Similar Scenario To The 1980s

To show that somewhat similar problems and comments relating to the male ad image continue, a few selected pieces from early 1990 are reviewed. These complement the previous remarks in this article which mostly focused upon the 1980s.

A *New York Times* article comments on the male image investigation. An early 1990 campaign for men's fragrance from Liz Claiborne may make one wonder if men's "masculinity is on the wane," according to Kim Foltz's piece, "In Ads, Men's Image Becomes Softer." Initially, she notes that "Madison Avenue is remaking its image of men." Since the majority of ads are still aimed at women, a growing number of advertisers by 1989 began to spend millions of dollars "to tell men that they can indeed be sensitive, caring, and not afraid to show insecurity." While there is still the Marlboro man and the fun-loving, back-slapping, macho-like beer pitches, "some advertising is now showing men cooking, washing dishes, and taking care of the children." Perhaps male ads have been "slow to change how men are portrayed," primarily because some ad agency clients are reluctant to abandon old concepts. They find it difficult "to believe men are really doing things like shopping in supermarkets," relates Allison Cohen, account planning director at Ally & Gargano.[63]

Penelope Queen, research director at Saatchi and Saatchi Advertising, notes that "as women become more independent, men are being given 'permission' to get in touch with aspects of themselves that they have had to deny and to take on roles they'd been told were 'not manly.'" She concludes: "Nonetheless, advertising is now beginning to reflect the changing roles." Perhaps a good illustration is Procter & Gamble's Cascade dishwasher power blurb which "shows two men having anxiety attacks before a dinner party because their dates are due at any minute and the glasses are 'covered with spots.'"[64]

Other examples are the Tylenol commercial which shows a father nursing his sick child and another spot for Ivory soap which features a father rushing home from work to play with his infant daughter. In a 7-Eleven pitch, two men are out walking, each pushing a child in a stroller. Eventually, as they approach the 7-Eleven store they

Changing Male Image in Advertising

push the strollers until they are racing. "We showed them engaged in a competition to make it easier for men to accept the concept of taking care of children," said Jack DiGiuseppe, Creative director at J. Walter Thompson (Chicago).[65]

In helping to set that new course, Dr. Farrell speaks out: "What is being created is the male 'Catch-22' " for "society still doesn't respect men who make a job of taking care of the home and children."[66] Dr. Farrell believes that while there are positive aspects in the relatively new male ad depictions, nonetheless, caution must be taken to guard against extreme portrayals.[67]

Although the following is somewhat of a departure from the male ad image problems, per se, still these findings may help to define and perhaps help to dispel poor gender image advertisement practices. Laura Shapiro's cover story in *Newsweek* on May 28, 1990 contends that, among other things, there are certain hazards of being male. Women are not the big societal problem, for after all, the nation is not overly burdened with too much empathy and altruism or with a plague of nuturance: "The problem is men—or more accurately, maleness." Jean Berko Gleason, professor of Psychology at Boston University, states: "Men are killing themselves doing all the things that our society wants them to do. At every age they're dying in accidents, they're being shot, they drive cars badly...they're two-fisted, hard drinkers....Maybe it's men's raging hormones, but I think it's because they're trying to be a *man*."[68]

In the early stages of childhood, prior to four years of age, relatively small amounts of gender differences or stereotyping exist. On the other hand, by age four or five, gender stereotypes develop with a "determination that makes liberal-minded parents groan in despair." Regardless of the origins, images of male aggressiveness and female nurturing seem to remain with us the rest of our lives. When a man is with a child, it is said they are playing, and not that he is nurturing it.[69] Furthering these gender notes, Kyle Pruett, psychiatrist at the Yale Child Study Center, says that "there are rules about being feminine, and there are rules about being masculine" as part of our living. Seemingly, one can argue forever about whether "those are good or bad societal influences," but children, "love to know the differences. It solidifies who they are."[70]

Beer ads tend to exploit male bonding images. Many are blatantly sexist is their approach. In early 1990, Budweiser featured a he-man campaign which seemed to aim at what Lippert expresses as "absolute studhorse, he-goat, megabulls" types: "These spots featured fantasy women, built to serve.

Copyright © by Bad Boys of Chicago. Used with permission.

Now, the use of fabulous babes is not unknown in beer advertising.... Even post-Hefner, Budweiser still serves up babes to the manliest of men."[71]

Macho ad stereotypes were still alive as 1990 was under way. Miller Brewing's annual college spring break advertising insert targeted 18-24 year old males, the main college beer-drinking crowd. The emphasis was on "drinking, sex, and advice on how to 'scam the babes.' "[72]

The adventurous macho-man depicted in advertising seems to have hit a new low in the controversial "bungee-jumping" Reebok television spot. Two men are shown standing on the edge of a bridge, 180 feet above a raging river, ready to jump: "One is wearing the new Pump from Reebok, the other is wearing Nikes. Both have elastic cords attached to their shoes. Several seconds after the men jump, the man wearing the Pump bounces back into view while the one wearing the Nikes disappears, leaving only his shoes bouncing at the end of the cord." NBC refused to run the commercial because it depicted a "reckless sport."[73]

The changes of the male ad image of the 1980s have been highlighted in a graduate research study. Erving Goffman's monograph, *Gender Advertisements*, explains that certain body language in ad photo poses was attributed only to women at the time, e.g. the so-called "bashful knee bend," the "licensed withdrawal," "mental drift," and "sexual availability and submissiveness." Now such poses can be found in male underwear ads. Chris Miller in her MA thesis asks: "Whatever happened to the jock in the Jockey ads? Does this mean Goffman's categories are shifting? Are men ready to see themselves as sex objects?" Miller, an anthropology graduate student in 1990 at Temple University, discovered that men like ads that show women as sex objects and ads that show men as "jocks," but they become nervous about those which feature men as sex objects. Women think that sexy bra ads were ridiculous and demeaning, but they like the images of openly seductive males who are displayed in sexy ads for men's underwear.[74]

A number of current "role-shifts are almost terrifying to some.... Many men are very confused." Men who are newly interested in child-rearing may play with kids more, take them to the park, and even change a diaper or two, but basically, "They haven't picked up the real drudgery at all" for "that is still left typically to the women." People are still trying to understand the aspects of why men are men and women are women. The introduction of men's studies in colleges is one of the latest attempts to understand some imaging male problems.[75]

Despite the premise expressed by some that there has been a declining male image, especially during the 1980s, a Gallup poll released in early 1990 indicates that nearly half of all adults polled believe that "U.S. men have the better life." In 1975 only one-third thought "men had it best." In fact, only 22% of adults polled in that Gallup survey believe women have a better life, but 21% believe men and women have a similar quality of life: "Women who came of age since the 1960s are particularly inclined to see it as a 'man's world.' " " Almost 63% of women polled between 18 and 49 years of age think men are better off, compared with only 40% of older women.[76]

A final comment on male image of the 1980s comes from Jeffrey Cohen, freelance writer for *TV Guide*, in late 1989. He gave examples of some ads demeaning males. If they "had been shown with the genders reversed, there would have been protests against the sexist portrayal of women—and rightly so." He succinctly summarizes his view: "But just because TV is making some effort to treat one gender fairly [females], must it bash the other?" One man on a 1989 Oprah Winfrey Show suggested that it was tough being a male in the 1980s. It seems that the idea that "a man can have problems with the male image presented by society isn't socially acceptable yet."[77]

Conclusion

The goal of this paper was to explore purported male advertising image changes, and possible reasons for these occurrences. The literature, interviews and other research resources present various views of male ad image portrayal.

Represented positions range from men's rights groups to male and female ad journalists. Pro-men advocates argue that men have been ridiculed by stereotyping such as fall-guys and bimbos. What many consider as insult, others accept as good-natured, tongue-in-cheek humor.

Sorting all the facts, opinions, comments, statistics and other data in this male ad image controversy can prove to be an exhausting task. The reader can, however, use this present study as a basis for his or her own conclusions of the issues. More research should be done before formulating a conclusive opinion. The 1990s will certainly present an opportunity to continue to investigate and analyze this topic.

Notes

[1] Jennifer Foote, "The Ad World's New Bimbos," *Newsweek* (January 25, 1988): 44.
[2] Foote, 44-45.

Changing Male Image in Advertising

[3] Martha T. Moore, "Men in Ads Play Dumb: Bimbo-Boys Sell," *USA Today* (June 7, 1989): 8-B.

[4] Moore, 8-B.

[5] Warren Farrell, *Why Men Are The Way They Are* (New York: McGraw, 1986): 27.

[6] Farrell, 29-30.

[7] "DeBeers Digs Deep to Mine New Markets," *Marketing & Media Decisions* (May 1981): 68-69, 128.

[8] Paul Sullivan, "Jewelry Market No Longer Diamond In The Rough," *Advertising Age* (March 14, 1985): 16.

[9] Lee Israel, "Aramis Image: From Boxes to People," *Advertising Age* (December 9, 1985): 30.

[10] Mary Jung, "Watchdog Group Lashes Out at Ads That Demean Men," *Media Marketing* (March 27, 1989): 2.

[11] Jung, 2.

[12] Jung, 21.

[13] Fred Hayward, telephone interview, February 18, 1988; Hayward, telephone interviews, September 29, 30 and October 3, 1989.

[14] Fred Hayward, "Male Bashing On The Rise," *Media & Values* 48 (Fall 1989): 16.

[15] Martha Helgerson, "Madison Avenue Tries to Build Men in Image It Wants," *Post-Bulletin Spectrum* [Rochester, MN] (April 12, 1985): 12, 14.

[16] Marion Widger, "Men Losing Their Appetites for 'Roles,'" *The Middlesex News* (February 24, 1985): 8-F; and a billboard in Chicago, Illinois, on the northwest corner of State and Huron Streets for Oro International Jewelers, "Tell Her In Gold," (April 27, 1990).

[17] Drew Jubera, "Stale Roles and Tight Buns," *Dallas Times Herald* (July 1, 1985): 4-C.

[18] Judera, 4-C.

[19] Michael Weisskoff, telephone interview, March 14, 1988; OASIS, "Stale Roles and Tight Buns," companion literature to media package, 1987.

[20] Weisskoff, telephone interview on February 15, 1988.

[21] Ibid.

[22] Ibid; OASIS, "Stale Roles and Tight Buns," companion releases, 1982, 1987.

[23] OASIS, "Stale Roles and Tight Buns," 1986: 7, and slide description: 60.

[24] Weisskoff, telephone interview on October 3, 1989; Weisskoff, telephone interview on March 14, 1988.

[25] Barbara Lippert, telephone interview, February 23, 1988.

[26] Lippert, telephone interview, March 13, 1989.

[27] Barbara Lippert, "New Fab's Bump and Grind Awash in Good, Clean Fun," *Adweek's Marketing Week* (April 20, 1987): 19.

[28] Barbara Lippert, "Drano Breaks Through With Some Bubbly Sex Appeal," *Adweek* (September 21, 1987): 30; Lippert, telephone interview, March 21, 1989.

[29] Barbara Lippert, "Advertising's New Hunks: A Post-Feminist 'Tat for a Tit,'" *Adweek's Marketing Week* (October 26, 1987): 60.

[30] Ibid., 60.

[31] Barbara Lippert, "Send In The Wimps," *Vogue* November 1988): 414. [M.F. Riche and M. Efrom references from Lippert article.]

[32] Lippert, telephone interview, March 21, 1989.

[33] Lippert, telephone interview, March 20, 1990.

[34] Hayward, telephone interview, February 24, 1990.

[35] Ibid.

[36] Warren Farrell, telephone interview, March 26, 1990.

[37] Valerie Mackie, telephone interview, March 13, 1989.

[38] Mackie, telephone interview, January 31, 1990.

[39] Jennifer Pendleton, telephone interview, February 16, 1988.

[40] Fred Danzig, telephone interview, February 22 1988.

[41] Danzig, telephone interview, March 14, 1989.

[42] Danzig, telephone interview, February 7, 1990.

[43] Ibid.

[44] Larry Doherty, telephone interview, February 17, 1988.

[45] Doherty, telephone interview, March 13, 1989.

[46] Doherty, telephone interview, January 31, 1990.

[47] Larry Edwards, telephone interview, February 16, 1989.

[48] "Voices of Authority: Male vs. Female," *Television/Radio Age* (September 29, 1986): 75; George Blooston, "The Voice of Authority," *Savvy* (June 1988): 12.

[49] Bob Goldsborough, telephone interview, January 31, 1990.

[50] Jack Nachbar, telephone interview, February 15, 1988.

[51] Ibid.

[52] Nachbar, telephone interview, March 20, 1990.

[53] Hayward, telephone interview, March 24, 1990.

[54] Hayward, letter to Sammy R. Danna, February 19, 1990.

[55] Ibid.

[56] Ibid.

[57] Ibid.

[58] Hayward, telephone interviews, September 29 and 30, October 3, 1989; television viewing by Sammy R. Danna, January-February 1990.

[59] Hayward interviews, September 29-October 3, 1989.

[60] Bob Garfield, telephone interview, February 5, 1990; Garfield, letter Sammy R. Danna, February 19, 1990.

[61] Ibid.

[62] Hayward, "Best and Worst Men's Images in Advertising," supplementary letter, February 19, 1990. [Exclusive release for this writing]

[63] Kim Foltz, "In Ads, Men's Image Becomes Softer," *New York Times*, March 26, 1990, C-12.

[64] Foltz, C-12.

[65] Foltz, C-12.

[66] Foltz, C-12.

[67] Warren Farrell, in an interview on March 26, 1990, San Diego (telephone).

[68] Laura Shapiro, "Guns and Dolls," *Newsweek*, May 28, 1990, 62, 65.

[69] Shapiro, 57, 58.

[70] Shapiro, 58.

[71] Barbara Lippert, "With Inflatable Fantasies, Bud Pumps Up Outdated Men," *Adweek*, March 19, 1990, 21.

[72] Teresa Riordan, "Miller Guy Life," *New Republic*, March 27, 1989, 16-17 (abstract).

[73] "Daring Reebok TV Ad Gets 2 Thumbs Down," (Knight-Ridder Newspapers), *Chicago Tribune*, March 21, 1990, Section 3, 1.

[74] Patricia McLaughlin, "Sex Adds to Ads," *Chicago Tribune*, April 29, 1990, Section 6, 5.

[75] Zay N. Smith, "What Is A Man?" *Chicago Sun-Times*, May 9, 1990, 39.

[76] Linda DeStafano and Diane Colasanto, "Public's View: Men Have the Better Life," *Chicago Sun-Times*, February 4, 1990, 5.

[77] Jeffrey Cohen, "Stop Bashing Men," *TV Guide* [commentary], August 12, 1989, 28-29.

Contributors

Karen Buzzard was born and raised in the Missouri Ozarks. She attended Drury College in Springfield, Missouri for her Bachelor of Arts, the University of Iowa at Iowa City for her Master of Arts, and the University of Wisconsin at Madison for her Ph.D. in Communications. She worked for two years as Director of Research at an independent UHF station in Philadelphia. Dr. Buzzard specializes in broadcast ratings and management. She is the author of, *Chains of Gold: Marketing the Ratings and Rating the Markets* (Scarecrow Press, 1990). She is currently an associate professor at Northeastern University in Boston and teaches courses in the area of broadcasting and communications management. She has been an active member of the Popular Culture Association for the past three years.

Richard N. Chapman received his Ph.D. from Yale University in 1976. A former Woodrow Wilson fellow, he has taught at Southeast Missouri State University and Wells College in Aurora, New York, where he was Chairman of the Humanities Division and Director of American Studies. He is presently Professor of History and Chairman of the History Department at Francis Marion College in Florence, South Carolina. He is the author of *Contours of Public Policy, 1939-1945* (1981) and a contributor to *Power and Responsibility: Case Studies in American Leadership* (1986). Awarded a National Endowment for the Humanities Fellowship for 1984-85, he is currently at work on a study of the career of the intellectual and reformer Stuart Chase.

Sammy R. Danna received his Ph.D. degree in Communication from the University of Missouri-Columbia. Dr. Danna holds three masters degrees in speech education, in secondary/higher education and in theology. In addition he completed all the doctoral degree coursework at the University of Illinois (Urbana-Champaign) in Rhetoric and Public Address. He has been a full Professor of Communication at Loyola University of Chicago since 1980. He is the author of over 70 articles, monographs and book chapters. Of these, 58 articles appeared in the old *Educational and Industrial Television* journal. Upon publication of his 50th piece in *E&ITV*, its management presented him with what it termed an "exclusive award" in the form of a specially designed plaque. Five monographs were written for the Freedom of Information Center at the University of Missouri-Columbia and two book chapters for *American Broadcasting*, 1975. Dr. Danna has delivered papers and chaired sessions at the Popular Culture Association national and regional Conventions since 1980. In addition, he has chaired the PCA Advertising Area since 1985.

Monroe Friedman is Professor of Psychology at Eastern Michigan University in Ypsilanti. Long active as a researcher and consultant, he has contributed more than a hundred articles and paper presentations to the field of consumer affairs. He is a past president of the American Council on Consumer Interest and a former editor of the *Journal of Consumer Affairs*. He has also served in Washington as a Congressional Fellow and a research consultant to the White House Office of Consumer Affairs, the U.S. General Accounting Office, the Consumer Interests Foundation, the Federal Trade Commission, and the National Science Foundation.

Rita C. Hubbard received her Ph.D. in Rhetoric and Communication from Temple University in 1982. She is currently Professor of Speech Communication and Chair of the Department of Arts and Communication at Christopher Newport College in Newport News, Virginia. Her earlier publications dealt with programmed speech communication textbooks, romance novels, and rhetorical control in society. She has served as associate editor of two journals, *Communication Education* and *Communication Quarterly*.

Margaret J. King has a Ph.D. in American Studies and M.A. in Popular Culture, with research experience at the East-West Center. She is a cultural specialist who writes about the popular arts, theme parks, museums, mass media, cross-cultural topics, and cultural trends. Experience includes museum development, freelance writing, editing with J.B. Lippincott and F.A. Davis, and assorted cultural research projects. Currently she teaches liberal arts subjects at the University of Maryland at Baltimore and at Thomas Jefferson University in Philadelphia.

Stephen L. W. Greene teaches journalism at San Jose State University. His twin interests are popular culture at the turn of the last century and the use

Contributors

of computers at the turn of yet another century. Greene first became interested in advertising when he had to sell a lot of it to maintain his weekly newspaper in Northern California. In academia, he has continued his quest for linage, albeit for non-pecuniary reasons.

Robert M. MacGregor is a Professor of Marketing at Bishop's University, Lennoxville, Québec. As a cultural analyst, his research interest includes racial and ethnic stereotyping.

Luigi Manca is Professor and Chair of the Department of Literature and Communications at Illinois Benedictine College in Lisle, IL. Born and educated in Italy (he received the title of Dottore in Filosofia from the Universitá degli Studi di Roma), Manca completed his Ph.D. in mass communications at the University of Iowa in 1981. His current research focuses on popular advertising images of the 1980s.

Joanne Morreale is Assistant Professor of Speech Communication at Northeastern University in Boston, MA. She received her B.A. at the University of Massachusetts, Amherst, and her Ph.D. from Temple University in Philadelphia. She is the author of *A New Beginning: A Textual Frame Analysis of the Political Campaign Film* (1991) and several articles on televisual communication.

Alfred C. Richard received his B.A. from the University of Maine. Graduate study for the Masters of Arts and Ph.D. was completed at Boston University. His Graduate Thesis "*The Panama Canal in American National Consciousness,*" was published by Garland Press in 1990. He is the author of *"The Tampico Incident: Connecticut Almost Goes to War"*, an article published in *Connecticut History*, Vol. 28, 1987; and also *The Hispanic Image on the Silver Screen* in two volumes forthcoming from Greenwood Press in 1991. He has taught the following courses at Central Connecticut State University: Latin American Survey, History of Mexico, Inter-American History, History of Brazil, Seminar in Latin American History, Directed Studies in various aspects of Latin American History, World Civilization, Western Civilization, History of American Life, and English History.

Marilyn M. Robitaille teaches courses in Children's Literature, Adolescent Literature, pedagogy, and composition and rhetoric at Tarleton State University in Stephenville, Texas. She has conducted workshops emphasizing the use of media in teaching composition, and her articles on related topics have appeared nationally in *English Journal* and in the documents of the Educational Resources Information Centers. She is currently finishing course work toward a Ph.D. in English with a concentration in Rhetoric at Texas Woman's University in Denton, Texas. She completed her master's work at the Bread Loaf School of English, Middlebury College where a course in popular culture shaped her ideas about the media.

Shay Sayre is a professor of Advertising, San Jose State University, San Jose, CA. She holds an Ed.D. in organizational leadership from the University of San Diego. A Fulbright-Hays scholar in Hungary, Sayre investigates the diffusion of Western culture into nations in transition to a free-market economy.

Gina Strumwasser is a professor of Art History at California State University, Fresno. She earned an A.B. in Sociology from the University of California, Berkeley in 1968 and a Ph.D. in Art History from UCLA in 1979. She has presented papers and has published articles on the way in which women are portrayed and perceived in art as well as on such artists as Jan van Eyck, Leonardo da Vinci and Rembrandt. She has traveled extensively in Western Europe and has organized and directed Art History programs in England, Italy and most recently, Egypt. She is currently responsible for Western Art History in the department of art and specializes in the area of Northern and Italian Renaissance and Baroque.

Thomas W. Whipple is Professor of Marketing at the James J. Nance College of Business Administration, Cleveland State University, Cleveland, Ohio. He received a B.S. in mathematics from Marietta College in 1965, a M.B.A. from Ohio University in 1967, and a Ph.D. in business administration from the State University of New York at Buffalo in 1971. Dr. Whipple has authored chapters in books, presented papers at academic conferences, and published articles in professional journals on the effectiveness and consequences of advertising. He co-authored a book titled *Sex Stereotyping in Advertising* in 1983 that received the Outstanding Academic Book Award from the Association of College and Research Libraries of the American Library Association.

Eric J. Zanot is an associate professor and head of the advertising sequence in the College of Journalism at the University of Maryland. He received his bachelor's and master's degrees from The Pennsylvania State University and his doctorate from the University of Urbana-Champaign. His professional experience includes work in public television and with two major advertising agencies. The article on subliminal advertising appearing in this book is one of many he has written on the topic. He has also made many presentations, lectures, speeches and appeared on radio and television to address this topic. His other research interests include the regulation of deceptive advertising and public attitudes toward advertising. Dr. Zanot is a member of the Association for Education in Journalism and Mass Communications, the American Academy of Advertising and the Popular Culture Association.

Tom Zelman is an Assistant Professor of English at the College of St. Scholastica, Duluth, Minnesota. He earned an A.B. in French from Rutgers University, an M.A. in English from the University of Michigan, and a Ph.D. in English from Indiana University. His article on metaphors of indeterminacy in Robert Frost's poetry will be published in the *South Carolina Review*. His article on Irish poet Eavan Boland will appear in *Twentieth-Century Literature*.